English Words
Second Edition

'Katamba brings words to life. So relaxed is his style that *English Words* often reads like a leisurely chat with an old friend. But don't be fooled . . . the data is used expertly to introduce a wide range of lexical issues and to provide deceptively sophisticated insights.'

Steven Jones, University of Central Lancashire, UK

'Anyone who has an interest in the systematic study of words will find this book entertaining and serious at the same time. The student of language will find the challenging exercises, the hyperlinks and the various well-chosen examples particularly stimulating for understanding the nature of language.'

Vincent Ooi, National University of Singapore

How do we find the right word for the job? Where does that word come from? Why do we spell it like that? And how do we know what it means?

Words are all around us, but we don't often think about them too deeply. In this highly accessible introduction to English words, the reader will discover what the study of words can tell them about the richness and complexity of our daily vocabulary and about the nature of language in general.

Assuming no prior knowledge of linguistics, the book covers a wide range of topics, including the structure and the meaning of words, how their spelling relates to pronunciation, how new words are manufactured and how the meaning changes with the passage of time. This revised and expanded second edition brings the study of words right up to date, looking at text messaging and email, and including new material on psycholinguistics and word meaning.

With lively examples from a range of sources – encompassing poetry, jokes, journalism, advertising and clichés – and including practical exercises and a fully comprehensive glossary, *English Words* remains an entertaining introduction to the study of words and will be of interest to anyone who uses them.

Francis Katamba is Professor of Linguistics at Lancaster University.

English Words

Structure, history, usage
Second edition

Francis Katamba

Routledge
Taylor & Francis Group

LONDON AND NEW YORK

First published 1994
by Routledge
Reprinted 1995, 1997, 2001, 2002

Second edition first published 2005
by Routledge
2 Park Square, Milton Park, Abingdon, Oxon OX14 4RN

Simultaneously published in the USA and Canada
by Routledge
270 Madison Avenue, New York, NY 10016
Reprinted 2005

Routledge is an imprint of the Taylor & Francis Group

© 1994, 2005 Francis Katamba

Typeset in Times New Roman by
Florence Production Ltd, Stoodleigh, Devon
Printed and bound in Great Britain by
Biddles Ltd, King's Lynn, Norfolk

British Library Cataloguing in Publication Data
A catalogue record for this book is available
from the British Library

Library of Congress Cataloging in Publication Data
Katamba, Francis, 1947–
    English words / Francis Katamba. – 2nd ed.
        p. cm.
    Includes bibliographical references and indexes.
    1. Lexicology. 2. English language–Etymology.
    3. English language–New words. 4. English language–Word
    formation. I. Title.
    PE1571.K38 2004
    423'.028–dc22   2003027962

ISBN 0–415–29892–X (hbk)
ISBN 0–415–29893–8 (pbk)

To Janet, Francis and Helen

Contents

List of illustrations   xi
Preface to the first edition   xiii
Preface to the second edition   xv
Acknowledgements   xvi
Key to symbols used   xviii
Abbreviations   xx

PART I
The nature and internal structure of words   **I**

1 Introduction   **3**

  1.1 Why study words?   3
  1.2 Overview of coming chapters   8

2 What is a word?   **10**

  2.1 Introduction   10
  2.2 Words are like liquorice allsorts   11
  2.3 Summary   25
    Exercises   25

3 Close encounters of a morphemic kind   **27**

  3.1 The quest for verbal atoms   27
  3.2 Close morphological encounters: zooming in on
    morphemes   27
  3.3 Morphemes and their disguises   31
  3.4 Freedom and bondage   43

3.5 Sound symbolism: phonaesthemes and
     onomatopoeia   44
3.6 Summary   47
     Exercises   48

4 **Building words**   **50**

4.1 Words and jigsaws   50
4.2 Know the pieces of the jigsaw   50
4.3 The main types of word-building: inflection and
     derivation   53
4.4 Derivation: fabricating words   56
4.5 Listing and institutionalisation   74
4.6 Keeping tabs on idioms   75
4.7 Clitics   77
4.8 Summary   81
     Exercises   82

PART II
Words in a wider context   **85**

5 **A lexicon with layers**   **87**

5.1 The nature of the lexicon   87
5.2 Morphological information in the lexicon   88
5.3 Syntactic information in the lexicon   88
5.4 Does it ring true? (phonological information)   89
5.5 Rendezvous with lexical phonology and
     morphology   90
5.6 Productivity, the time-warp and cranberries   100
5.7 Peeping beyond the lexicon   104
5.8 Base-driven stratification   105
5.9 Summary   109
     Exercises   110

6 **Word meaning**   **113**

6.1 Introducing meaning   113
6.2 Word-meaning   114
6.3 Sense and componential analysis   117
6.4 Semantic relations   118
6.5 Semantic fields   125
6.6 Semantic prototypes: the birdiness rankings   127

6.7 *Beyond the lexicon*   129
6.8 *Summary*   130
     Exercises   130

PART III
A changing, expanding lexicon   **133**

7 A lexical mosaic: sources of English vocabulary   **135**

7.1 *The nature of borrowing*   135
7.2 *Scandinavian loanwords*   150
7.3 *The French influence*   151
7.4 *Words from other modern European languages*   158
7.5 *Loanwords from non-European languages*   159
7.6 *The Germanic inheritance*   162
7.7 *Summary*   164
     Exercises   165

8 Words galore: innovation and change   **168**

8.1 *A verbal bonanza*   168
8.2 *Jargon*   168
8.3 *Slang*   169
8.4 *Rhyming slang*   170
8.5 *Clichés and catch-phrases*   172
8.6 *A rose by any other name*   173
8.7 *Clipping*   180
8.8 *Acronyms and abbreviations*   183
8.9 *Fads and copycat formations*   184
8.10 *Back-formation*   185
8.11 *Blends*   186
8.12 *Geek-speak: internet slang and jargon*   186
8.13 *Euphemism*   190
8.14 *Summary*   193
      Exercises   194

9 Should English be spelt as she is spoke?   **197**

9.1 *Writing systems*   197
9.2 *Is the English orthography mad?*   197
9.3 *Morphological signposts in the spelling*   212
9.4 *Lexical signposting in the spelling*   213

9.5 *Spelling reform*   214
9.6 *Is speech degenerate writing?*   220
9.7 *Email and text messaging: imo email & txt r gr8*   222
9.8 *Summary*   228
     Exercises   228

PART IV
Modelling the mental lexicon   **233**

10 Speech recognition   **235**

10.1 *A mind full of words*   235
10.2 *Modelling the mental lexicon*   240
10.3 *Speech recognition*   244
10.4 *Speech recognition models*   253
10.5 *Summary*   261
      Exercises   262

11 Speech production   **264**

11.1 *Modelling speech production*   264
11.2 *Slips of the tongue as evidence for the model*   268
11.3 *Selecting words*   276
11.4 *Aphasia*   283
11.5 *Summary*   289
      Exercises   290

      Glossary   292
      Notes   301
      Bibliography   302
      Name Index   312
      Subject Index   315

Illustrations

[1.2]	Lewis Carroll's Humpty Dumpty	6
[2.11]	'Waiter, do you serve shrimps?' joke	20
[3.18]	Spike Milligan's 'On the Ning Nang Nong'	46
[4.7]	Passage from Roald Dahl's *The BFG*	55
[5.5]	Sample derivation no. 1 showing hierarchical strata	94
[5.6]	Sample derivation no. 2 showing hierarchical strata	95
[5.7]	Sample derivation no. 3 showing hierarchical strata	96
[6.5]	Semiotic triangle	115
[6.9]	Semantic features	117
[6.13]	Co-hyponym hierarchy	119
[6.20]	Extract from the *Cambridge Learner's Dictionary* showing polysemy	123
[6.24]	Semantic fields: colour terms	126–7
[6.25]	Birdiness rankings	128
[6.30]	'On her Birthday Sarah felt like a nineteen year old' greetings card	132
[7.7]	Foreign words in the history of English (numbers in use)	143
[7.8]	Foreign words in the history of English (percentages)	143
[8.28]	'Quidditch injuries' cartoon	191
[8.29]	'Electric chair' cartoon	193
[9.1]	Get around in English: how to pronounce the **th** sound	198
[9.13]	Spike Milligan's 'Questions, Quistions & Quoshtions'	209–10
[9.21]	'Beg Parding': English children's rhyme	215
[9.22]	Reformed English spellings	218
[9.28]	Top 10 smileys	226

[9.29]   Eazy-E: 'It's on (Dr Dre) 187um Killa' webpage
         advertisement   231
[10.19] The Cohort model of word recognition   256
[10.20] The TRACE model of speech perception   258
[11.1]   An overview of language production processes   265
[11.27] Fragment of a lexical network   278
[11.28] General knowledge questions and phonological
         processing   282
[11.29] 'Again Mariner and Butcher are trying to work
         the oracle' cartoon   283
[11.30] The brain and language processing   284–5

Preface to the first edition

This book developed out of a course on English words that I have taught at Lancaster over the last few years. It is intended to arouse curiosity about English words and about language in general, especially among students who are not intending to specialise in linguistics.

Is it not strange that we spend so many of our waking hours talking and yet we know so little about words? Putting words under a microscope and peering at them seems to be a dead boring and absolutely unrewarding subject. Most people know more about sport, cars, computers, gardening, virtually anything than they know about words. If you are one of them, then read on.

This book was written for you. It is intended to disabuse you of the false impression that investigating words is tedious, dry and totally unenjoyable. *English Words* takes you on a voyage of discovery during which you find out how words are structured, how they convey meaning, how their spelling relates to pronunciation, how new words are manufactured, how the meaning of words changes as time passes and how words are imported from other languages. Finally, in the concluding chapter we marvel at the ability you and I have to store tens of thousands of words in our minds and to retrieve the right words instantaneously in conversation. All this is exciting stuff.

Traditionally, the student is not offered a single course or coursebook that covers all the various topics that I have listed above. My aim in departing from normal practice by covering such a wide range of topics in one book is to provide a synthesis of what linguists and students of neighbouring disciplines such as psychology have found out about words. So, this book gives a panoramic view of words in the English language. I think there is some virtue in making sure that students do not concentrate so hard on seeing the trees that they miss the forest.

Another feature of the book is that it is primarily a descriptive study of words in the English language. It is only very occasionally that the structure of words in other languages is discussed.

No previous knowledge of linguistics is assumed. I keep linguistic theory and jargon mostly in the background and focus on the description. Studying the contents of this book will not turn you into a morphologist, but it will teach you a lot of things about English.

Your involvement in learning about English words is important. You will not be invited to watch all the interesting things about words from a distance as a mere spectator. Plenty of examples and exercises are provided for you to do some of the investigations yourself.

It is my pleasure to thank many people who have helped me in various ways during the preparation of this book. First, I acknowledge the help of my family. The writing and preparation of the book would have been an even more arduous task without their constant support and active help in hunting for examples and illustrations.

I am also grateful to various other people whose comments, advice and support have been very useful. I thank Claire L'Enfant, Senior Editor at Routledge, who started it all when she invited me to undertake this project and would not take no for an answer. In addition, I would like to thank the editorial and design staff at Routledge, in particular Beth Humphries and Emma Cotter for their advice and help in the preparation of this book. Next, I would like to thank in a special way first-year undergraduates on *Course LING 152: English Words* at Lancaster over the last couple of years who have been such co-operative, critical and really excellent guinea pigs.

I am also grateful to a number of colleagues and friends. I thank Jenny Thomas, Mick Short and Keith Brown, who commented on part of an early draft. And I thank Ton That Ai Quang from whom I received the Vietnamese data. Finally, above all, I am indebted to Dick Hudson and an anonymous American reader who went through the entire manuscript thoroughly and provided numerous useful comments and suggestions on matters of substance and presentation. The book is much better in every way than it would otherwise have been without their assistance. Any imperfections that still remain are my responsibility.

Francis Katamba
Lancaster, 1993

Preface to the second edition

In preparing the second edition I have had the benefit of a lot of feedback from teachers who have used this book. To them all I am very grateful. I will single out Steven Jones of the University of Central Lancashire who urged me to produce a second edition of the book and offered many useful suggestions. In the light of the feedback, the book has been significantly modified. There is more emphasis on psycholinguistics and there is updated coverage of expansion and evolution of the English lexicon, taking into account the impact of mobile phone and internet technologies.

I would also like to thank my publishers, Christabel Kirkpatrick and Kate Parker at Routledge, for their patience, helpfulness and professionalism.

Francis Katamba
Lancaster, 2004

Acknowledgements

American Psychological Association, The and the authors James, Lori E. and Burke, Deborah M., for the figure 'Example of presentation of general knowledge questions and phenological processing' from the *Journal of Experimental Psychology: Learning, Memory and Cognition*, vol. 26/6 © 2000.

CartoonStock, for permission to reproduce cartoons 'We've had a lot of these "quidditch" injuries since "Harry Potter" was released!' and 'Just an idea, but we could do these at once if we had an electric sofa'.

Crystal, David (1997) *The Cambridge Encyclopedia of Language*, 2nd edn. Cambridge: Cambridge University Press. Brain diagrams from p. 263 copyright © Cambridge University Press. Reproduced with permission.

Dahl, Roald (1982) *The BFG*. London: Jonathan Cape. Illustration by Quentin Blake reprinted by permission of The Random House Group Ltd.

Emotional Rescue Ltd, for permission to reproduce greetings card 'On her Birthday Sarah felt like a nineteen year old'.

Faber and Faber Ltd, for permission to reproduce 'On the Ning Nang Nong' and 'Questions, Quistions & Quoshtions' by Spike Milligan.

Fantoni, B. (1984) *Private Eye's Colemanballs 2*. London: *Private Eye/* André Deutsch. Martin Tyler cartoon by Bill Tidy copyright © Pressdram Limited 2003.

Harley, T. (2001) *The Psychology of Language: From Data to Theory*, 2nd edn. Hove: The Psychology Press. Figure from p. 229 reproduced with permission.

James, Lori E. and Burke, Deborah M. (2000) 'Phonological Priming Effects on Word Retrieval and Tip-of-the-Tongue Experiences in Young and Older Adults'. *Journal of Experimental Psychology: Learning, Memory, and Cognition*, 26 (6): 1378–91. Figure 2 from p. 1382 reproduced with permission.

Lee Gone Publications, for permission to reproduce *How To Be British* (postcard no. 20: 'How to Pronounce the *th*') © LGP, Brighton (www.lgpcards.com).

McClelland, J. M. and Elman, J. L. (1986) 'The TRACE model of speech perception'. *Cognitive Psychology* 18: 1–86. Figure 2 from p. 9 reproduced with permission from Elsevier.

Simpson, James (1979) *A First Course in Linguistics*. Edinburgh: Edinburgh University Press. Permission to reproduce Figure 39 from p. 189.

Young, J. and Young, P. (1981) *The Ladybird Book of Jokes, Riddles and Rhymes*. Loughborough: Ladybird Books. Permission to reproduce the 'Shrimp' joke and illustration from p. 40. Copyright © Ladybird Books Ltd.

Every effort has been made to trace and contact copyright holders. The publishers would be pleased to hear from any copyright holders not acknowledged here so that this acknowledgements page may be amended at the earliest opportunity.

Key to symbols used

Symbols for phonemes

A key word for each phoneme is given, first in ordinary spelling and then in phonemic transcription. The phonemic transcription represents the pronunciation in British Received Pronunciation.

Vowels

/ɪ/	sit	/sɪt/	/eɪ/	eight	/eɪt/
/e/	set	/set/	/aɪ/	pie	/paɪ/
/æ/	sat	/sæt/	/ɔɪ/	toil	/tɔɪl/
/ʌ/	mud	/mʌd/	/ɪə/	beer	/bɪə/
/ɒ/	dog	/dɒg/	/ɔə/	bore	/bɔə/
/ʊ/	good	/gʊd/	/ʊə/	boor	/bʊə/
/ə/	send<u>er</u>	/sendə/	/əʊ/	low	/ləʊ/
	<u>a</u>bove	/əbʌv/	/aʊ/	town	/taʊn/

/iː/	seed	/siːd/
/ɑː/	bar	/bɑː/
/ɔː/	saw	/sɔː/
/uː/	zoo	/zuː/
/ɜː/	fur	/fɜː/
/eə/	bare	/beə/

Consonants

/tʃ/	chest	/tʃest/	/m/	mail	/meɪl/
/dʒ/	jest	/dʒest/	/n/	nail	/neɪl/
			/ŋ/	long	/lɒŋ/
/j/	yes	/jes/	/l/	leap	/liːp/
/w/	win	/wɪn/	/r/	rip	/rɪp/

/f/	fan	/fæn/	/p/	pan	/pæn/
/v/	van	/væn/	/b/	ban	/bæn/
/θ/	thin	/θɪn/	/t/	tan	/tæn/
/ð/	then	/ðen/	/d/	did	/dɪd/
/s/	seal	/siːl/	/k/	kit	/kɪt/
/z/	zeal	/ziːl/	/g/	get	/get/
/ʃ/	ship	/ʃɪp/			
/ʒ/	measure	/meʒə/			
/h/	hop	/hɒp/			

Non-phonemic symbols

[ʔ] Glottal stop as in *water* /wɔːʔə/ as said in accents where between vowels the *t* 'can be swallowed'.

[ɫ] Dark l.

[l] Clear l.

ˌ (Under a consonant) denotes syllabic consonant as in *kettle* [ketɫ]

Other symbols

ā The symbol ‾ over a vowel indicates that it is a long vowel.

˙ A raised dot indicates that the preceding vowel is stressed (in examples from *OED*).

< Is derived from.

> Becomes, develops into.

ˋ Marks main stress on the following syllable.

ˈ Marks secondary stress.

* An asterisk shows that a given form is disallowed.

/ / Slashes indicate a *broad* or phonemic transcription which only shows phonemes.

[ ] Square brackets indicate a *narrow* (i.e. detailed) transcription that shows allophones.

~ This indicates that forms alternate.

→ Rewrite as; or becomes (depending on context).

( ) Optional items are put in parenthesis.

Small capitals

Small capitals are used for technical terms when first introduced and occasionally thereafter to highlight their technical sense.

Abbreviations

Adj.	adjective
Adv.	adverb
Af.	Affix
Ag.	agent
Det.	determiner
FLH	Full Listing Hypothesis
LP	lexical phonology
ME	Middle English
N	noun
NP	noun phrase
Obj.	object
OE	Old English
OED	*Oxford English Dictionary*
ON	Old Norse
P	pronoun
Pat.	patient
PP	prepositional phrase
Pres.	present
RP	received pronunciation
RDUES	Research and Development Unit for English Studies
S	sentence
Sing.	singular
Subj.	subject
V	verb
V_{en}	verb ending in -en (past participle)
V_{ing}	verb ending in -ing (present participle)
VP	verb phrase

Part I

The nature and internal structure of words

The opening chapter introduces the main themes of the book. The next chapter examines and clarifies the concept 'word'. Chapter 3 investigates the basic elements of word structure and Chapter 4 explores how complex words are built.

Chapter 1

Introduction

1.1 Why study words?

Imagine a life without words! Trappist monks opt for it. But most of us would not give up words for anything. Every day we utter thousands and thousands of words. Communicating our joys, fears, opinions, fantasies, wishes, requests, demands, feelings – and the occasional threat or insult – is a very important aspect of being human. The air is always thick with our verbal emissions. There are so many things we want to tell the world. Some of them are important, some of them are not. But we talk anyway – even when we know that what we are saying is totally unimportant. We love chitchat and find silent encounters awkward, or even oppressive. A life without words would be a horrendous privation.

It is a cliché to say that words and language are probably humankind's most valuable single possession. It is language that sets us apart from our biologically close relatives, the great primates. (I would imagine that many a chimp or gorilla would give an arm and a leg for a few words – but we will probably never know because they cannot tell us.) Yet, surprisingly, most of us take words (and more generally language) for granted. We cannot discuss words with anything like the competence with which we can discuss fashion, films or football.

We should not take words for granted. They are too important. This book is intended to make explicit some of the things that we know subconsciously about words. It is a linguistic introduction to the nature and structure of English words. It addresses the question, 'what sorts of things do people need to know about English words in order to use them in speech?' It is intended to increase the degree of sophistication with which you think about words. It is designed to give you a theoretical grasp of English word-formation, the sources and evolution of English vocabulary and the way in which we store words and retrieve them from the mind.

I hope a desirable side effect of working through *English Words* will be the enrichment of your vocabulary. This book will help to increase, in a very practical way, your awareness of the relationship between words. You will be equipped with the tools you need to work out the meanings of unfamiliar words and to see in a new light the underlying structural patterns in many familiar words which you have not previously stopped to think about analytically.

For the student of language, words are a very rewarding object of study. An understanding of the nature of words provides us with a key that opens the door to an understanding of important aspects of the nature of language in general. Words give us a panoramic view of the entire field of linguistics because they impinge on every aspect of language structure. This book stresses the ramifications of the fact that words are complex and multi-faceted entities whose structure and use interacts with the other modules of the grammar such as PHONOLOGY, the study of how sounds are used to represent words in speech; SYNTAX, the study of sentence structure; and SEMANTICS, the study of meaning in language.

In order to use even a very simple word, such as *frog*, we need to access various types of information from the word-store which we all carry around with us in the MENTAL LEXICON or DICTIONARY that is tucked away in the mind. We need to know:

[1.1] 1 its shape, i.e. its PHONOLOGICAL REPRESENTATION /frɒg/ which enables us to pronounce it, and its ORTHOGRAPHIC REPRESENTATION *frog*, if we are literate and know how to spell it (see the Key to symbols used on pages xvii–xix);
2 its grammatical properties, e.g. it is a noun and it is countable – so you can have one *frog* and two *frogs*;
3 its meaning.

But words tend not to wear their meaning on their sleeve. Normally, there is nothing about the form of words that would enable anyone to work out their meaning. Thus, the fact that *frog* refers to one of these guys 🐸 simply has to be listed in the lexicon and committed to memory by brute force. For, typically, the relationship between a LINGUISTIC SIGN like the word *frog* and its meaning is ARBITRARY. Other languages use different words to refer to this small tailless amphibian of the genus Rana. In French it is called *(la) grenouille*. In Malay they call it *katak* and in Swahili *chura*. None of these words is more suited than the others to the job of referring to this creature.

And, of course, within a particular language, any particular pronunciation can be associated with any meaning. So long as speakers accept that sound–meaning association, they have a kosher word. For instance, *convenience* originally meant 'suitability' or 'commodiousness', but in the middle of the nineteenth century a new meaning of 'toilet' was assigned to it and people began to talk of 'a public convenience'. In the early 1960s the word acquired the additional new meaning of 'easy to use, designed for hassle-free use' as in *convenience food*.

As Humpty Dumpty pointed out to Alice, we are the masters and words are our servants. We can make them mean whatever we want them to mean. The only thing missing from Humpty Dumpty's analysis is the social dimension. Any arbitrary meaning assigned to a word needs to be accepted by the speech community which uses the language. Obviously, language would not be much use as a means of communication if each individual language user assigned a private meaning to each word which other users of the language did not recognise. Apart from that, it is instructive to listen in on the lesson on the nature of language that Humpty Dumpty gave to Alice ([1.2] on p. 6).

Let us now consider one further example. All competent speakers of English know that you can add -*s* to a noun to indicate that it refers to more than one entity. So, you say *cat* when referring to one and *cats* if there is more than one. If you encountered in the blank in [1.3a] an unfamiliar word like *splet* (which I have just made up), you would automatically know from the context that it must have the plural form *splets* in this position since it is specified as plural by *all*. Further, you would know that the plural of *splet* must be *splets* (rather than *spletren* by analogy to *children* or *spleti* by analogy to *stimuli*). You know that the majority of nouns form their plural by adding the regular plural suffix or ending -*s*. You always add -*s* unless express instructions are given to do otherwise. There is no need to memorise separately the plural form of most nouns. All we need is to know the rule that says 'add -*s* for plural'. So, without any hesitation, you suffix -*s* to obtain the plural form *splets* in [1.3b]:

[1.3] a   We put all the big _____ on the table.
       b   We put all the big *splets* on the table.

[1.2]

'As I was saying, that *seems* to be done right – though I haven't time to look it over thoroughly just now – and that shows that there are three hundred and sixty-four days when you might get unbirthday presents –'

'Certainly,' said Alice.

'And only *one* for birthday presents, you know. There's glory for you!'

'I don't know what you mean by "glory",' Alice said.

Humpty Dumpty smiled contemptuously. 'Of course you don't – till I tell you. I meant "there's a nice knock-down argument for you!"'

'But "glory" doesn't mean "a nice knock-down argument",' Alice objected.

'When *I* use a word,' Humpty Dumpty said in a rather scornful tone, 'it means just what I choose it to mean – neither more nor less.'

'The question is,' said Alice, 'whether you *can* make words mean so many different things.'

'The question is,' said Humpty Dumpty, 'which is to be master – that's all.'

(Carroll 1982: 274)

The study of word-formation and word-structure is called MORPHOLOGY. Morphological theory provides a general theory of word-structure in all the languages of the world. Its task is to characterise the kinds of things that speakers need to know about the structure of the words of their language in order to be able to use them to produce and to understand speech.

We will see that, in order to use language, speakers need to have two types of morphological knowledge. First, they need to be able to analyse existing words (e.g. they must be able to tell that *frogs* contains *frog* plus *-s* for plural). Usually, if we know the meanings of the elements that a word contains, it is possible to determine the meaning of the entire word once we have worked out how the various elements relate to each other. For instance, if we examine a word like *nutcracker* we find that it is made up of two words, namely the noun *nut* and the noun *cracker*. Furthermore, we see that the latter word, *cracker*, is divisible into the verb *crack* and another meaningful element *-er* (roughly meaning 'an instrument used to do X'), which, however, is not a word in its own right. Numerous other words are formed using this pattern of combining words (and smaller meaningful elements) as seen in [1.4]:

[1.4] $[[\text{tea}]_{\text{Noun}}\text{-}[\text{strain-er}]_{\text{Noun}}]_{\text{Noun}}$
$[[\text{lawn}]_{\text{Noun}}\text{-}[\text{mow-er}]_{\text{Noun}}]_{\text{Noun}}$
$[[\text{can}]_{\text{Noun}}\text{-}[\text{open-er}]_{\text{Noun}}]_{\text{Noun}}$

Given the frame $[[\underline{\hspace{2cm}}]_{\text{Noun}}\text{-}[\underline{\hspace{2cm}} \text{er}]_{\text{Noun}}]_{\text{Noun}}$, we can fill in different words with the appropriate properties and get another compound word (i.e. a word containing at least two words) which is also a noun. Try this frame out yourself. Find two more similar examples of compound words formed using this pattern.

Second, speakers need to be able to work out the meanings of novel words constructed using the word-building elements and standard word-construction rules of the language. Probably we all know and use more words than are listed in dictionaries. We can construct and analyse the structure and meaning of old words as well as new ones. So, although many words must be listed in the dictionary and memorised, listing every word in the dictionary is not necessary. If a word is formed following general principles, it may be more efficient to reconstitute it from its constituent elements as the need arises rather than permanently commit it to memory. When people make up new words using existing words and word-forming elements, we understand them with ease – providing we know what the elements they use to form those words mean and providing the word-forming rules that they employ are familiar. This ability is one of the things explored in morphological investigations. A challenging question which morphology addresses is, 'how do speakers know which non-occurring or non-established words are permissible and which ones are not?' Why is *hovercraftful* allowed while *hoverment is not?

Morphology provides a general theory of word-formation applicable to any language but, as mentioned earlier, this book focuses on word-formation in English. Its objective is to provide a description of English words designed to make explicit the various things speakers know, albeit in an unconscious manner, about English words. The emphasis will be on the description of English words from a variety of perspectives rather than the elaboration of morphological theory. So, data and facts about English words are brought to the fore and the theoretical and methodological issues are kept in the background for the most part. The use of formal notation has also been kept to a minimum in order to keep the account simple.

1.2 Overview of coming chapters

At the very outset we need to establish the nature of the subject we are going to be examining. The rest of the chapters in this part deal with the nature and internal structure of words. Chapter 2 clarifies what we mean by 'word'; Chapter 3 investigates the basic elements of word structure; and Chapter 4 explores the construction of complex words. In the course of the discussion traditional morphological concepts of structural linguistics are introduced and extensively exemplified.

Morphology is not a stand-alone module. So, Part 2 puts words in the wider context. Chapter 5 introduces Lexical Phonology and Morphology, a theory where phonological and morphological rules have an intimate relationship. For Chapter 5 we stay in the lexicon and consider words from the point of view of meaning. (Although there is not a single chapter devoted to the behaviour of words in the syntax, throughout the book there are frequent discussions of syntactic patterns formed by words.)

Part 3 highlights the dynamic nature of the lexicon. The vocabulary of English is constantly changing and expanding. Chapter 7 discusses the effects of the massive infusion of words from other languages over the centuries and in Chapter 8 attention shifts to the ways in which the vocabulary has expanded by using the internal resources of the language. The last chapter in the part (Chapter 9) looks at the relationship between words in speech and in writing. Is writing simply a mirror of speech – and an apparently distorting one in the case of English? Why is English spelling not altogether transparent? The answers provided have an evolutionary slant. We consider historical changes in the sound pattern of English that are not reflected in the orthography due to its conservatism. We also consider the effect on spelling of technological advances such as the invention of printing (and the decision by Caxton to set up a printing press in London in 1476). The part ends with an account of the impact of the internet and mobile phone texting language on written English in our day.

The final part is devoted to the MENTAL LEXICON. Here we pull together the various strands developed in earlier chapters. We address questions like: 'What does knowing a word mean?'; 'How do we manage to store such a vast number of words in the mind and to retrieve just the right one instantaneously in speech?'; and 'How do we go from an abstract concept to physically uttering words when we speak?'. To tackle these questions we use psycholinguistic models of speech recognition in Chapter 10, and of speech production in Chapter 11.

I have already stressed the point that morphology is not a self-contained module of language. Any discussion of word-formation touches on other areas of linguistics, notably phonology and syntax, so I have provided a key to the list of pronunciation symbols at the beginning of the book. I have also included at the end a glossary of linguistic terms (many of them from other branches of linguistics) which might be unfamiliar. But still I may have missed out some terms that you might be unsure about. If you encounter any unfamiliar technical terms that are not explained in this book, I suggest that you consult a good dictionary of linguistics like Crystal (2002). Sometimes it is useful to present data using phonetic notation. A key to the phonetic symbols used is to be found on pp. xvii–xix.

After this introductory chapter, all chapters contain exercises. Several of the analytical exercises require you to look up words and parts of words in a good dictionary like the *Oxford English Dictionary (OED)*. Access to such a dictionary is essential when you work through this book. This is a practical way of learning about the structure of English words (and may also be a useful way of enriching your vocabulary).

Chapter 2

What is a word?

2.1 Introduction

Often we find it very difficult to give a clear and systematic account of everyday things, ideas, actions and events that surround us. We just take them for granted. We rarely need to state in an accurate and articulate manner what they are really like. For instance, we all know what a game is. Yet, as the philosopher Wittgenstein showed, we find it very difficult to state explicitly what the simple word *game* means. Tennis, tig, football and chess are all games. But we are hard pressed to say what they have in common.

The same is true of the term *word*. We use words all the time. We intuitively know what the words in our language are. Nevertheless, most of us would be hard pushed to explain to anyone what kind of object a word is. If a couple of Martian explorers (with a rudimentary understanding of English) came off their space-ship and stopped you in the street to enquire what earthlings meant by the term WORD, what would you tell them? I suspect you might be somewhat vague and evasive. Although you know very well what words are, you might find it difficult to express explicitly and succinctly what it is that you know about them.

The purpose of this chapter is to try to find an answer to the question, what is a word? It is not only Martian explorers curious about the way earthlings live who might want to know what words are. We too have an interest in understanding words because they play such an important role in our lives. As we saw in the last chapter, it is impossible to imagine human society without language. And, equally, it is impossible to imagine a human language that has no words of any kind and to understand the nature of language without gaining some understanding of the nature of words. So, in this chapter we will clarify what we mean when we use the term 'word'. This clarification is essential if our investigations are to make any headway for, as you will see presently, we mean quite a few very different things when we talk of words.

A standard definition of the word is found in a paper written in 1926 by the American linguist Leonard Bloomfield, one of the greatest linguists of the twentieth century. According to Bloomfield, 'a minimum free form is a word'. By this he meant that the word is the smallest meaningful linguistic unit that can be used on its own. It is a form that cannot be divided into any smaller units that can be used independently to convey meaning. For example *child* is a word. We cannot divide it up into smaller units that can convey meaning when they stand alone.

Contrast this with the word *childish* which can be analysed into *child-* and *-ish*. While the *child* bit of *childish* is meaningful when used on its own (and hence is a word), the same is not true of *-ish*. Although according to the *Oxford English Dictionary (OED)* *-ish* means something like 'having the (objectionable) qualities of' (as in *mannish, womanish, devilish, sheepish, apish* etc.), there is no way we can use it on its own. If someone shouted to you in the street, 'Hey, are you *-ish?*', you might smile bemusedly and think to yourself, 'Isn't he weird!' In the next chapter we will take up the question of what to do with pieces of words that cannot be used meaningfully on their own. But for the moment we will focus exclusively on words.

2.2 Words are like liquorice allsorts

When we talk of words we do not always mean exactly the same thing. Like liquorice allsorts, words come in all sorts of varieties. We will start our discussions by distinguishing the different senses in which we use the term 'word'.

2.2.1 Word forms

Let us use the term WORD-FORM to describe the physical form which realises or represents a word in speech or writing. Consider the words in the following extract from T. S. Eliot's poem:

[2.1] Half-past one,
      The street-lamp sputtered,
      The street-lamp muttered,
      The street-lamp said, 'Regard that woman

Who hesitates towards you in the light of the door
Which opens on her like a grin . . .'
('Rhapsody on a windy night' in Eliot (1963))

In written English, words are easy to recognise. They are preceded by a space and followed by a space. Using this criterion, we can say that there are thirty-one words (i.e. word-forms) in the extract from 'Rhapsody'. We will call word-forms like these which we find in writing ORTHOGRAPHIC WORDS. If you look again at the extract, you might wonder if some of the hyphenated orthographic words are 'really' individual words. Many people would hyphenate *half-past* as Eliot does but not *street-lamp*. They would write *street lamp* as two separate words, with a space between them. What would you do?

The use of hyphens to indicate that something is a complex word containing more than one word-like unit is variable, largely depending on how transparent the compound nature of a word is. Shakespeare wrote *today* as *to-day* and *tomorrow* as *to-morrow*:

[2.2] a To-morrow, Caesar,
I shall be furnished to inform you rightly . . .
(Anthony and Cleopatra, I, iv)

b O! that we now had here
But ten thousand of those men in England
That do not work to-day.
(Henry V, IV, iii)

Hyphenating *to-day* and *to-morrow* is less common now, probably because most speakers are unaware of the compound nature of these words. *Today* comes from Old English *tō dæġ* 'to + day' and *tomorrow* is from Middle English *to mor(e)we* (i.e. to (the) morrow) – *to-* can be traced back ultimately to a form that meant 'this' in Indo-European. Note in passing that three major periods are distinguished in the history of the English language: Old English (conventionally abbreviated as OE) was spoken *c.*450–1100; Middle English (conventionally abbreviated as ME) was spoken *c.*1100–1500 and Modern English from 1500 to the present.

Generally, the use of the hyphen in such words that are no longer seen as compounds is in decline. The hyphen tends to be mostly used in compounds that are regarded as fairly new words. Many well-established words that are transparently compounded, e.g. *schoolboy*, are normally written without a hyphen. Of course, judgements as to what is an established word vary greatly. There are few firm rules here. For instance, in the *OED* both *seaway* and *sea-way* are shown to be accepted ways of writing the word pronounced as /siːweɪ/. Similarly, the compilers of the *OED* show variation in the way they enter both hyphenated *first-rate* and *first rate* written as two words separated by a space.

Interestingly, hyphenation is also used creatively to indicate that an idea that would normally be expressed by a phrase is being treated as a single word for communicative purposes because it has crystallised in the writer's mind into a firm, single concept. Thus, for example, the expression *simple to serve* is normally a phrase, just like *easy to control*. But it can also be used as a hyphenated word as in *simple-to-serve recipe dishes* (*M&S Magazine* 1992: 9). Similarly, on page 48 of the same magazine, the writer of an advertising feature uses the phrase 'fresh from the farm' as a hyphenated word in 'fresh-from-the-farm eggs'.

But for creative hyphenation you are unlikely to find anything more striking than this:

[2.3] On Pitcairn there is little evidence of the *what-we-have-we-hold, no-surrender*, the *Queen's-picture-in-every-room* sort of attitude.
>   (Simon Winchester in *The Guardian* magazine, 12 June 1993: 27; italic added to highlight the compounds)

The Research and Development Unit for English Studies (RDUES) at the University of Liverpool is producing a database of neologisms in journalistic English taken from *The Independent* newspaper of London. They include numerous examples of complex hyphenated compound words such as:

[2.4] Love explains to Allure magazine why she loves the schizophrenia of LA: You've got your Moorish next to your Mediterranean next to your modern next to your British ex-patriate next to your aspiring starlet next to your *ex-madam-now-action-movie-transsexual* post-op next to your triple-A writer ex-crackhead Spanish-Chinese nursery owner.
>   (RDUES 1999)

Rephrase – *ex-madam-now-action-movie-transsexual* without using a hyphenated compound. Which version is more effective? Why?

What we have established is that, as a rule, orthographic words have a space on either side of them. But there are cases where this simple rule of thumb is not followed. There is a degree of flexibility in the way in which words are written down: being, or not being, separated by a space is in itself not a sure sign of word status. Some orthographic words which are uncontroversially written as one unit contain two words within them. They are compound words like *firstrate*, *seaway*, *wheelbarrow* and *teapot*. Furthermore, there are forms like *they're*, *hadn't* and *I'm* which are joined together in writing yet which are not compound words. When you scratch the skin, you see immediately that *they're* and *I'm* are really versions of the pairs of words *they are* and *I am*. Our theory needs to say something about awkward customers like these. Since the issues they raise are complex, we will postpone discussion of them until section (4.7). Finally, there are words which are compounded (and maybe hyphenated as in [2.3] and [2.4] above) as a one-off to crystallise a particular meaning.

So far we have only considered orthographic words, i.e. recognisable physical written word-forms. Obviously, words as physical objects exist not only in writing, but also in speech. We will now briefly turn to word-forms in spoken language. We will refer to them as PHONOLOGICAL WORDS.

The challenge of word recognition arises in an even more obvious way when we consider speech (see Chapters 10 and 11). Words are not separated distinctly from each other. We do not leave a pause between words that could be equated to a space in writing. (If we did that, conversation would be painfully slow! Just try speaking to one of your friends today leaving a two-second gap between words. See how they react.) In normal speech words come out in a torrent. They overlap. Just as droplets of water cannot be seen flowing down a river, individual words do not stand out discretely in the flow of conversation. So they are much harder to isolate than words in writing. None the less, we are able to isolate them. If you heard an utterance like:

[2.5] The cat slept in your bed.
    /ðə kæt slept in ˈjɔː bed/
            Notes: ˈ shows that the following syllable is stressed; phonemic transcription is written between slant lines.

you would be able to recognise the six phonological words that have been written in PHONEMIC TRANSCRIPTION, i.e. transcription which shows the PHONEMES. Phonemes are sounds that contrast word meaning in a particular language, e.g. in English /p/ and /b/ are distinct phonemes since they distinguish words like *pat* and *bat*. In this book phonemic transcriptions and references to pronunciation will be based on RECEIVED PRONUNCIATION (RP), the prestige accent of standard British English – the variety popularly known as the Queen's English or BBC English.

An intriguing question that linguists and psychologists have tried to answer is: how do people recognise words in speech? We will address this question in detail in section (10.3). For now let us simply assume that phonological words can be identified. Our present task will simply be to outline some of their key properties. To do this it will be useful to distinguish between two types of words: the so-called CONTENT WORDS and FUNCTION WORDS. Content words are the nouns, verbs, adjectives and adverbs which contain most of the REFERENTIAL (or COGNITIVE MEANING) of a sentence. This roughly means that they name individuals and predicate of them certain properties. They tell us, for instance, what happened or who did what to whom, and in what circumstances. An example will make the point clear. In the old days, when people sent telegrams, it was content words that were mainly (or exclusively) used. A proud parent could send a message like *Baby girl arrived yesterday* which contained two nouns, a verb and an adverb. Obviously, this is not a well-formed, grammatical sentence. But its meaning would be clear enough.

Function words are the rest – prepositions, pronouns, conjunctions, articles and so on. They have a predominantly grammatical role. A telegram containing only the words *She it and for us* would convey little idea of what the intended interpretation was. This is not to say that function words are superfluous. Without them sentences are usually ungrammatical. A sentence like **Nelly went town*, which lacks the preposition *to*, is not permitted. We have to say *Nelly went to town*.

In English, one of the syllables of a content word is more prominent than the rest because it receives MAIN STRESS. Main stress is preceded by `'`:

[2.6] *Initial stress*   *Medial stress*   *Final stress*

Initial stress	*Medial stress*	*Final stress*
'acrobat	a'nnoying	ca'hoots
'kingfisher	de'molish	gaber'dine
'patriarchate	Chau'cerian	hullaba'loo

Main stress can fall on only one syllable in a word. The location of main stress is part of the make-up of a word and is not changed capriciously by individual speakers. You cannot decide to stress *hullabaloo* on the first syllable on a Monday (`*hullabaloo*) and on the final syllable for the rest of the week (*hullaba`loo*).

However, in some cases, if we wish to contrast two related words, we can shift stress from its normal position to a new position. This can be seen in `*vendor* and *ven`dee* which normally are stressed on the first and second syllable respectively. But if the speaker wants to contrast these two words both words might be stressed on the final syllable as I heard an estate agent do in a radio interview.

[2.7] It is *ven`dor*, not the *ven`dee* who pays that tax.

This example illustrates well the point that a word is allowed just one stress. Stress can be shifted from one syllable to another, but a word cannot have two main stresses. We could not have *`*ven`dor* and *`*ven`dee* where the two syllables received equal stress. Stress has to do with relative prominence. The syllable that receives main stress is somewhat more prominent than the rest, some of which may be unstressed or weakly stressed. By contrast, function words are normally unstressed. We can say *Nelly went to town* with no stress on *to* unless we wish to highlight *to* for contrastive purposes, e.g. *Nelly went `to town (and not away from town)*.

It is easy to see how stress can function as a valuable clue in determining whether two content words are a single compound word or two separate words. The nouns *street* and *lamp* are both stressed when they occur in isolation. But if they appear in the compound `*street-lamp*, only the first is stressed. The stress on *lamp* is suppressed.

Stress is not the only phonological clue. In addition to stress, there are rules regulating the positions in which various sounds may occur in a word and the combinations of sounds that are permissible. These rules are called PHONOTACTIC RULES. They can help us to know whether we are at the beginning, in the middle or at the end of a word. A phonological word must satisfy the requirements for words of the spoken language. For instance, while any vowel can begin a word, and most consonants can appear alone at the beginning of a word, the consonant [ŋ] is subject to certain restrictions. (This consonant is spelled *ng* as in *long* (see the key to symbols used on page xviii). In English words [ŋ] is not allowed to occur initially although it can occur in other positions. Thus, [ŋ] is allowed internally and at the end of a word as in [ˈlɒŋɪŋ] *longing* and [lɒŋgə] *longer*. But you could not have an English word like *ngether* *[ŋeðə], with [ŋ] as its first sound. However, in other languages this sound may be found word-initially as in the Chinese name *Ng* [ŋ] and the Zimbabwean name Nkomo [ŋkomo].

There are also phonotactic restrictions on the combination of consonants in various positions in a word in the spoken language. As everyone knows, English spelling is not always a perfect mirror of pronunciation. So when considering words in the spoken language it is important to separate spelling from pronunciation (see Chapter 9). You know that *a knock-kneed knight* is pronounced /nɒk niːd naɪt/ and not */knɒk kniːd knaɪt/.

Similarly, other stop-plus-nasal combinations like *tm* /tm/ and *dn* /dn/ are allowed at the end of a word (e.g. *bottom* /bɒtm/ and *burden* /bɜːdn/), but these consonant clusters are not permitted at the beginning of a word. Putative words like */tmɪs/ (*tmiss*) and */dnel/ (*dnell*) are just impermissible. In the spoken language we recognise as English words only those forms that have the right combination of sounds for the position in the word where they occur.

Moreover, even when a sound or combination of sounds is allowed, often a somewhat different pronunciation is used depending on the position in which it occurs in a word. This can be seen in the pronunciation of the *l* sound in RP in different positions in a word. Compare the initial *l* with the final *l* in the following:

[2.8]

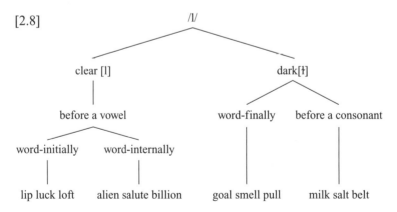

The *l* sound is always made with the blade of the tongue against the teeth-ridge, with the sides lowered to allow air to escape. But there is a subtle difference. When *l* is in word-final position or when it is followed by another consonant (as it is in the last two columns), besides the articulatory gestures mentioned above, the back of the tongue is also simultaneously raised towards the soft palate (or velum). This type of *l* is called dark or velarised *l* ([ɫ]). But when *l* is followed by a vowel, regardless of whether it is at the start of a word or word-internal, no velarisation takes place. This latter type of *l* is called clear or non-velarised *l* ([l]). Thus, the kind of *l* we hear gives an indication of where in a word it appears. Note the use of square brackets. They are used to enclose ALLOPHONES, i.e. variants of a phoneme. Allophones are different sounds, e.g. [l] and [ɫ], that occur in different contexts which all represent the same phoneme /l/. Note the convention of writing phonemes between slant lines (e.g. /lɪp/, /belt/) and allophones between square brackets (e.g. [lɪp], [beɫt].)

With regard to spelling too, the situation is not chaotic, although the relationship between letters and phonemes is not always straight-forward, as the silent *k* of *knee* /niː/ demonstrates. We recognise as English words only those orthographic words that conform to the spelling conventions of English. If you saw the word *zvroglen* you would treat it as a foreign word. The letter combination *zvr* is not English.

2.2.2 Words as vocabulary items

We need to distinguish between words in the sense of word-form as opposed to words as vocabulary items. Let us revisit the examples in [2.1] on pp. 11–12. If we are considering word-forms, we can see that the hyphenated word-form *street-lamp* occurs three times. So, if we were counting different word-forms, we would count *street-lamp* three times. However, if we were counting distinct words, in the sense of distinct VOCABULARY ITEMS we would only count it once.

The distinction between word-forms and vocabulary items is important. Very often, when we talk about words what we have in mind is not word-forms, but something more abstract – what we will refer to here as LEXEMES (i.e. vocabulary items). Anyone compiling a dictionary lists words in this sense. So, although the word-forms in each of the columns in [2.9] below are different, we do not find each one of them given a separate entry in an English dictionary. The first word in each column is listed under a heading of its own. The rest may be mentioned under that heading, if they do not follow a regular pattern of the language – e.g. *write, written* (past participle), *wrote* (past tense). But, if they do follow the general pattern (e.g. *washes, washing, washed; smile, smiling, smiled*), they will be left out of the dictionary altogether. Instead, the grammar will be expected to provide a general statement to the effect that verbs take an *-ing* suffix, which marks progressive aspect, and an *-ed* suffix that marks both the past tense and the past participle and so on.

[2.9] WASH	TAKE	BRING	WRITE
wash	take	bring	write
washes	takes	brings	writes
washing	taking	bringing	writing
washed	took	brought	wrote
washed	taken	brought	written

In [2.9] each lexeme (i.e. vocabulary item) that would be entered in a dictionary is shown in capital letters and all the different word-forms belonging to it are shown in lower-case letters.

The examples in [2.9] are all verbs. But, of course, lexemes can be nouns, adjectives or adverbs as well. You will find examples from these other word classes listed in [2.10].

[2.10]	*Noun*	*Adjective*	*Adverb*
a	MATCH	KIND	SOON
	match	kind	soon
	matches	kinder	sooner
b	GOOSE	BAD	WELL
	goose	bad	well
	geese	worse	better

In [2.10] we have three pairs of lexemes: the nouns *match* and *goose*; the adjectives *kind* and *bad*; and the adverbs *soon* and *well*. In each case the word-forms belonging to each lexeme in [2.10a] follow a general pattern for words of their type and need not be listed in the dictionary. But all the ones in [2.10b] are irregular and must be listed in the dictionary.

The lexeme is an abstract entity that is found in the dictionary and that has a certain meaning. Word-forms are the concrete objects that we put down on paper (orthographic words) or utter (phonological words) when we use language. The relationship between a lexeme and the word-forms belonging to it is one of REALISATION or REPRESENTATION or MANIFESTATION. If we take the lexeme *write*, which is entered in the dictionary, for example, we can see that it may be realised by any one of the word-forms *write*, *writes*, *writing*, *wrote* and *written* which belong to it. These are the actual forms that are used in speech or appear on paper. When you see the orthographic words *written* and *wrote* on the page, you know that, although they are spelt differently, they are manifestations of the same vocabulary item WRITE.

The distinction between word-forms and lexemes which I have just made is not abstruse. It is a distinction that we are intuitively aware of from an early age. It is the distinction on which word-play in puns and in intentional ambiguity in everyday life depends. At a certain period in our childhood we were fascinated by words. We loved jokes – even awful ones like [2.11]

[2.11]

'Waiter, do you serve shrimps?'
'We serve anyone, sir.
We don't mind what size you are!'

Source: J. and P. Young (1981) *The Ladybird Book of Jokes, Riddles and Rhymes*

The humour, of course, lies in recognising that the word-form *shrimp* can belong to two separate lexemes whose very different and unrelated meanings are nonetheless pertinent here. It can mean either 'an edible, long, slender crustacean' or 'a tiny person' (in colloquial English). Also, the word *serve* has two possible interpretations. It can mean 'to wait upon a person at table' or 'to dish up food'. Thus, word-play exploits the lexical ambiguity arising from the fact that the same word-form represents two distinct lexemes with very distinct meanings.

In real-life communication, where there is potential ambiguity, we generally manage to come to just one interpretation without too much difficulty by selecting the most appropriate and RELEVANT interpretation in the situation. Suppose a 20-stone super heavyweight boxer went to Joe's Vegan Restaurant and asked the waiter for a nice shrimp curry and the waiter said in reply, 'We don't serve shrimps', it would be obvious that it was shrimps in the sense of crustaceans that was intended. If, on the other hand, a little man, barely five feet tall and weighing a mere seven stone, went to a seafood restaurant and saw almost everyone at the tables around him tucking into a plateful of succulent shrimps, and thought that he would quite fancy some himself, he would be rightly offended if the waiter said, 'We do not serve shrimps.' It is obvious in this situation that shrimps are on the menu and are dished up for consumption. What is not done is serving up food to people deemed to be puny.

Serious literature is not above using puns. For instance, the First World War poet Siegfried Sassoon gives the title 'Base details' to the poem in which he parodies cowardly generals who stay away at the base, at a safe distance from the action, and gladly speed young soldiers to their death at the front. The word-form *base* in the title represents two distinct lexemes here whose meanings are both relevant: (i) *Base details* are details of what is happening at the $base_{(Noun)}$ (meaning 'military encampment'), and (ii) *Base details* are particulars of something that is $base_{(Adj.)}$ (meaning 'reprehensibly cowardly, mean etc.'). See Chapter 6 for further discussion of word meaning.

2.2.3 Grammatical words

Finally, let us consider the word from a grammatical perspective. Words play a key role in syntax as sentences contain arrangements of words. A word, in the sense of a lexical item with a certain meaning plus certain syntactic and morphological properties, is referred to as a GRAMMATICAL WORD (cf. lemma in section (11.1)). Often words are required to have certain properties if they serve certain syntactic purposes. Thus, although in [2.12a] we have the same sense of the same lexeme (*play*) realised by the same word-form (*played*), we know that this word does at least two quite different grammatical jobs in the sentence of which it is a part:

[2.12] a She played the flute.   b She took the flute.
        She has played the flute.   She has taken the flute.

If you compare the sentences in [2.12], you will see that in [2.12a] the verb *play* is realised by the word-form *played* regardless of whether it simply indicates that the action happened in the past as in the first example or that an action was (recently) completed as in the second example. Contrast this with the situation in [2.12b] where these two grammatical meanings are signalled by two different forms. *Took* indicates that the action happened in the past while *taken* (after *has/had*) indicates that the action is complete. In *She played the flute* and *She took the flute* the words *played* and *took* are described grammatically as the 'past tense forms of the verbs *play* and *take*'. By contrast, in *She has played the flute* and *She has taken the flute* we describe *played* and *taken* as the 'past participle' of *play* and *take*.

Linguists use the term SYNCRETISM to describe situations such as that exemplified by *played* where the same word-form of a lexeme is used to realise two (or more) distinct grammatical words that are represented separately in the grammatical representations of words belonging to some other comparable lexemes. The phenomenon of syncretism is one good reason for distinguishing between word-forms and grammatical words. It enables us to show that words belonging to the same lexeme and having the same form in speech and writing can still differ.

A further example should make the ideas of grammatical words and syncretism even clearer. Consider the verbs in the following sentences:

[2.13] a You hit me.   (= you hit me some time in the past)
                          or
                          (= you hit me habitually)

       b You cut it.   (= you cut it some time in the past)
                          or
                          (= you cut it habitually)

As the paraphrases show, the word-form *hit* belonging to the lexeme *hit* can represent either the present tense or the past tense form of the verb. In other words, there is syncretism. We have two different grammatical words $hit_{[+verb, +present]}$ and $hit_{[+verb, +past]}$ but a single word-form. The same analysis also applies to *cut*. It can represent either the present or past tense of the verb *cut*.

Syncretism is not limited to verbs. It can apply to other word classes (e.g. nouns) as well:

[2.14] a The wolf killed a sheep and one deer.
    b The wolf killed two sheep and three deer.

In these two sentences, although the word-form *sheep* belongs to the same lexeme and is unchanged in form, we know that its grammatical value is not the same. In [2.14a] it realises the word with the grammatical properties of noun and singular, but in [2.14b] it represents a plural form. Likewise, the same word-form *deer* represents a singular noun in [2.14a] and a plural noun in [2.14b].

What can we say about the word as an entity that functions as a grammatical unit in the syntax of a language? As mentioned already, the (grammatical) word is normally defined as the MINIMAL FREE FORM that is used in the grammar of a language. Let us now put some flesh on this terse and somewhat cryptic statement.

By free form we mean an entity that can stand on its own and act as a free agent; it is an element whose position in a sentence is not totally dictated by other items. In order to explain what 'freedom' means in this context, we need to take on board two ancillary ideas: POSITIONAL MOBILITY and STABILITY. Although words are not the smallest grammatical units used to construct sentences (see the discussion of morphemes in the next chapter), at the level of sentence organisation the rules of sentence formation treat words as unanalysable units. Often it is possible to change the order in which words appear in a sentence and still produce a well-formed sentence. Words enjoy considerable positional mobility. However, the elements inside a word do not enjoy such mobility. While syntactic rules can transport words to new places in a sentence, they cannot shift in the same way elements that are found inside words. Moving words around in the following produces grammatical sentences with basically the same meaning, but with somewhat different emphasis:

[2.15] a This old industrialist revisited Lancaster, fortunately.
 b Fortunately, this old industrialist revisited Lancaster.
 c Lancaster, this old industrialist revisited, fortunately.
 d Fortunately, Lancaster was revisited by this old
   industrialist.

Evidently, the position of words in a sentence is not rigidly fixed. They can, and often do, get moved around if the communicative needs of the speaker or writer require it. However, the interior of a word is a no-go area for syntactic rules. They are strictly barred from manipulating elements found inside a word. As far as syntax is concerned, words are indivisible units that cannot be split and whose internal units are inaccessible (see Matthews 1991; Lyons 1968; Di Sciullo and Williams 1987).

The word as a grammatical unit shows stability (or INTERNAL COHESION). The order of elements inside a word is rigidly fixed. If the elements of a sentence are shifted, certain meaningful units (in this case *re-visit-ed* and *fortun-ate-ly*) all move en bloc, and their order always remains unchanged. The internal structure of the word cannot be tampered with. We are not allowed to perform operations that would yield words like *ed-visit-re, *ate-fortun-ly etc. We will return to this point on pp. 30–1.

The definition of the word includes the term 'minimal' for a good reason. This is intended to separate words from phrases like *this old industrialist*. Like words, phrases can occur in isolation and they can be moved from one position to another (as we have seen in [2.15]). But the expression *this old industrialist* is not a minimal form since it contains smaller forms capable of occurring independently, namely *this, old* and *industrialist*. Furthermore, the sequence *this old industrialist* does not have the kind of internal cohesion found in words. It can be interrupted by other words, e.g. *this wealthy old industrialist; this very wealthy, old, benevolent industrialist*.

The assumption that the grammatical word is 'a minimum free form' works well as a rule of thumb. But it encounters difficulties when confronted by a COMPOUND WORD like *wheelbarrow* which contains the words *wheel* and *barrow* which can stand alone. In such cases it is clear that the word is not the smallest meaningful unit that can be used on its own. It is for this reason that the definition of the word as the unit on which purely syntactic operations can be performed is preferable. In the case of compounds this definition works. The interior of a compound is a syntactic no-go area. Syntactic rules are not allowed to apply separately to words that make up a compound. Thus, for example, although the nouns *wheel* and *barrow* can be modified by the adjective *big* ([*big barrow*], [*big wheel*]), and although we can talk of [*big wheelbarrow*], in which case *big* modifies the entire compound, there is no possibility of saying *wheel* [*big barrow*], with the adjective only modifying the second element of the compound word.

2.3 Summary

In this chapter we have established that, normally, the term 'word' is used ambiguously. To avoid the ambiguity, we need to distinguish between three different types of word:

1   a word-form (i.e. a particular physical manifestation of at least one lexeme); in speech it is called a phonological word and in writing an orthographic word;
2   a lexeme (i.e. vocabulary item);
3   a grammatical word (i.e. a unit of grammatical structure that has certain morphological and syntactic properties) (see lemma in section (11.3.1)).

In the coming chapters, in cases where the relevant sense of the term 'word' is clear from the context I will not spell out whether it is the word as a vocabulary item, grammatical word, phonological or orthographic form that is being dealt with. But, where it is not clear, I will indicate the sense in which I am using this term. We are now in a position to consider in detail the internal structure of words. That is the task of the next chapter.

Exercises

1   Comment on the problems you encounter in determining the number of words in the following nursery rhyme. Relate your answer to the different senses in which the term 'word' is used.

> The grand old Duke of York
> He had ten thousand men.
> He marched them up to the top of the hill,
> Then he marched them down again.

> When they were up, they were up,
> And when they were down, they were down,
> And when they were only half way up
> They were neither up nor down.

2   Determine the number of words in the internet pages below. Comment on any difficulties that you encounter and explain how you resolve them.

  a   http://www.grooms-hearing.co.uk/aftercareservice.htm
  b   www.ReggaeAmbassadors.org
  c   Yahoo! Groups: englandsupporters
  d   http://www.chocolatelovers.net/

3   Which ones of the italicised word-forms in the following sentences belong to the same lexeme? What difficulties, if any, have you had in determining whether word-forms belong to the same lexeme?

  a   She *saw* him *saw* through that plank of wood.
  b   *Bill* will pay the *bill.*
  c   I saw *Farmer* near your *farm* again this morning.
  d   Jan looked *pale* when she walked towards the *pail.*
  e   I am *sick* of your claiming to be *sick* all the time.
  f   I was looking at the *book* when she *booked* the ticket.

4   Using at least two fresh examples, show how syncretism can be used to support the distinction between word-forms and grammatical words.

5   Identify the compound words in the list below. Justify your answer.

  a   weapons of wealth
       destruction (WWD)
  b   backward
  c   steadfast
  d   exercise book
  e   stay-at-home
  f   understand
  g   jurisdiction
  h   greenhouse
  i   in your face
  j   men in grey suits
  k   multiplex
  l   middle-aged ladette wannabes

Chapter 3

Close encounters of a morphemic kind

3.1 The quest for verbal atoms

We saw in the last chapter that the word is the smallest meaningful unit of language that can function independently in the grammar. A word can be used on its own, without appending it to some other unit. Thus, in the word *childish* we can isolate *child* and use it on its own because it is a word in its own right. But we cannot use *-ish* as a stand-alone unit, for *-ish* is not a word.

While recognising that words are the smallest meaningful units which function independently in the grammar, we also need to recognise that words can be decomposed into smaller units that are also meaningful. Our task in this chapter is to explore the internal structure of words in order to gain some understanding of the basic units which are used to form words.

3.2 Close morphological encounters: zooming in on morphemes

Originally 'morphology' meant the study of biological forms. But nineteenth-century students of language borrowed the term and applied it to the study of word-structure. In linguistics MORPHOLOGY is the study of the formation and internal organisation of words.

Let us begin our morphological analysis by considering eight words (not altogether randomly chosen):

[3.1] hope   soon   mend   boil   safe   leaf   word   elephant

Obviously all the words in [3.1] have a meaning, but lack internal structure. We cannot identify any smaller units that are themselves meaningful which occur inside them. If a Martian stopped you in a street near the local zoo and enquired what *phant* in *elephant* or *ca* in *catapult* means, you would think she was asking a most bizarre question that did not merit an answer. Or you might condescendingly explain that, of course, in each case the whole word means something, but its parts cannot be said to mean anything on their own. Though somewhat puzzled, the Martian might accept your explanation.

But, being the persistent type, let us suppose she enquired further whether the words in [3.2] were also indivisible into smaller meaningful units:

[3.2] childish	hopeless	sooner	mended
cats	re-boil	unsafe	ex-wife

You would have to give a different answer. You would need to tell your interrogator, who by now would be getting increasingly bewildered, that the words in [3.2] can be divided into smaller units of meaning as shown in [3.3]:

[3.3] child-*ish*	hope-*less*	soon-*er*	mend-*ed*
cat-*s*	*re*-boil	*un*-safe	*ex*-wife

The part of the word that is not italicised can function independently in the grammar of English. Indeed, each of the non-italicised chunks is a word (i.e. vocabulary item) that is listed as such in the dictionary. By contrast, the italicised bits, though meaningful (and their meanings can be indicated as shown in [3.4]), cannot function on their own in the grammar.

[3.4] -ish	'having the (objectionable) qualities of'	child-ish = 'having the qualities of a child'
-less	'without X'	hopeless = 'without hope'
-er	'more X'	sooner = 'more soon'
-ed	'past'	mended = 'mend in the past'
-s	'plural'	cats = 'more than one cat'
re-	'again'	re-boil = 'boil again'
un-	'not X'	unsafe = 'not safe'
ex-	'former'	ex-wife = 'former wife'

What we have done to the words in [3.4] can be done to thousands of other words in English. They can be decomposed into smaller units of meaning (e.g. *re-* 'again') or grammatical function (e.g. *-ed* 'past').

The term MORPHEME is used to refer to the smallest unit that has meaning or serves a grammatical function in a language. Morphemes are the atoms with which words are built. It is not possible to find sub-morphemic units that are themselves meaningful or have a grammatical function. Thus, given *-less* or *un-*, it would make no sense to try to assign some identifiable meaning to any part of these forms. Of course, it is possible to isolate the individual sounds /l-ɪ-s/ or /ʌ-n/, but those sounds in themselves do not mean anything.

We have now established that words are made up of morphemes. But how do we recognise a morpheme when we see one? Our definition of the morpheme as the smallest unit of meaning (or grammatical function) will be the guiding principle. Any chunk of a word with a particular meaning will be said to represent a morpheme. That is how we proceeded in [3.3] and [3.4] above.

Morphemes tend to have a fairly stable meaning which they bring to any word in which they appear. If we take *re-* and *un-*, for example, they mean 'again' and 'not' respectively – not just in the words we have listed above, but also in thousands of other words. Usually morphemes are used again and again to form different words. Thus *re-*, meaning 're-do whatever the verb means', can be attached before most verbs to yield a new word with a predictable meaning (e.g. *re-run*, *re-take*, *re-build* etc.). In like manner, *un-* meaning 'not X' (where X stands for whatever the adjective means) can be attached to various adjectives (e.g. *un-real*, *un-clean*, *un-happy* etc.) to yield a new word with a predictable negative meaning.

The segmentation of words into morphemes is not a trivial and arcane pastime indulged in by linguists to while away the time on a wet Bank Holiday afternoon. It is something that is important for all users of language. During your lifetime, you will probably encounter hundreds of thousands of different words. Many of these words will be new to you. For no matter how extensive your vocabulary is, you will inevitably come across words that are unfamiliar. It is impossible for anyone to know all the words that are found in English.

So, what do you do when faced with an unfamiliar word? Reach for a good dictionary? Perhaps. But this is not always feasible. Nor is it always necessary. Very often you just figure out what the strange word means using the context, together with your knowledge of the meaning of the morphemes which the word contains. You normally do this subconsciously. What we are doing here is making explicit your tacit knowledge of word-structure.

Imagine this scenario. In 1992, a newspaper report on the war in the Bosnian republic states that what we are witnessing is the *Lebanonisation* of Bosnia. Suppose you have not encountered the word *Lebanonisation* before. Would you understand what the writer is saying? Probably you would – without looking it up in any dictionary. How would you do it? The answer is simple. By using your knowledge of the world – in particular history (*Balkanisation*) – and your knowledge of current affairs (the 1975–90 civil war in Lebanon) plus your knowledge of the principles of word-formation you are able to work out the meaning of *Lebanonisation*.

Let us focus on principles of word-formation. You know that *-ize/-ise* is used when talking about nations to mean 'to make X', e.g. from *America* we get *Americanise*, from *Korea* we get *Koreanise*, from *Kenya* we get *Kenyanise* etc. By attaching *-(an)ise* we turn a noun into a verb. So, given the noun *Lebanon* we can form the verb *Lebanonise*. Next, from the verb *Lebanonise*, we can create a new noun by adding *-ation* (which forms nouns of action).

If you know that various warlords created warring fiefdoms that destroyed the Lebanese state during the civil war that raged in Lebanon in the 1970s and 1980s, you will know that the Croats, Muslims and Serbs engaged in the Bosnian conflict risk doing the same to the Bosnian state in the 1990s. *Lebanonisation* is the act of 'turning a country into another Lebanon'. Thus, our knowledge of word-structure contributes to our understanding of the meaning of unfamiliar words.

We have demonstrated that words can be decomposed into morphemes. Now we are going to see that words have INTERNAL STRUCTURE. A simple way of showing this is to analyse words like *uncanny* and *unhappy*. From these words we can derive *uncannier* and *unhappier*. If you analyse *unhappier*, you will see that extracting the correct meaning 'more [not happy]' (i.e. sadder) rather than the incorrect one 'not [more happy]' (i.e. not happier) depends on the way we group together the morphemes. In the first analysis, where *unhappier* is interpreted as *sadder*, the meaning 'not' conveyed by *un-* is bracketed together with *happy* [unhappy] as one unit and this is intensified by the *-er* suffix. In the alternative second analysis, *happy* and *-er* are bracketed together as a unit [happier] (i.e. more happy) which then is negated by [un-] to give 'not more happy', which is incorrect. When someone is *unhappier*, it does not mean they are simply less happy, it means rather that they are not happy at all. They are sad. This shows that morphemes in a word with several morphemes may be grouped together in different ways for semantic purposes. The way in which this is done has semantic consequences. Conceivably, morphemes could be thrown together higgledy-piggledy to form a word. So long as you had the right morphemes, a well-formed word would pop out. But that is definitely not the case. Words have internal structural groupings, as we have seen.

Furthermore, the sequencing of morphemes in a word may be subject to restrictions. Take a word like *ungovernability* which contains four morphemes, namely *un-*, *govern*, *abil*, *ity*. Everyone who knows this word knows that these four morphemes must appear in the order in [3.5a]. Any other order is strictly forbidden:

[3.5] a un-govern-abil-ity
      b *govern-abil-un-ity
      c *ity-un-abil-govern
      d *abil-un-ity-govern
      e *un-govern-ity-abil etc.

Clearly, knowing a word means not just knowing the morphemes it contains, but also the rigid order in which they are allowed to appear. We will return to this point in section (4.4).

To sum up the discussion so far, words are built using morphemes. If we know how morphemes are used to form words, we do not need to be unduly flustered when we come across a strange word. Usually it is possible to work out the meaning of a strange word if it contains familiar morphemes.

3.3 Morphemes and their disguises

The identification of morphemes is not altogether straightforward. This is because there is no simple one-to-one correspondence between morphemes and the speech sounds that represent them. In this section we will attempt to unravel the complexities of the relationship between morphemes and the actual forms (sounds of groups of sounds) by which they are manifested in speech.

3.3.1 Allomorphs: morph families

Any physical form that represents a morpheme is called a MORPH. The forms *-ish*, *-less*, *-er*, *-ed*, *-s*, *re-*, *un-* and *ex-* in [3.4] on p. 28 are all morphs. Morphological analysis begins with the identification of morphs, i.e. forms that carry some meaning or are associated with some grammatical function. In *asparagus* there is just one morph but in all the words in [3.4] there are two.

It is important not to confuse morphs with SYLLABLES. When we talk of morphs we have in mind sounds that can be related to a particular meaning or grammatical function (e.g. plural or past tense). However, when we talk of syllables all we have in mind are chunks into which words can be divided for the purposes of pronunciation.

This is not an abstruse distinction. We are not being pedantic. It is a distinction that matters to ordinary people because human languages are organised in such a way that the construction of units that are meaningful is normally in principle separate from the construction of strings that are pronounceable. Thus, for rhythmical effect, nursery rhymes often use nonsense syllables like '*Deedle, deedle*' in '*Deedle deedle dumpling my son John*' which do not represent anything meaningful.

Alternatively, a sound representing a morpheme may not be a syllable in its own right, e.g. by itself, the *-s* which represents the plural morpheme is not a syllable. The word *cats* has two morphemes, *cat* and *-s*, but it is all just one syllable. The single syllable *cats* realises two morphemes. The converse situation, where several syllables realise a single morpheme, is equally possible. Thus, the trisyllabic and quadrisyllabic word-forms *elephant* and *asparagus* both realise just a single morpheme.

The nature of the relationship between sounds and morphemes is intriguing. At first sight, it might look reasonable to assume that morphemes are made up of PHONEMES. We might be tempted to think, for instance, that *horse*, the English morpheme with the meaning 🐎 is made up of the phonemes /hɔːs/. But we have several kinds of evidence showing that this is not the case.

First, if morphemes were *made up* of phonemes, a given morpheme would be uniquely associated with a given phonological representation. In reality, the same morpheme can be realised by different morphs (i.e. sounds or written forms). Morphs which realise the same morpheme are referred to as ALLOMORPHS of that morpheme.

The INDEFINITE ARTICLE is a good example of a morpheme with more than one allomorph. It is realised by the two forms *a* and *an*. The sound at the beginning of the following word determines the allomorph that is selected. If the word following the indefinite article begins with a consonant, the allomorph *a* is selected, but if it begins with a vowel the allomorph *an* is used instead:

[3.6] a   a dictionary   b   an island
          a boat   an evening
          a pineapple   an opinion

Hence the incorrectness of the sentence marked with an asterisk in [3.7]:

[3.7] a   I spent *an* evening with them.
          *I spent *a* evening with them.
      b   I spent *the* evening with them.

Allomorphs of the same morpheme are said to be in COMPLE-MENTARY DISTRIBUTION. This means that they do not occur in identical contexts and therefore they cannot be used to distinguish meanings. In other words, it is impossible to have two otherwise identical utterances that differ in their meanings depending on the allomorph of a morpheme that is selected. So, because *a* and *an* both realise the same indefinite article morpheme, it is impossible to have two sentences like those in [3.7a] above which are identical in all ways, except in the choice of *a* or *an*, but mean different things.

Complementary distribution presupposes the more basic notion of DISTRIBUTION. Distribution is to do with establishing the environments in which the morpheme which we are investigating occurs and the allomorphs by which it is realised in those different contexts. In other words, by distribution we mean the total set of distinct linguistic contexts in which a given form appears, perhaps in different guises. For instance, the indefinite article has the distribution: *a* before consonants (e.g. *a tree*) and *an* before vowels (e.g. *an eagle*).

As mentioned already, such functionally related forms which all represent the same morpheme in different environments are called allomorphs of that morpheme. Another way of putting it is that allomorphs are forms that are phonologically distinguishable, but which, none the less, are not functionally distinct. In other words, although they are physically distinct morphs with different pronunciations, allomorphs do share the same function in the language.

To summarise, allomorphs of a morpheme are in complementary distribution. This means that they cannot substitute for each other. Hence, we cannot replace one allomorph of a morpheme by another allomorph of that morpheme and change meaning.

For our next example of allomorphs we will turn to the plural morpheme. The idea of 'more than one' is expressed by the plural morpheme using a variety of allomorphs including the following:

[3.8]   *Singular*   *Plural*
   a rad-ius   radi-i
      cactus   cact-i
   b dat-um   dat-a
      strat-um   strat-a
   c analys-is   analys-es
      ax-is   ax-es
   d skirt   skirt-s
      road   road-s
      branch   branch-es

Going by the orthography, we can identify the allomorphs -*i*, -*a*, -*es* and -*s*. The last is by far the most common.

Try and say the batch of words in [3.8d] aloud. You will observe that the pronunciation of the plural allomorph in these words is variable. It is [s] in *skirts*, [z] in *roads* and [ɪz] (or for some speakers [əz]) in *branches*. What is interesting about these words is that the selection of the allomorph that represents the plural is determined by the last sound in the noun to which the plural morpheme is appended.

We have already seen that, because allomorphs cannot substitute for each other, we never have two sentences with different meanings which solely differ in that one sentence has allomorph X in a slot where another sentence has allomorph Y. Compare the two sentences in [3.9]:

[3.9] a They have two cats.   b They have two dogs.
         [ðeɪ hæv tuː kæt-*s*]   [ðeɪ hæv tuː dɒg-*z*]
         *[ðeɪ hæv tuː kæt-*z*]   *[ðeɪ hæv tuː dɒg-*s*]

We cannot find two otherwise identical sentences which differ in meaning simply because the word *cats* is pronounced as [kæt-s] and *[kæt-z] respectively. Likewise, it is not possible to have two otherwise identical sentences with different meanings where the word *dogs* is pronounced as [dɒgz] and *[dɒgs]. In other words, the difference between the allomorphs [s] and [z] of the plural morpheme cannot be used to distinguish meanings.

3.3.2 Contrast

Different morphemes CONTRAST meanings but different allomorphs do not. If a difference in meaning is attributable to the fact that one minimal meaningful unit has been replaced by another, we identify the morphs involved as manifestations of distinct morphemes. So, in [3.7] on p. 33 the indefinite article realised by *a* or *an* is a distinct morpheme from the definite article realised by *the* since a semantic difference is detectable when *a* or *an* is replaced with *the*.

A further example of contrast is given in [3.10]:

[3.10] a   I unlocked the door.   b   She is untidy.
           I re-locked the door.

The two sentences in [3.10a] mean very different things. Since they are identical except for the fact that where one has *un-* the other has *re-*, the difference in meaning between these two sentences is due to the difference in meaning between the morphemes realised by *re-* (meaning 'do again') and *un-* (meaning 'reverse the action').

Now, contrast the *un-* of *unlocked* with the *un-* of *untidy*. In both cases we have the same morph *un-* (which is spelt and pronounced in exactly the same way). But it is obvious that *un-* represents different morphemes in these two word-forms. In *I unlocked the door* the morph *un-* found in *unlocked* realises a reversive morpheme which is attached to verbs – it reverses the action of locking. But in *untidy* it realises a negative morpheme attached to adjectives – *untidy* means 'not tidy'. (If a person is *untidy*, it does not mean that at some earlier point they were tidy and someone has reversed or undone their tidiness.)

If morphemes were made up of phonemes a simple correlation of morphs with morphemes is what we would find. But, in fact, it is quite common for the same phonological form (i.e. morph) to represent more than one morpheme. It is from the context that we can tell which morpheme it represents. This is the second piece of evidence against the assumption that morphemes are composed of phonemes.

The complex relationship between morphemes and the allomorphs that represent them gives us a window through which we can glimpse one of the most fascinating aspects of language: the relationship between FORM and FUNCTION. In linguistics we explore the form of various elements of language structure, e.g. words and sentences, because it is important to know how they are constructed. However, form is not everything. We are also interested in knowing what linguistic elements are used for, what function they serve.

Just consider for a moment this non-linguistic analogy. Imagine a friend returns from a foreign vacation with two beautiful ornamental glass containers with a globular shape and gives one to you as a present and keeps the other for herself. She does not tell you what your present is used for. She uses hers as a vessel for containing wine at the table – she got the idea of buying these containers when she was served wine in a similar container in a fancy restaurant. You do not know this. You look at your present and decide to put it on the table as a container for cut fresh flowers. She calls hers a flagon, for that is what she is using it as. You call yours a vase.

Are these objects 'flagons' or 'vases'? Which one of you is right? I am not being evasive if I say that both of you are right. For, although the two objects are identical as far as their form – their physical properties – is concerned, they are very different with regard to the functions that they serve in your two households.

There are numerous linguistic parallels. What is physically the same linguistic form can be used to represent distinct morphemes. In order for forms to be regarded as allomorphs belonging to the same morpheme, it is not sufficient for them to have the same form – to be pronounced or written in the same way. They must also have the same grammatical or semantic function. The significance of this point was hinted at in the discussion of *un-* in *unlocked* and *untidy* when we showed that the same morph can represent different morphemes. It should become even more obvious when you consider the form *-er* in the following:

[3.11] a think ~ thinker   drive ~ driver
           sweep ~ sweeper   sell ~ seller
        b cook ~ cooker   compute ~ computer
           propel ~ propeller   erase ~ eraser
        c London ~ Londoner   northern ~ northerner
           New York ~ New Yorker   Highlands ~ Highlander

The same form, -er, represents three different meanings and hence has to be assigned to three distinct morphemes. In [3.11a] it forms an agentive noun from a verb, with the meaning 'someone who does X' (i.e. whatever the verb means). In [3.11b] the same -er forms an instrumental noun from a verb, with the meaning 'something used to X' (i.e. to do whatever the verb means). Finally, in [3.11c] the same -er form is attached to a noun referring to a place to mean 'an inhabitant of'.

Clearly, the same form does serve different functions here. So, it realises different morphemes. This is further evidence that should quickly disabuse us of the assumption that morphemes are made up of morphs. Not only can a single morpheme have several allomorphs (as in the case of the plural morpheme), the same morph (e.g. -er) can represent different morphemes. There is no simple one-to-one matching of morphemes with morphs.

3.3.3 The right mask

We saw in section (3.3.1) that many morphemes are realised by a variety of allomorphs in different contexts. The question we will address now is this: how is the distribution of those allomorphs determined? In other words, how do speakers select the right allomorph to use in a given situation? We will see that normally the choice of allomorph is not arbitrary. There is a number of general principles that guide speakers in choosing one allomorph rather than another. These factors may be phonological, grammatical or lexical. We will explore these factors in turn.

3.3.3.1 Phonologically conditioned allomorphs

Some morphemes (e.g. *cut* and *day*) are unproblematic. They do not have different allomorphs that represent them in different environments. The dictionary entries of morphemes like these and the actual forms that represent them in different situations do not differ significantly. If all English morphemes were like that, English morphology would be a very dull subject.

In fact, many morphemes have several allomorphs. In the vast majority of cases, the distribution of these allomorphs is determined by phonological factors. For instance, given a base with certain phonetic characteristics, a particular allomorph of the affix morpheme has to be selected. Or, conversely, in some cases when a certain affix is present, a base with particular phonetic characteristics must be selected. This sounds abstract. Let us get down to earth.

A standard example of the PHONOLOGICALLY CONDITIONED choice of allomorphs is the regular plural of English nouns. The plural morpheme is represented by *-s* or *-es* in the orthography but has three different manifestations in the spoken language: /s/ as in /hæts/ *hats*, /z/ as in /dʌvz/ *doves*, and /ɪz/ as in /bædʒɪz/ *badges*. Because the alternation between /s/, /z/, and /ɪz/ is regular, we can incorporate a rule in the grammar (and we will be doing that below) which predicts how the plural is realised.

The rules whose job it is to account for the alternations in the representation of morphemes are called MORPHOPHONEMIC RULES. Normally a morphophonemic rule will say, 'Morpheme M is to be realised by allomorph X in this context, by allomorph Y in that context, and by allomorph Z in some other context' etc. The allomorph with the widest distribution is usually taken as the UNDERLYING REPRESENTATION (also called the UNDERLYING FORM or BASE FORM).

[3.12] *Phonologically   conditioned   allomorphs   of   the   plural morpheme*

a   Underlying /-z/ is realised as [-s] in the surface representation if a stem ends in a voiceless consonant which is not a STRIDENT CORONAL. (A STRIDENT CONSONANT is a hissing sound also called a sibilant, e.g. /s, z/ and a CORONAL is a consonant made with the tip or the blade of the tongue raised to approach or touch either the teeth ridge or the hard palate, or both.)
This means that /-z/ is realised as [-s] after /p t k f θ /.

	Underlying representation	*Surface representation*
maps	/mæp-z/	[mæps]
sheets	/ʃiːt-z/	[ʃiːts]
weeks	/wiːk-z/	/wiːks/
chief	/tʃiːf-z/	/tʃiːfs/
oaths	/əʊθ-z/	/əʊθs/

b   Underlying /-z/ is realised as [-z] if a stem ends in a voiced sound which is not a strident coronal, e.g. the consonants /b d g v ð m n ŋ l r w/ or any vowel.

	Underlying representation	*Surface representation*
tubs	/tʌb-z/	[tʌbz]
lads	/læd-z/	[lædz]
mugs	/mʌg-z/	[mʌgz]
groves	/grəʊv-z/	[grəʊvz]
lathes	/leɪð-z/	[leɪðz]
brooms	/bruːm-z/	[bruːmz]
tons	/tʌn-z/	[tʌnz]
songs	/sɒŋ-z/	[sɒŋz]

c   Underlying /z/ is realised as [-ɪz] if a stem ends in a consonant which is both (i) strident and (ii) coronal. This means that /-ɪz/ is the allomorph selected after /s z ʃ ʒ tʃ dʒ/, with /ɪ/ inserted to separate the coronal sibilant of the stem from that of the suffix.

	Underlying representation	*Surface representation*
glasses	/glaːs-z/ → /glaːs-ɪz/	[glaːsɪz]
cheeses	/tʃiːz-z/ → /tʃiːz-ɪz/	[tʃiːzɪz]
ashes	/æʃ-z/ → /æʃ-ɪz/	[æʃɪz]
bridges	/brɪdʒ-z/ → /brɪdʒ-ɪz/	[brɪdʒɪz]
finches	/fɪntʃ-z/ → /fɪntʃ-ɪz/	[fɪntʃɪz]
charges	/tʃɑːdʒ-z/ → /tʃɑːdʒ-ɪz/	[tʃɑːdʒɪz]

ASSIMILATION is the process whereby sound becomes more similar to another sound in its neighbourhood. So, voiceless final consonants in the stem require the voiceless fricative allomorph /s/ while voiced final consonants go with the voiced fricative /z/. However, where following this procedure would result in two sibilants being right next to each other, the vowel /ɪ/ (or /ə/ (schwa) in some dialects) is inserted between the last consonant and the suffix (as in *glasses* /glaːsɪz/ or /glaːsəz/).

Assimilation is normally the reason for the phonological conditioning of allomorphs. A morpheme may have more than one mask. It may masquerade as one of several allomorphs when the sounds that represent it are modified so that they become more like some other sound(s) in the environment where it appears. An allomorph wearing a suitable phonological mask is chosen to suit each set of phonological circumstances.

The phonological modification, as mentioned at the beginning of this chapter, can affect bases as well as affixes. So far we have seen a suffix with several phonologically conditioned allomorphs. Now we will look at bases that change when an affix is attached.

In some nouns which end in a labio-dental voiceless fricative, e.g. /f/, the final consonant gets voiced to [v] when the plural suffix /-z/ is present. The voicing is much more common with the nouns ending in /f/:

[3.13]	Plural	Genitive
wife	wives	wife's
calf	calves	calf's
thief	thieves	thief's

In [3.13] the final sound of the noun stem ending in /f/ shows two contrasting behaviours when /-z/ is suffixed. If the -s represents the plural of the noun as in *wives* (< *wife* (singular)) the final /-f/ changes to /v/. But where the -s represents the genitive morpheme as in *his wife's career*, no such change takes place (*his wive's career*) (see Swadesh and Voeglin 1939). This is not usual. It is common to find differing patterns of phonological behaviour depending on the morphological context in which an allomorph appears.

There is a change in progress in the way nouns ending in /f/ form their plural. The direction of change is towards eliminating the allomorph of the root with the sound /v/ so that we only have the /f/ form. *Hooves* and *rooves* are being supplanted by *hoofs* and *roofs* as the plurals of *hoof* and *roof*. There are many nouns ending in /f/ whose last sound never changes in the plural, namely *chiefs* /tʃiːfs/ (*/tʃiːvz/), *laughs* /lɑːfs/ (*/lɑːvz/), *beliefs* /bɪliːfs/ (*/bɪliːvz/). The ongoing elimination of the /f/ ~ /v/ alternation (in *hooves* etc.) is a way of making a quirky part of the system fall into line.

To sum up, the behaviour of /f/-final nouns illustrates two properties of morphophonemic rules:

1 Morphophonemic rules tend to be exception ridden. They rarely apply to all forms with the appropriate phonological properties. In this respect morphophonemic rules differ from purely allophonic rules found in phonology. ALLOPHONIC RULES (which have the job of specifying the phonetic realisation of phonemes) apply automatically and blindly wherever the requisite phonetic

environment that triggers the alternation is present. For instance, any /l/ following a vowel in the same syllable is realised as [ɫ] (see [2.8] p. 17).

2   Morphophonemic rules are triggered by the presence of certain morphemes. They are tied rules which are only permitted to operate if certain morphological information sets them off. Thus, for example, in the data in [3.13] above, if suffix /-z/ represents the plural morpheme, it assimilates the voicing of the last sound of the stem, but if it represents the genitive (as in *the wife's career*), it does not.

3.3.3.2 Phonology in the back seat: lexical and grammatical conditioning

The selection of allomorphs of *root morphemes* is sometimes determined not by the phonological environment but rather by the grammatical context in which the morpheme occurs. Different allomorphs of the root may be used depending on the grammatical word of which it forms part. I will illustrate this by contrasting the base form, the past tense form and the past participle form of the following verbs:

[3.14]	*Base*	*Past tense*	*Past participle*
a	jump	He *jump-ed* yesterday.	He has *jump-ed*.
	call	He *call-ed* yesterday.	He has *call-ed*.
b	ride	He *rode* yesterday.	He has *ridden*.
	drive	He *drove* yesterday.	He has *driven*.
c	sing	He *sang* yesterday.	He has *sung*.
	stink	He *stank* yesterday.	He has *stunk*.

In [3.14a] regular verb stems like *jump* remain unchanged in all three columns. The formation of the past tense and the past participle is simply accomplished by the suffixation of *-ed*. This contrasts with the verbs in [3.14b] and [3.14c] where the grammatical word that is realised by the word-form dictates the allomorph of the stem that is used. Thus in [3.14b] we see the base form *ride* (as in *I ride*). But, if *ride* is in the past tense, it must be realised as *rode* and, if it is the past participle that is required, then the form selected is *ridden*. Similarly, in [3.14c] the base form of *sing* is *sing* (as in *I sing*). But, if *sing* is in the past tense, it must be realised as *sang* and, if it is the past participle that is required, then the form selected is *sung* and so on. This is a case of the selection allomorph of the root being solely conditioned by grammatical factors. Hence it is called GRAMMATICAL CONDITIONING.

The converse is also possible. The selection of INFLECTIONAL AFFIXES may be determined by the presence of a particular lexical root morpheme. Hence this is called LEXICAL CONDITIONING. A classic example of this in English is the way in which *ox* forms its plural as *oxen* rather than **oxes*. Phonologically and grammatically comparable words like *fox ~ foxes* and *box ~ boxes* form their plurals using the regular /-z/ suffix – we certainly do not get **foxen* and **boxen*. In the grammar and phonology of modern English, there is nothing that explains why *ox* has *oxen* as its plural. The suffix *-en* singles out this particular word. In other words, *-en* is a lexically conditioned allomorph of the plural morpheme.

Our final example involves nouns which remain unchanged in the plural:

[3.15] *Singular*: sheep, deer, equipment, aircraft
        Plural: sheep, deer, equipment, aircraft

If a farmer said to you *I lost one sheep but my neighbour lost 200 sheep last year*, you would know that *sheep* is singular in '*one sheep*' but plural in '*200 sheep*', although the same word-form *sheep* is used in both cases. The plural of *sheep* and other words of this ilk is formed by adding a ZERO SUFFIX, as it were. In spite of the absence of any overt number marking, such nouns can function as plurals. A child acquiring English needs to recognise and memorise, word by word, the set of nouns which take zero, rather than the standard /-z/ suffix, because the distribution of the zero plural suffix is lexically conditioned.

3.3.3.3 Madness without method: suppletion

Occasionally, there is no method in the madness. This is so in a tiny minority of cases when SUPPLETION takes place. Then the choice of the allomorphs of a root morpheme that serve in different grammatical contexts is phonologically arbitrary: the allomorphs in question bear no phonological resemblance to each other.

That is what happens in the case of the verb *go*, which has *went* as its past tense form and *gone* as its past participle. The forms *good*, *better* and *best*, which belong to the adjective *good*, also show suppletion since the relationship between the morphs representing the root morpheme is phonologically arbitrary. It would plainly make no sense to claim that there is single underlying representation in the dictionary from which *go* and *went* or *good* and *better* are derived. The best we can do is to content ourselves with listing these allomorphs together under the same entry in the dictionary.

Normally, the word-forms representing the same lexeme show some phonetic similarity (see [3.14] for example). However, when suppletion occurs, the word-form that realises a lexeme bears no reasonable resemblance to the other word-forms representing the same lexeme.

Mercifully, the majority of words follow general rules (for example adding the suitable phonologically conditioned allomorph of the plural /-z/ suffix) and word-forms belonging to the same lexeme are phonologically similar to some degree. Acquiring a language for the most part involves working out these general rules rather than using brute force to commit morphemes and their allomorphs to memory.

3.4 Freedom and bondage

When we classify morphemes in terms of where they are allowed to appear, we find that they fall into two major groupings. Some morphemes are capable of occurring on their own as words, while other morphemes are only allowed to occur in combination with some other morpheme(s) and cannot be used by themselves as independent words.

Those morphemes that are allowed to occur on their own in sentences as words are called FREE MORPHEMES, while those morphemes that must occur in the company of some other morphemes are called BOUND MORPHEMES. In [3.16] the bound morphemes are italicised.

[3.16] pest   pest(i)-*cide*
        modern   *post*-modern-*ist*
        child   child-*ish*
        pack   *pre*-pack-*ed*
        laugh   laugh-*ing*

The free morphemes in [3.16] can all be manipulated by syntactic rules; they can stand on their own as words. By contrast, it is impossible to use the forms -*cide*, *post*-, -*ist*, -*ish*, *pre*-, -*ed* or -*ing* independently.

So far, all the examples of free morphemes that function as roots that we have encountered have been content words (see p. 15). However, not all free morphemes are content words. Some are employed to indicate grammatical functions and logical relationships rather than to convey lexical or cognitive meaning in a sentence. Hence such words are called FUNCTION WORDS. They include words such as the following:

[3.17] articles: *a/an, the*
       demonstratives: e.g. *this, that, these, those*
       pronouns: e.g. *I, you, we, they; my, your, his, hers,*
                            who etc.
       prepositions: e.g. *in, into, on to, at, on* etc.
       conjunctions: e.g. *and, or, but, because, if* etc.

In ordinary language use such words are extremely common. But on their own they would not convey a lot of information. If you received a telegram like *But it my on to the in* you might suspect that the sender either had a strange sense of humour or was not mentally sound.

3.5 Sound symbolism: phonaesthemes and onomatopoeia

In the vast majority of words, the relationship between sound and meaning is arbitrary (see p. 4). There is no reason why a particular sound, or group of sounds, should be used to represent a particular word, with a particular meaning. If someone asked you what [b] in *bed* or [str] in *strange* meant, you would think they were asking a very odd question. As a rule, sounds *qua* sounds do not mean anything.

However, the general principle that says that the link between sound and meaning in words is arbitrary is occasionally dented. This happens in two sets of circumstances. First, certain individual sounds, or groups of sounds, which do not represent a specific enough meaning to be called morphs nevertheless appear to be vaguely associated with some kind of meaning. Such sounds are called PHONAESTHEMES.

As our first example of a phonaestheme, let us take the RP vowel [ʌ] (which is historically descended from [ʊ], the vowel that is still used in words like *dull* and *hut* in the north of England). This phonaestheme is found in words associated with various kinds of dullness or indistinctness, e.g. *dull, thud, thunder, dusk, blunt, mud, slush, sludge, slump* etc. Obviously, the vowel [ʌ] *per se* does not mean 'dull'. If it did, *dim*, which contains the vowel [ɪ], would not be a virtual synonym for *dull*.

Many words which mean 'to talk indistinctly' contain one or more occurrences of the labial consonant [m], which is made with the lips firmly closed, preventing clear articulation. That way, the very act of pronouncing the word iconically mimics a key aspect of its meaning. You can see this if you watch yourself in a mirror saying words like *mumble, murmur, mutter, muted, grumble* etc. It is probably not an accident that these words also contain the phonaestheme [ʌ]. Similarly, the sound [ʌmp] (spelled *-ump*) as in *clump, dump, bump, lump* and *hump* is often found at the end of words which are associated with heaviness and clumsiness, although no one would wish to suggest that *-ump* in itself represents the ideas of heaviness and clumsiness. Interestingly, here again we have the vowel [ʌ] followed by the labial consonants [mp].

Observe also that, whereas [ʌ] tends to have associations of heaviness or dullness, the high front vowels [iː] and [ɪ] frequently occur as phonaesthemes in words associated with smallness, as in *wee, teeny-weeny, lean, meagre, mini, thin* and *little*. (The fact that *big* has the opposite meaning just goes to show that phonaesthemes only represent a tendency.)

Second, and more importantly, in addition to phonaesthemes, there are onomatopoeic words in which a direct association is made between the sounds of a word-form and the meaning that it represents. In cases of ONOMATOPOEIA, the sounds (*qua* sounds and not as morphs) symbolise or reflect some aspect of the meaning of the word that they represent. So, if speakers of any language want an onomatopoeic word for the noise a cat makes, they will not choose a noise like *bimbobam* – except, perhaps, in the land of the Ning Nang Nong.

The words for sounds made by various animals, e.g. *neigh, miaow, moo* etc., are the most obvious examples of onomatopoeia. But there are others such as *roar, crack, clang, bang, splash, swish, whoosh, buzz, hiss, cheep, bleep, gurgle, plop* and *plod*. In the case of onomatopoeic words, the relationship between sound and meaning is to some extent ICONIC. The sounds mimic an aspect of the meaning of the linguistic sign much in the same way that

[3.18]

On the Ning Nang Nong

On the Ning Nang Nong
Where the cows go Bong!
And the Monkeys all say Boo!
There's a Nong Nang Ning
Where the trees go Ping!
And the tea pots Jibber Jabber Joo.
On the Nong Ning Nang
All the mice go Clang!
And you just can't catch 'em when they do!
So it's Ning Nang Nong!
Cows go Bong!
Nong Nang Ning!
Trees go Ping!
Nong Ning Nang!
The mice go Clang!
What a noisy place to belong,
Is the Ning Nang Ning Nang Nong!

Spike Milligan

this iconic sign for a restaurant ✗ represents – an aspect of the meaning 'eat' which a restaurant is all about. This symbol is still conventional to some degree. To people who eat with chopsticks, it might not be immediately obvious why this sign represents a restaurant (rather than a cutlery shop), but once it is pointed out the link can be seen quite easily.

Onomatopoeic words are iconic in so far as they directly reflect some aspect of the meaning of what they stand for. So, conventionally in English cows go 'moo' and horses go 'neigh' and bees go 'buzz'. That is why Spike Milligan's nonsense poem 'On the Ning Nang Nong' is bizarre.

To be onomatopoeic, the sound must imitate to some degree an aspect of the noise made by the bird or animal. But exactly what is imitated will vary from language to language. An English cock will say *cockadoodledoo* and a Russian cock *kukuriku*, but in Uganda a cock may say *kookolilookoo*. (These differences are not attributable to dialectical variation among the males of the *Gallus domesticus* species.) Onomatopoeic words are not purely and simply formed by mimicking precisely the meanings that they convey. To some extent onomatopoeic words are also moulded by linguistic convention. That is why in different places in the world different onomatopoeic words may be used for the same animal or bird noise.

3.6 Summary

In this chapter we have established that words have internal structure. They are built using morphemes which are put together following rigid principles that determine how they are arranged. While the elements of a sentence enjoy a considerable degree of mobility, the morphemes in a word do not.

A basic distinction was drawn between morphemes that are free and capable of occurring independently as words in their own right, and others that are bound which must always be attached to some other morphemes in words. Bound morphemes are incapable of occurring in isolation as self-standing words and so cannot be manipulated directly by rules of the syntax.

In doing morphological analysis, the principles of contrast and complementary distribution play a key role. If morphs (i.e. forms) contrast meaning, they represent distinct morphemes. But if morphs cannot contrast meaning, they are grouped together as allomorphs of the same morpheme.

In principle, the relationship between morphemes and morphs is indirect. It involves representation, not composition. Hence, on the one hand, the same morph may represent different morphemes and, on the other hand, the same morpheme may be represented by distinct allomorphs.

Many morphemes have several allomorphs. The selection of allomorph may be conditioned by phonological, grammatical or lexical factors. Normally, phonological conditioning is due to assimilation: the allomorph that occurs in a particular context is the one that is most similar to the sounds found in neighbouring forms. Very occasionally, allomorphs may be selected arbitrarily (suppletion).

Normally the relationship between a linguistic sign like a morpheme and its meaning is arbitrary. However, in a minority of cases, sound symbolism (in the shape of phonaesthemes and onomatopoeia) plays a role in word-formation. In such cases the relationship between the sign and its meaning is to some extent iconic.

Exercises

1   Using at least one fresh illustrative example, explain what is meant by:

a   morpheme   g   suppletion
b   allomorph   h   zero suffix
c   complementary distribution   i   assimilation
d   phonological conditioning   j   morphophonemics
e   lexical conditioning   k   phonaesteme
f   grammatical conditioning

2   List the meanings associated with the form -er in *faster, Icelander, cooker, louder, sprinkler, grater, baker, milliner, astrologer, washer, buyer, sender* and *pensioner*. Give a suitable descriptive label to each meaning. (If in doubt, consult a good dictionary.)

3   Identify the morphemes in the words below and determine which ones are free, and which ones are bound. In some cases the choice will not be clear-cut. Explain the grounds for your decision.

beds	manly	pedestrian
bedding	mannish	pedal
bedrooms	manhood	pedestal
bedfellows	manager	pedate
unenthusiastically	managers	biped
servility	management	tripod
servant	mismanaged	millipede
server	foothold	centipede
served	footpaths	expedition
services	footlights	expedite
servicing	footman	impede
toiletology	footsteps	impediment
external	paternal	ether
externalise	paternalism	ethereal
externally	paternity	ethernet

4   Account for the pronunciation of the past tense and plural suffixes in the following words. Make your statement as general as possible.

a   watched owned obeyed opted rushed whizzed
b   rocks trees dances midges trends laughs

5   Study these words and answer the questions that follow:

alumni	vertebrae	automata
stimuli	larvae	phenomena
loci	algae	criteria

a   All the words above have been imported into English from other languages. With the help of a good dictionary, find out where they came from.
b   Write down the singular form of each noun.
c   Identify the plural suffix in each noun.
d   Determine whether the selection of the appropriate plural allomorph in these words is phonologically, grammatically or lexically conditioned.

Chapter 4

Building words

4.1 Words and jigsaws

Word manufacture is not a task we leave to experts. We all do it. This chapter surveys techniques of word-formation. Just as anyone putting together a jigsaw must realise that the different pieces go in positions where their shape fits, anyone assembling words must also realise that the various morphemes available in a language can only be used in certain places where they fit. That is not to say there is no room for creativity and innovation. Most words are institutionalised and have to be listed in dictionaries, but others are novel, possibly used as a one-off.

4.2 Know the pieces of the jigsaw

We established in Chapter 3 that words have internal structure. In this section we will consider in some detail the various elements used to create that structure. We will begin with a discussion of roots in section (4.2.1); this will be followed by a treatment of affixes in section (4.2.2).

4.2.1 Roots are the core

A ROOT is a morpheme which forms the core of a word. It is the unit to which other morphemes may be added, or, looked at from another angle, it is what remains when all the affixes are peeled away (for a different view see Giegerich 1999: 88). All roots belong to one of the LEXICAL CATEGORIES, i.e. they belong to the word classes of noun, adjective, verb or adverb. Here are some examples:

[4.1] *Noun*	*Adjective*	*Verb*	*Adverb*
bell	big	bring	now
child	black	eat	soon
tree	good	love	here
lion	strong	think	very

We saw in the last chapter that many words contain a free morpheme, which may occur on its own with nothing appended to it. The vast majority of root morphemes that are capable of appearing on their own are CONTENT WORDS, i.e. nouns, verbs, adjectives and adverbs (see section 2.2.1).

We also saw that there are very many morphemes which are always kept in bondage. These are the bound morphemes, which are totally barred from occurring independently. Many roots fall into this category. Examples of BOUND ROOTS are provided in [4.2a] below. In each case the root is italicised and separated from the rest of the word (which may contain one or more morphemes).

[4.2] a *sanct-* 'holy'   *vir-* 'man'   *tox-* 'poison'   *loc-* 'place'
        *sanct-*ify   *vir-*ile   *tox-*in   *loc-*al
        *sanct-*um   *vir-*il-ity   *tox-*ic   *loc-*ate
        *sanct-*uary   *vir-*ago   non-*tox-*ic   dis-*loc-*ate
        *sanct-*ity   trium-*vir-*ate in-*tox-*ic-ate   *loc-*um

      b *region-al*   *civil-*ity   *glor(y)-*ify
        season-al   *banal-*ity   *person-*ify
        emotion-al   *solemn-*ity   *solid-ify*

The data in [4.2b] illustrate another important point. Some of the forms to which affixes are attached are fully fledged words in their own right. There is a need for a common term to refer to forms, be they bound roots or self-standing words, to which affixes may be attached. The term BASE is used to meet this need. Any form to which affixes are appended in word-formation is called a base. Bases to which affixes are added can be bound roots like *loc-* in *loc-al*, *loc-um*, *loc-us* or independent words like *season* in *season-al*. They can also be forms which already contain other affixes, e.g. [[*loc-al*]-*ity*], [[*loc-al*]-*ism*].

An issue raised by the segmentation of words into morphemes is what counts as a morpheme. I suspect that *sanct-*, *vir-* and *tox-* do not jump at you as obvious examples of morphemes in the same way that *govern* does because their meanings are not immediately obvious. An etymological dictionary, or a knowledge of Latin, might help to persuade you that these are indeed recognisable morphemes. But your intuitions as a speaker of English would probably not enable you to reach that conclusion. So the question arises of how to treat such awkward cases. If a form was recognisable at some time in the past as a morpheme, does that mean that for ever more it should be recognised as a morpheme? Where do we draw the line between forms whose analysis is only of historical or etymological relevance and those whose analysis is well motivated in the synchronic study of the language? We will just note this tricky problem for the moment and defer tackling it until section (5.6).

4.2.2 Affixes are for appending

It is clear that many words are complex. They are made up of a root together with other morphemes. Any morphemes that are appended to the root are called AFFIXES. We shall discuss affixes in a preliminary way in this section and return to them in more detail in section (4.4.1).

Affixes can be attached before or after the base. For instance, using the root *polite* as our base, we can form the new lexical items by adding -*ness* to give *polite-ness* ('the property of being polite') or -*ly* to give *polite-ly* ('in a polite manner'). An affix that is appended after the base (e.g. -*ness* and -*ly*) is called a SUFFIX, while an affix that goes before the base, as *im-* does in *im-polite*, is called a PREFIX.

In some languages affixes are not just placed before or after the base. Some are inserted inside it. Such affixes are called INFIXES. Thus, in the Tagalog language of the Philippines, the infix -*um*- is placed after the initial consonant of the root to mark 'non-future tense':

[4.3]	*Base*		*Infixed form*	*Non-future (present or past) tense*
a	bili	'buy'	b-um-ili	'buy/bought' (not 'will buy')
b	sulat	'write'	s-um-ulat	'write/wrote' (not 'will write')
c	basa	'read'	b-um-asa	'read/read' (not 'will read')

English has no bound infix morphemes. But, in expressive language, expletives can be inserted into other words as in:

[4.4] a My ex now lives in Minne-bloody-sota.
       b That was fan-*bleeding*-tastic!

Several more colourful four-letter words could also be infixed. Can you think of some?

You will observe that there are phonological factors that play a role here. The base will normally have at least three syllables. (Hence *Stu-bloody-pid* is not acceptable). The infix itself is normally two syllables long and is placed immediately before the syllable of the base that carries the main stress of the word (see Bauer 1983: 90).

Up to now all the word-building elements we have encountered have been morphs that represent a morpheme; they have all been entities associated with some meaning. This is not always the case. Sometimes, morphological forms that do not represent any meaning are used in word-building in the same way that blank fillers are put in by a joiner to occupy space when cupboards or doors do not quite fill the entire space available. We will call such 'blanks' FORMATIVES. For instance, the adjective-forming suffix -al is attached directly to *region* to form *regional* and to *politic* to form *political*. However, when -al is suffixed to some other bases a bridging formative is needed. Thus, in the case of *contract* we get *contractual*. The meaningless formative -u- must intervene between the base *contract* and the suffix -al. We cannot just say *contractal.

4.3 The main types of word-building: inflection and derivation

We have seen above the types of morphemes that are available. Now we will consider how they are deployed. We will see that word-building processes fall into two broad categories: INFLECTION and DERIVATION. Typically inflection contributes a morpheme that is required in order to ensure that the word has a form that is appropriate for the grammatical context in which it is used. For instance, if we have a third person subject, a present tense verb agreeing with it must take the -s ending; anything else is forbidden:

[4.5] She run*s* her business very efficiently.
      *She run her business very efficiently.
      *She running her business very efficiently.

To take another example, a monosyllabic adjective (e.g. *tall*, *nice*, *short* etc.) or a disyllabic adjective with a weak second syllable (e.g. *clever*, *thirsty*, *dirty* etc.) must take the comparative degree of suffix -*er* if it is followed by *than* indicating comparison. Failure to use the -*er* ending results in ungrammaticality:

[4.6] John is tall*er* than Jane. (*John is tall/tallest than Jane.)
He is dirt*ier* than Robin. (*He is dirty/dirtiest than Robin.)
I am short*er* than you. (*I am short/shortest than you.)

OBLIGATORINESS is an important feature of inflection. In [4.5] the choice of the verb form ending in -*s* and in [4.6] the choice of the adjective ending in -*er* is not a matter of personal preference. It is mandatory. The application of an inflectional process is automatically triggered if the right syntactic conditions obtain. Can you diagnose what is wrong with the extract from Roald Dahl's *The BFG* in [4.7] beside the spelling and punctuation? (See also section (4.4.1).)

Whereas inflection is driven by the requirement to form a word with the appropriate form in a particular grammatical context, derivation is motivated by the desire to create new lexical items using pre-existing morphemes and words. When you need a new word (in the sense of vocabulary item), you do not usually need to make it up from scratch. It is possible to create new lexical items by recycling pre-existing material. This is derivation. It takes one of these forms: AFFIXATION, CONVERSION, STRESS PLACEMENT or COMPOUNDING.

Derivation enables us to add new lexical items to the OPEN WORD-CLASSES of noun, or adjective, verb and adverb. These are the classes that contain the so-called content words (see section (2.2.1)). We are extremely unlikely to create new words belonging to classes like pronouns, articles or prepositions. Hence these classes are said to be CLOSED. It is extremely unlikely that one fine morning you will wake up with the inspired idea that English needs some new articles – the same boring *the*, *a/an* have been around too long – and coin a dozen fresh articles as a public service.

Not everyone would characterise derivation in the way that I have, contrasting derivation which produces new lexical items with inflection which produces grammatical words. Many linguists restrict the term derivation to the creation of new lexical items by adding affixes (including 'zero' ones: see p. 42). They explicitly distinguish it from compounding, which combines two bases containing root morphemes to form a new lexical item.

[4.7]

I HAS RITTEN A BOOK AND IT IS SO EXCITING NOBODY CAN PUT IT
DOWN. AS SOON AS YOU HAS RED THE FIRST LINE YOU IS SO HOOKED
ON IT YOU CANNOT STOP UNTIL THE LAST PAGE. IN ALL THE CITIES
PEEPLE IS WALKING IN THE STREETS BUMPING INTO EACH OTHER
BECAUSE THEIR FACES IS BURIED IN MY BOOK AND DENTISTS IS
READING IT AND TRYING TO FILL TEETHS AT THE SAME TIME BUT
NOBODY MINDS BECAUSE THEY IS ALL READING IT TOO IN THE
DENTISTS CHAIR. DRIVER IS READING IT WHILE DRIVING AND CARS IS
CRASHING ALL OVER THE COUNTRY. BRAIN SURGEONS IS READING
IT WHILE THEY IS OPERATING ON BRAINS AND AIRLINE PILOTS IS
READING IT AND GOING TO TIMBUCTOO INSTEAD OF LONDON. FOOT-
BALL PLAYERS IS READING IT ON THE FIELD BECAUSE THEY CAN'T PUT
IT DOWN AND SO IS OLIMPICK RUNNERS WHILE THEY IS RUNNING.

EVERYBODY HAS TO SEE WHAT IS GOING TO HAPPEN NEXT IN MY BOOK
AND WHEN I WAKE UP I IS STILL TINGLING WITH EXCITEMENT AT BEING
THE GREATEST RITER THE WORLD HAS EVER KNOWN UNTIL MY MUMMY
COMES IN AND SAYS I WAS LOOKING AT YOUR ENGLISH EXERCISE BOOK
LAST NITE AND REALLY YOUR SPELLING IS ATROSHUS SO IS YOUR
PUNTULASHON.

I prefer a two-way distinction between inflection on the one hand, and a broadly defined category of derivation on the other, because it highlights clearly the fact that essentially all word-formation boils down to one of two things: either the creation of lexical items, the province of derivation, or the creation of grammatical words, the province of inflection. It should be pointed out, however, that there are other (marginal) methods of forming lexical items that fall outside derivation (see Chapter 8).

4.4 Derivation: fabricating words

Most of the words you use in a day have been part of the English language for a long time. But that does not necessarily mean that you have memorised all of them. In many cases, and to varying degrees, we can reconstitute words we encounter as the need arises, or even occasionally coin new ones. What makes this possible is our mastery of the rules of word-formation. Confronted with a complex word, you will often be able to deconstruct it using your knowledge of word structure.

How can knowledge of word-structure be represented? We can represent the structure of a complex word such as *teachers*, *Americanisation*, *governmental* and *ungovernability* in two ways. We can use LABELLED BRACKETS as in [4.8] or a TREE DIAGRAM as in [4.9]. Either way, we want to show which morphemes in the word go together, and what string of morphemes forms the input to each word-formation process. Further we need to know the word-class to which the resulting word belongs.

[4.8] *Labelled brackets*
     $[teach]_V er]_N s]_N$
     $[Americ(a)]_N an]_{Adj.} is]_V ation]_N$
     $[[govern]_V ment]_N al]_{Adj.}$

[4.9] *Tree diagrams*

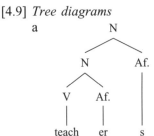

b

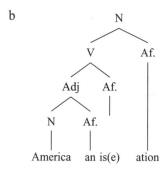

c

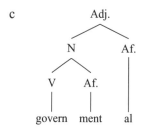

Note: af. = affix

Many complex words that contain multiple affixes have internal structure. When a base that contains one or more affixes is used as an input to a process that attaches more affixes, certain morphemes go more closely together than others and form a subgrouping.

4.4.1 Affixation: prefixes and suffixes

Probably the commonest method of forming words (in the sense of lexical terms) is by AFFIXATION. Affixes have already been introduced in section (4.2.2). We will now briefly examine their characteristics and return to them in more detail in Chapter 5.

The meanings of many affixes are not altogether transparent. It may be necessary sometimes to look them up in an etymological dictionary (like the *OED* or Skeat 1982). This of course raises questions about what we are doing when we divide words up into morphemes. To what extent is the morphological segmentation of words a historical exercise? In this chapter we will concentrate on the identification of morphemes and leave this awkward question to one side until section (5.6).

It is possible to group together affixes in different ways depending on one's purposes. For instance, we can classify affixes on the basis of their meaning. We can recognise a class of negative prefixes, e.g. *im-* (*im-possible*), *un-* (*un-necessary*), *dis-* (*dis-approve*), *non-* (*non-combatant*) etc. Alternatively, we could group affixes together on the basis of their phonological properties. It has been shown that affixes fall into two major classes: some are NEUTRAL while others are NON-NEUTRAL in their effects. Neutral affixes do not trigger a modification of the base to which they are attached; non-neutral ones do (see section (5.5.1)).

Normally, prefixes are stress neutral. Thus, in [4.10] stress falls on the same syllable in the word regardless of their presence or absence.

[4.10] *Stress-neutral prefixes*

 be- (forming derivative verbs with the general meaning of 'around')
  beset, besmear, becloud, bedarken, bejewel
 co-/con-/com- 'together'
  co-operate, co-habit, co-appear, co-opt, combine, conspire
 ex- 'former'
  ex-miner, ex-wife, ex-leader, ex-director, ex-pupil, ex-pilot
 mis- 'wrongly, badly'
  mis-understand, mis-manage, mis-read, mis-take, mis-inform, mis-allocate
 mal(e)- 'bad(ly)'
  malcontent, malpractice, maladjusted, malefactor, malevolent, maladroit
 re- 'again'
  re-think, re-take, re-play, re-examine, re-issue
 un- 'negative'
  unexciting, unhappy, uncomfortable, unwise, unmanageable, uncool
 dis- 'negative' (with adjectives)
  dishonest, dishonourable, discomfortable
 dis- 'negative, reversive' (with verbs)
  disallow, disagree, disapprove, dislike, disaffirm, disbelieve, disarm
 in- 'negative' (with adjectives)
  inarticulate, inactive, inept, inevitable, intangible, innumerable

un- 'negative' (with adjectives)
unoriginal, unusual, unseemly, unripe, unpleasant,
unsavoury, unreliable
un- 'reversive' (with verbs)
undo, unblock, unpack, unravel, unpick, unseat, unroll,
unsaddle

Next, let us survey derivational suffixes. Coverage is not meant to be comprehensive by any means, but it should be sufficient to provide a reasonably good picture of derivational affixation. In [4.11] I have provided a representative sample of derivational suffixes together with their general meaning, the grammatical class of bases that they attach to and the grammatical class of the resulting word. Discussion of the phonological effects of suffixes will be taken up in Chapter 5.

[4.11] DERIVATIONAL SUFFIXES
    a *Verb → Noun*
        -ation   'derives nouns of action from verbs':
                don-ation, reconcili-ation, regul-ation
        -ant   'person who does whatever the verb means':
                inhabit-ant, protest-ant, occup-ant
        -ant   'instrument that is used to do whatever the verb means':
                lubric-ant, stimul-ant, intoxic-ant
        -er   'person who does whatever the verb means':
                teach-er, build-er, paint-er
        -er   'instrument that is used to do whatever the verb means':
                cook-er, strain-er, drain-er
        -ing   'act of doing whatever the verb indicates':
                learn-ing, sav-ing, wait-ing
        -ist   'derives agent nouns from verbs – one who does X':
                cycl-ist, typ-ist, copy-ist
        -ion   'derives nouns of condition or action from verbs':
                eros-ion (from *erode*), corros-ion (from *corrode*), persuas-ion (from *persuade*), radiat-ion, promotion
        -ment   'the result or product of the action of the verb; the instrument used to perform the action of the verb':
                pave-ment, appoint-ment, pay-ment

-*ery*   'derives nouns indicating a place where animals are kept or plants grown':
catt-ery, pigg-ery, orang-ery, shrubb-ery

-*ery*   'derives nouns indicating place where the action specified by the verb takes place':
bak-ery, brew-ery, fish-ery, refin-ery

-*ee*   '(passive) person who undergoes action indicated by the verb':
employ-ee, detain-ee, pay-ee, intern-ee

b *Verb → Adj.*

-*ing*   'in the process or state of doing whatever the verb indicates':
wait-ing (as in *waiting car*) stand-ing (as in *standing passengers*)

-*ise/-ize* 'to bring about whatever the adjective signals':
real-ise, neutral-ise, fertil-ise, immun-ise

-*ive*   'having the tendency to X; having the quality character of X; given to the action of X-ing':
act-ive, pens-ive, evas-ive, representat-ive

-*able*   'able to be X-ed':
read-able, govern-able; manage-able, do-able

-*ing*   'the act of doing whatever the verb signifies':
sing-ing, fight-ing, writ-ing

c *Noun → Verb*

-*ate*   'derives verbs from nouns':
regul-ate, capacit-ate, don-ate

-*ise/-ize* 'to bring about whatever the noun signals':
colon-ise, American-ise, computer-ise

-*ise/-ize* 'put in the place or state indicated by the noun':
hospital-ise, terror-ise, jeopard-ise

d *Noun → Adj.*

-*al*   'pertaining to X':
autumn-al, dent-al, division-al, tradition-al

-*ate*   'derives adjectives denoting state':
intim-ate, accur-ate, obdur-ate
(There is normally a corresponding noun ending in -*acy*, e.g. intim-acy, accur-acy, obdur-acy.)

-*ish*   'having the (objectionable) nature, qualities or character of X':
lout-ish, fiend-ish, child-ish

-less	'without X':
	joy-less, care-less, fear-less
-ful	'filled with X':
	joy-ful, care-ful, fear-ful, cheer-ful
-(i)an	'associated with whatever the noun indicates':
	Chomsky-an, suburb-an, Trinidad-(i)an, reptil-(i)an
-some	'forms adjectives from verbs, having quality X':
	quarrel-some, trouble-some, tire-some

e *Adj.* → *Verb*

-ate	'cause to become, do etc. whatever the adjective indicates':
	activ-ate (< active) equ-ate (< equal)
-ise	'cause to become whatever the adjective indicates':
	modern-ise, steril-ise, stabil-ise, civil-ise

f *Adj.* → *Noun*

-ness	'forms a noun expressing state or condition':
	good-ness, fair-ness, bitter-ness, dark-ness
-ity	'forms a noun expressing state or condition':
	timid-ity, banal-ity, pur-ity, antiqu-ity
-ship	'state or condition of being X':
	hard-ship
-ery	'having the property indicated by the adjective':
	brav-ery, effront-ery, trick-ery

g *Adj.* → *Adv.*

-ly	'forms adverbs from adjectives':
	usual-ly, busi-ly, proud-ly, loud-ly

h *Noun* → *Noun*

-aire	'to be possessed of X':
	million-aire, doctrin-aire, solit-aire
-acy	'derives a noun of quality, state or condition from another noun or adjective (normally the base to which it is added also takes the nominal suffix *-ate*)':
	advoc-acy, episcop-acy, intim-acy, accur-acy, obdur-acy

-*er*   'a person who practises a trade or profession connected to the noun':

marin-er, geograph-er, football-er, haberdash-er, hatt-er

-*ery*   'derives nouns indicating general collective sense "-ware, stuff"':

machin-ery, crock-ery, jewell-ery, pott-ery

-*let*   'derives a diminutive noun':

pig-let, is-let, riv(u)-let

-*ling*   'derives a diminutive noun from another noun':

duck-ling, prince-ling, found-ling

-*hood*   'quality, state, rank of being X':

boy-hood, sister-hood, priest-hood

-*ship*   'state or condition of being X':

king-ship, craftsman-ship, director-ship, steward-ship

-*ism*   'forms nouns which are the name of a theory, doctrine or practice':

femin-ism, capital-ism, Marx-ism, structural-ism

-*ist*   'adherent to some -*ism*, a protagonist for X, an expert on X' (usually a base that takes -*ist* also takes -*ism*):

femin-ist, capital-ist, Marx-ist, structural-ist

i   *Adj. → Adj.*

-*ish*   'having the property of being somewhat X':

narrow-ish, blu-ish, pink-ish

j   *Verb → Verb*

-*er*   'adds frequent or iterative meaning to verbs':

chatt-er, patt-er, flutt-er

Having studied [4.11], I suggest that you now find one fresh example of a word that contains each of the suffixes listed. Afterwards identify two non-neutral suffixes which affect the location of stress in the base to which they are attached and two neutral ones that do not. This will give you a taste of the challenge posed by suffixes for morphological theory by the interaction between word-formation rules and phonological rules. We will take up that challenge in the next chapter.

Let us now turn to INFLECTIONAL SUFFIXES. English has not got much inflection, being essentially an isolating language, i.e. a language whose simple noncompound words normally contain just one morpheme (e.g. *cut, walk, snow*). The little inflection that it has consists of suffixes rather than prefixes. [4.12] contains a sample of common inflectional suffixes.

[4.12] a

Verbal suffixes	Function	Example
-s	3rd person, singular, present	He snore-s
-ing	progressive aspect (denoting action in progress)	He is snor-ing
-ed	past tense	He snor-ed

b *Noun suffixes*

-s	noun plural marker	road-s

c *Adj. suffixes*

-er	comparative adjective/adverb	slow-er, soon-er
-est	superlative adjective/adverb	slow-est, soon-est

A base to which inflectional affixes are added is called a STEM. Singling out stems from other bases in this fashion enables us to highlight the distinction between inflection and derivation. This is important, as we will see in sections (11.2.2) and (11.4.1), not only for the way linguists describe language but also for the way in which the brain processes words. So the bases in *road-s, government-s* and *schoolboy-s* are all stems since they are followed by the plural inflectional suffix *-s*. Of course, the internal structure of these stems is different: *road* is a simple root, *govern-ment* is a complex one, containing as it does the derivational suffix *-ment*; and *schoolboy* is also complex since it is a compound word.

Although until now we have treated inflection and derivation separately, it does not mean that they are mutually exclusive. Both derivational and inflectional morphemes may be found in the same word. In that event, derivational morphemes are attached first and any inflectional morphemes are added later, as it were. That is why, when both inflectional and derivational morphemes are present, the inflectional morphemes are on the outer fringes of the word, as you can see in [4.13]. In other words, derivation can create the input to inflection. A new lexeme that has been yielded by derivation can subsequently undergo inflection in order to ensure that the word has the appropriate grammatical properties for the syntactic position in which it occurs.

Similarly, if both compounding and inflection take place, as a rule compounding is carried out first. So, the inflectional morpheme is appended on the outer margins to the second element of the compound, which is on the right ([4.14a]). Finally, if a compound stem which includes an affixed base is inflected, as in [4.14b], again the inflectional morpheme appears on the margin, as the element of the word furthest to the right:

[4.13] *Inflection of stems with derivational suffixes*
   de-regul-at(e)-*ed* (*de-regul-*ed*-ate)
   perfect-ion-ist-*s* (*perfect-*s*-ion-ist)

[4.14] a *Inflection of compound stems*
   bed-room-*s* (*bed-*s*-room)
   wind-surf-*ing* (*wind-*ing*-surf)

b *Inflection of compound stems (including a derived base)*
   foot-ball-er-*s* (*foot-*s*-ball-er)
   trouble-shoot-er-*s* (*trouble-*s*-shoot-er)

Thus, inflectional morphemes tend to be more peripheral than derivational morphemes in a word, not only in English but also in other languages (see Katamba 1993).

4.4.2 Conversion

In English very often lexical items are created not by affixation but by CONVERSION or ZERO DERIVATION, i.e. without any alteration being made to the shape of the input base. The word-form remains the same, but it realises a different lexical item.

Conversion of verbs into nouns and nouns into verbs is extremely productive in English. Usually the same word-form can be used as a verb or a noun, with only the grammatical context enabling us to know which category it belongs to. Thus, *jump* in the two sentences below is exactly the same in form but it belongs to two different lexemes. In [4.15a] *jump* is the non-finite form of the verb 'jump' while in [4.14b] it is the singular form of the noun *jump*.

[4.15] a The pig will jump over the stile!
      b What a jump!

In *What a jump!* the verb is converted into a noun by 'zero derivation', i.e. without using any affix. What enables us to know whether
the word is a noun or a verb is the position that it occupies in the
sentence. If we see the subject *the pig* and the auxiliary verb *will*
before the word *jump*, we know it must be a verb. But when *jump*
occurs after the indefinite article *a* we know it must be a noun.

In [4.16] I have listed some common examples of forms that are
subject to noun-to-verb or verb-to-noun conversion. It is not difficult to think of situations where these words may be used either as
nouns or as verbs:

[4.16] light   bridge   seat   kick
        fish   bus   dog   lift
        farm   police   smear   finger
        smell   skin   rain   paper

Conversion is not restricted to nouns and verbs. Adjectives too
can undergo conversion. For instance, the word-form *green* realises
an adjective in [4.17a] and a noun in [4.17b]:

[4.17] a The Green Party first had political clout in the 1980s.
      b The Greens first had political clout in the 1980s.

Likewise, some adverbs are formed from adjectives without any
perceptible change in shape:

[4.18] a She is a *fast* runner. (*fast*$_{\text{Adj.}}$)
          She runs very *fast*. (*fast*$_{\text{Adv.}}$)

Slow has even more possibilities. It can be an adjective, an adverb,
a verb or a noun:

[4.19] a He is a slow bowler. (*slow*$_{\text{Adj.}}$)
      b Go slow. (*slow*$_{\text{Adv.}}$)
      c Slow the car! (*slow*$_{\text{Verb}}$)
      d *Mr Slow* is a popular children's book. (*slow*$_{\text{Noun}}$)

The widespread use of conversion shows the importance of the criterion of syntactic function in determining word-class membership

in English. Very often it is by its function rather than by its morphological form that we tell the word-class to which a word belongs.

4.4.3 Stress placement

The interaction of grammar and phonology in the derivation of disyllabic words should be noted. Stress falls on the first syllable if the word surfaces as a noun and on the second syllable if it surfaces as a verb:

[4.20]   *Stress on prefix*   *Stress on first syllable of*
                                   the base
         a   NOUN   VERB
             ˈconduct   conˈduct
             ˈconvert   conˈvert
             ˈexport   exˈport

In some cases, in addition to the stress change, there is also a change in the vowels, e.g. *record* /ˈrekɔːd/(noun) vs. *record* /rɪˈkɔːd/ (verb). Here we will ignore such phonological changes, which are not important for our present purposes.

4.4.4 Compound parade

The third method of forming new lexical items is to use COMPOUND-ING. In this section I will present a brief outline of compounding in English. For more extensive coverage of compounds see Marchand (1969), Adams (1973, 2001), Roeper and Siegel (1978), Selkirk (1982), Lieber (1983), Bauer (1983) and Katamba (1993).

As mentioned already, a compound is formed by combining two bases, which may be words in their own right, to form a new lexical item. This is shown in [4.21a] where the two bases are separated by a hyphen:

[4.21] a   shop-steward   ink-pot
            room-mate   road-show
            moon-light   shoe-string

        b   strong-mind = ed   book-sell = er
            old-fashion = ed   market-garden = er
            time-honour = ed   script-writ = er

As we saw at the end of section (4.4.1), compounding and affixation are by no means incompatible. An affixed base may serve as input to a compounding process, and vice versa. In [4.21b], the suffix is separated by '=' from the base.

Compounds differ in their structure. The majority of English compounds are nouns. Common types of noun compounds include the following:

[4.22]

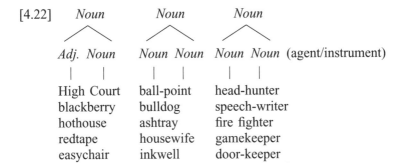

Noun	*Noun*	*Noun*
Adj. Noun	*Noun Noun*	*Noun Noun* (agent/instrument)
High Court	ball-point	head-hunter
blackberry	bulldog	speech-writer
hothouse	ashtray	fire fighter
redtape	housewife	gamekeeper
easychair	inkwell	door-keeper

Let us now turn to examples of adjectival compounds. Some are listed in [4.23]:

[4.23]

$N + V_{en}$	$Adj. + V_{ing}$	$Adj. + V_{en}$
crestfallen	hard-working	clear-sighted
waterlogged	good-looking	hard-featured
heartbroken	easygoing	soft-hearted
frost-bitten	fast-growing	new-born

> *Note*: *Ven* is the past participial form of the verb. It is the verb form that ends in *-en* or *-ed* after *has*, e.g. in *It has eaten* or in *It has wounded*.

An interesting property of most compounds is that they are HEADED. This means that one of the words that make up the compound is syntactically dominant. In English the head is normally the item on the right hand of the compound. The syntactic properties of the head are passed on to the entire compound. Thus, in our examples above, if we have a compound like *easychair* which is made up of the adjective *easy* and the noun *chair*, syntactically the entire word is a noun. This applies to all the words in the left-hand column in [4.22].

Furthermore, the syntactic head is usually also the semantic head of the compound. The non-head element in the compound specifies more narrowly some characteristic of the head. So, an *easychair* is a type of *chair* and a *bulldog* is a kind of *dog* etc. If a compound contains a semantic head, it is called an ENDOCENTRIC COMPOUND. Unfortunately, at the semantic level headedness is not consistently applied. A minority of compounds have no semantic head. Take *turncoat* and *head-hunter*. Literally, a *turncoat* is a person who 'turns his or her coat'. But the word means 'renegade'. A *head-hunter* at one time might literally have hunted people for their heads. Today's head-hunter works in a recruitment firm that searches for top executive talent. Such words are examples of EXOCENTRIC COMPOUNDS.

Let us now turn to the phonology of compounds. As mentioned in Chapter 2, compounds typically have one word that receives the main word stress while the other word is relatively less prominent. Contrast the stress pattern of the compound nouns in [4.24a] and in the noun phrases containing the same words in [4.24b]:

[4.24] a *Compound*　　　　　　b *Phrase*
　　　　　ˈWhite 'House　　　　　'white ˈhouse
　　　　　ˈgreen 'fly　　　　　　'green ˈfly
　　　　　ˈwet 'suit　　　　　　'wet ˈsuit
　　　　　ˈhot 'dog　　　　　　'hot ˈdog
　　　　　ˈblack 'bird　　　　　'black ˈbird

　　　　Note: ˈ = main (or primary) stress and ' = secondary stress.

Normally in compound nouns primary stress falls on the first word and the second word gets secondary stress, as in the ˈ*White* '*House* (the residence of the US President in Washington) and the other words in [4.24a]. However, in the phrases in [4.24b] like '*white* ˈ*house* (as opposed to any house that is painted green, purple or pink) the reverse is true. The second word receives primary stress, and the first word gets secondary stress.

Another aspect of compounding that has interested linguists in recent years is the place of compounds in the lexicon. The question that has been raised is whether or not compounds should be listed in the dictionary. The consensus is that compounding is very widely and productively used in word-formation and many headed compound words do not need to be listed in the dictionary because their meanings are so transparent that they can be worked out using standard rules in the grammar.

COMPOSITIONALITY holds the key. Normally we can work out the meaning of the whole from the meanings of its parts. If we know the meanings of the smaller units which the larger unit contains, we can work out the meaning of the whole. In syntax we do not need to list sentences with their meanings since they are predictable from the meanings of the words they contain and the grammatical and semantic relationships between them. If we know what the words mean, using our knowledge of syntactic and semantic rules we can work out the meanings of sentences, even ones we have not previously encountered like *The unicorn kicked the yeti* and *The yeti was kicked by the unicorn*. Similarly, in morphology, where the meaning of compound words is compositional, we do not need to list them in the dictionary.

Following Selkirk (1982), I shall argue that the same rules that characterise the structure of sentences are used to construct and interpret transparent, compositionally formed compounds such as those in [4.25]. The examples and the analysis are based on Marchand (1969):

[4.25] a watchmaker   b fishing rod   c writing table
       road-sweeper   frying pan   waiting room
       bookseller   carving knife   dining room
       speech-writer   sewing machine   ironing board

All the examples in [4.25] are DEVERBAL COMPOUND NOUNS, i.e. noun compounds formed from verbs. Their structure is like that of a sentence fragment where the verb is in construction with a noun (or more precisely a NP: noun phrase) which has a very intimate syntactic and semantic relation with it. Semantically, the NP has a role like agent, instrument or patient vis-à-vis the verb (see Selkirk 1982).

In the *bookseller* type of compound in [4.25a], the NP refers to someone whose role is that of AGENT, i.e. the person who does whatever the verb signifies. The head, which is the element on the right in the compound, is a noun derived from a verb by adding the *-er* suffix which forms nouns denoting agents. Corresponding to the compound *bookseller* is the clause 'someone who sells books'; corresponding to *watchmaker* is the clause 'someone who makes watches' etc.

In the *fishing rod* type of deverbal noun compound in [4.25b], the head NP on the right of the compound denotes an INSTRUMENT used to perform whatever action is designated by the verb. The element on the left that tells us in more specific terms about the head is a GERUNDIVE NOUN which is derived from the verb by suffixing *-ing*. A *fishing rod* is in a very literal sense a 'rod used for fishing'. The instrumental interpretation serves us well in the rest of the examples. A *frying pan* is 'a pan used for frying', a *carving knife* is 'a knife used for carving' etc.

The final set of examples found in [4.25c], which includes *writing table*, is similar in structure to the examples in (b). Again we have a gerundive noun as the non-head constituent on the left of the compound. What is different here is the semantic relationship between the gerundive and the head NP following it. Whereas in column (b) the head NP that follows the gerundive functions as the instrument used to do whatever the verb that underlies the gerundive denotes, in column (c) the head NP indicates the LOCATION where the action or event or state designated by the verb underlying the gerundive takes place. A *writing table* is 'a table at which one writes', a *waiting room* is 'a room where one stays while waiting' etc. There is a sentence which corresponds to each one of these verbal compounds. The reason for this is that verbal compounds are derived from sentences.

Now, the number of grammatical sentences in English (or any other language) is unlimited. So, it would be futile to try to memorise *all* the sentences that are sanctioned by the rules of English grammar. The same is true of verbal compounds, since they have sentences as their source. It would be futile to attempt to list all verbal compounds. So, speakers master a system of grammatical rules that allows them both to construct and to understand an indefinitely large number of sentences. One refinement is necessary: often the general interpretation of compounds provided by the grammar requires a little fine tuning. For instance, given a deverbal compound noun with a locative meaning, e.g. *waiting room*, the grammar enables us to determine that it is a room where people wait. But it will not enable us to know that it is a room in a public place like a railway station designated especially for that purpose.

A major part of the rule system in the grammar consists of PHRASE STRUCTURE RULES whose job is to define CONSTITUENT STRUCTURE. By constituent structure we mean word groupings that form coherent units called PHRASES on which syntactic rules operate. Some simplified phrase structure rules are shown below.

[4.26] a S → NP VP
      b NP → (Det.) N (PP)
      c VP → V (NP) (PP)
      d PP → P NP
      Notes: 1 The arrow → is to be interpreted as 'consists of'.
              2 Parentheses indicate that the presence of an item
                 is optional. The rest of the abbreviations are
                 listed on p. xx.

Often it is more convenient to show the information conveyed in phrase structure rules using a PHRASE STRUCTURE TREE. Such trees express more explicitly the 'hierarchical' nature of syntactic structure. Syntactic organisation is like Chinese boxes, with smaller units contained in bigger units.

The first three phrase structure rules [4.26] can be re-stated as shown in [4.27].

[4.27] a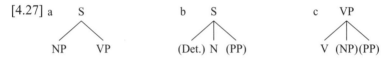

It says in [4.27a] that a sentence contains two constituents, a NP and a VP; [4.27b] says that a NP can contain a noun on its own or a noun together with either or both a determiner and a PP. In [4.27c] we see that a VP must contain a verb which may be followed by either a NP or a PP, or both a NP and a PP.

In the dictionary, words are entered with a word-class label like N for noun, Adj. for adjective, V for verb and P for preposition. A word belonging to the appropriate class is selected to fill a slot below N, V, P etc. In other words, below N we put a noun, below V we put a verb, and so forth. We can represent a whole sentence in a tree diagram as shown in [4.28]:

[4.28]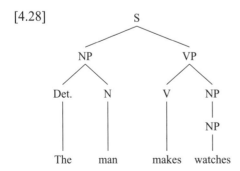

Phrase structure rules and phrase structure trees are not to be seen merely as a statement of the constituent structure of a given sentence but as very general rules for GENERATING, i.e. enumerating, an indefinitely large number of sentences with the same structure. *The man makes watches* is analogous to *The girl loves tennis, The chicken lays eggs, The student hates exams* etc. All these sentences and thousands more are generated by [4.28] if the appropriate words are provided.

At no cost, we can use the rules that produce sentences to produce compound words. Selkirk (1982) has proposed that in morphology we should characterise the structure of compounds by harnessing the phrase structure rules used in syntax. We can represent the structure of the deverbal compounds we have discussed using these phrase structure trees:

[4.29] Deverbal compounds

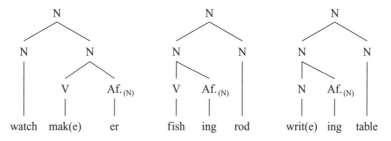

To conclude, the fact that deverbal compounding usually operates in a predictable way means that it is not necessary to list all the compounds in the lexicon and memorise them. Just as it is possible to use phrase structure rules in syntax to produce an indefinitely large number of sentences, it is also possible, when dealing with lexical items, to use phrase structure rules in morphology to produce an indefinitely large number of compound words. Morphology is no different to syntax in the rules it employs for this purpose.

4.4.4 Wishy-washy and razzle-dazzle words

Sapir (1921: 76) observed that nothing is more natural than the prevalence of REDUPLICATION – the repetition of the base of a word in part or in its entirety. He observed that, though rare, reduplication is found in English, e.g.:

[4.30] pooh-pooh   goody-goody   wishy-washy
   sing-song   roly-poly   harum-scarum

Later on, Thun (1963) showed that reduplication is less marginal than is commonly assumed. He listed and examined about 2,000 reduplicative words in standard English and in various dialects. As seen above, syntactic considerations are normally paramount in compounding and phonological aspects do not have a major role. In this regard, reduplicatives (compound words formed by reduplication) are different. The most significant property of these words is that word-formation is driven by phonological factors.

There are two main types of reduplicatives: RHYME MOTIVATED COMPOUNDS and ABLAUT MOTIVATED COMPOUNDS (see Bauer 1983). Rhyme here means what it means in poetry: the vowels and any consonant(s) that appear after it in the last syllable are identical, while ablaut means a change in the root vowel. (Usually ablaut signals a change in grammatical function, e.g. the $o \sim e$ alternation in $long_{(Adj.)}$ vs. $length_{(Noun)}$ marks a difference in word-class.) These labels for the two categories of reduplicative compounds highlight the fact that the repetition of the bases in compounds of this kind involves copying the rhyme in so-called rhyme motivated compounds, and copying the consonants and altering the vowel in ablaut motivated compounds.

Some rhyming compounds are formed by joining bases which are both pre-existing words as in *Black-Jack* and *brain-drain*. Probably more common, however, are rhyming compounds where one (or both bases) is not an independent word, as in [4.31]:

[4.31] *Rhyme motivated compounds*
   nitwit   helter-skelter   namby-pamby
   titbit   hobnob   higgledy-piggledy
   nitty-gritty   teeny-weeny   hurly-burly

Finally, there are ablaut motivated compounds in which one or both bases may not be an independent word:

[4.32] *Ablaut motivated compounds*
    tip-top   riff-raff   ding-dong   shilly-shally
    tick-tock   tittle-tattle   wibble-wobble   dingle-dangle
    ping-pong   dilly-dally   flip-flop   mish-mash

4.5 Listing and institutionalisation

Morphological theory provides the tools for analysing 'real' words like *shopkeeper* and *conversations* which are listed in dictionaries and which probably most competent, adult speakers of English know. But, if it stopped at that, it would be failing in its task of characterising the nature of speakers' lexical knowledge. For our knowledge of English vocabulary goes far beyond the INSTITU-TIONALISED words listed in dictionaries. You know thousands of words listed in dictionaries. And you also know an indefinitely large number of words that have not been documented by lexicographers, although they have occurred in speech or writing. Further, you have the ability to comprehend many POTENTIAL WORDS that have not yet occurred.

Obviously, a very considerable number of words must simply be memorised. If a word is made up of a single morpheme (e.g. *zebra*, *tree*, *saddle*), there is no way one can work out its meaning. However, as mentioned in our earlier discussion of compositionality in section (4.4.4) (see also section (5.1)), if a word contains several morphemes and if you know what the morphemes mean, you are usually able to work out what the word as a whole means, even if you have never encountered it before. (See the discussion of *Lebanonisation* in section (3.2) p. 30.) The same point is illustrated by the non-institutionalised word *Hollywoodisation*, which I heard in a radio discussion in which someone lamented 'the growing Hollywoodisation of the Cannes Film Festival'.

Word manufacture can be faddish. A word, especially one that captures the spirit of the times, may spawn numerous imitations. Take the 1980s word *yuppie*, which was formed by adding the suffix spelled as *-y* or *-ie* to the initial letters of either 'Young Urban Professional Person' or 'Young Upwardly Mobile Professional Person'. It spawned imitations like *yuppify*, *yuppiedom*, *yupette*, *buppie* ('black yuppie'), *guppie* ('gay yuppie') etc. (Ayto 1999: 573).

Let me add *re-yuppification* and *deyuppification*. I expect you not to have encountered these words before now. They are NONCE WORDS (words expressly coined for the first time and apparently used once) that are not yet institutionalised. Nevertheless, I am confident that you have figured out their meaning instantly. You analysed them as containing the prefix *re-* (again), the root *yuppie* and the suffixes *-fic* meaning 'make' and *-ation*, which derives nouns of action. You knew that *re-yuppification* of a neighbourhood means turning it into a yuppie environment again. *Deyuppification* was equally easy to analyse. The prefix *de-* is a reversive verbal prefix meaning the undoing of whatever the verb means. So, you figured that, if *deyuppification* happened, the yuppies (or their lifestyle) would be removed from the neighbourhood. Many complex MORPHOLOGICAL OBJECTS are compositional. They need not be listed in the lexicon since their meaning can be worked out by anyone who knows the meaning of their constituent elements. In this words such as *deyuppification* differ from simple morphological objects (morphemes or simple words, e.g. *-ful*, *-ly*, *-less*, *zebra*), which must be listed in the dictionary and memorised since they contain no clues to their meanings.

Many of the nonce, non-institutionalised words are compounds (see section (2.2.1)). If a speaker wants to express an idea which would normally be expressed by a syntactic phrase in a manner that heightens its concreteness and salience, it is possible as a one-off, hyphenated compound. The newspaper columnist Melanie Phillips manufactured the word '*anything-goes-as-long-as-you-can-get-away-with-it-culture*' which is an excellent example of this phenomenon:

[4.33] Public life has fallen into disrepute and the cynicism of the people knows no bounds. It's the anything-goes-as-long-as-you-can-get-away-with-it-culture, and it is as prevalent in the corridors of Whitehall as in the joyriders' ghettos.

(Phillips 1993)

At the other end of the spectrum old words go out of use, e.g. *wone* meaning 'home, abode' is now obsolete. If I said to you '*Where is your wone?*' you would have no idea what I was talking about. Then there is also the problem of separating the dialectal and the archaic words from obsolete ones, e.g. *porret* ('young leek or onion'). While *wone* is obsolete, *porret* survives in dialectal use but it is very rare. The line between 'dialectal and very rare' and 'obsolete' is a fine one.

4.6 Keeping tabs on idioms

Words like *tree* or *zebra* which contains just one morpheme must be listed in the dictionary as their meaning cannot be inferred from their configuration. In this respect morphology differs from syntax.

Typically, sentences do not need to be listed since they are compositional, while many words need to be listed in the dictionary because they are not compositional (see Di Sciullo and Williams 1987). Compare the sentences below:

[4.34]

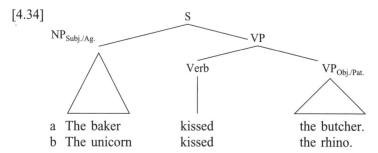

a The baker   kissed   the butcher.
b The unicorn   kissed   the rhino.

Notes: NP = noun phrase; Subj. = subject; VP = verb phrase;
        Obj. = object
        Ag. = agent (i.e. the individual or entity that instigates the action)
        Pat. = patient (i.e. the individual or entity that undergoes the action)
        △ A triangle is placed above constituents whose internal structure is not important for our present purposes.

Although you almost certainly have never seen or heard the sentence in [4.34b], you had no difficulty understanding it because you were able to work out which words form syntactic constituents, and what their semantic relationships are. Hence, since sentences are formed compositionally, they do not have to be listed.

The trouble is that it is sometimes possible to create new lexical items by converting syntactic phrases into word-like vocabulary items. A consequence of this is to upset the neat distinction that we have drawn between words, as listed morphological objects, and sentences, as unlisted syntactic objects. Syntactic phrases used as lexical items are called IDIOMS. Idioms are peculiar in that they are non-compositional syntactic phrases. Their meanings cannot be deduced from the meanings of the words they contain (see Di Sciullo and Williams 1987; Katamba 1993).

As you can see in [4.35], the structure of idioms is similar to the structure of ordinary syntactic phrases. The example in italic is idiomatic and the plain one is not:

[4.35] a

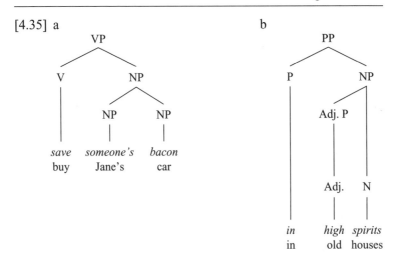

Obviously, knowing the grammatical structure and the meaning of the words in these idiomatic expressions is no help in understanding what the idioms mean. The meanings of these idioms must be listed in the dictionary along the lines shown in [4.36]:

[4.36] *Idiom*   *Gloss*
     a *save someone's*   'save someone a lot of
        bacon   trouble'
     b *in high spirits*   'slightly drunk and excited'

An indefinitely large number of syntactic phrases can be turned into idioms by assigning them idiosyncratic, non-compositional meanings. This is one of the ways in which a limitless supply of lexical items is assured, and another reason why all the lexical items of a language cannot be listed in a dictionary.

4.7 Clitics

There is a class of bound morphemes which are attached at the margins of words but which are not affixes. Such morphemes are called CLITICS. They cohabit with a word to form a single word-form without getting into a deep relationship with it. For instance, they can easily move from one word to another within a phrase if the syntactic conditions are right. The number of word-forms containing clitics is unlimited.

There are two classes of clitics:

[4.37]   *Class 1 clitics*

These always occur as appendages to words. They are totally incapable of appearing on their own as independent words. The GENITIVE ' *'s*' (as in *a farmer's wife*) is the only example of this kind of clitic in English.

Class 2 clitics

These are forms which are capable of appearing as independent words in some cases but are also used as dependent appendages to words. This is exemplified by the reduced auxiliary verbs, e.g. *'re, 'm, 'll, 'd* (as in *they're, I'm, I'll, they'd*, which are derived from *are, am, will* or *shall*, and *had*). Also similar is the reduced negative *n't* (as in *hadn't*), which is short for *not*.

The thing that all clitics have in common is some phonological deficiency which debars them from functioning as independent phonological words. In English, it is crucial for a phonological word to have a vowel. (There are no vowel less words like *tpngs, *tvmrk or *s.) Clitics do not qualify for word status because they lack vowels. The requirement that words must contain vowels is inviolable. To become pronounceable any form like *'ll* or *'d* must be annexed to a word. The word to which a clitic is appended is called a HOST.

We will now take a closer look at the two types of clitic in turn, starting with the class 1 type of clitic, i.e. the genitive *'s*:

[4.38]   a   the farmer's wife
         b   a day's work

The genitive *'s* construction in English is used to indicate that a noun (to be precise, NP) on the left which hosts the *'s* is a syntactic modifier which specifies more narrowly the meaning of the noun on the right which is the head of the entire NP. The exact semantic value of the *'s* genitive construction varies, as you can see from the following examples based on Quirk and Greenbaum (1973):

[4.39]   GENITIVE *'s*   PARAPHRASE
         a *Possessive genitive*
           the farmer's cattle   the cattle belonging to the farmer

the farmer's tractor   the tractor belonging to the
                            farmer
the farmer's wife   the wife of the farmer

b *Genitive of origin*
the farmer's messenger the messenger sent by the farmer
the farmer's story   the story told by the farmer

c *Genitive of measure*
two years'   imprisonment lasting for
   imprisonment   two years
a day's journey   a journey lasting one whole day.

Frequently the noun on the left is the possessor of the entity that
is on its right which functions as the head of the entire NP, as
in [4.39a]. 'Possessor' is a misleading term for this relationship in
many cases. Often the meaning of this construction is not one of
'owning'. The farmer may own the cattle and tractor, but not the
wife. She is his partner, not his chattel. The genitive in this latter
case indicates a relationship, not possession.

The fact that the *'s* genitive is not necessarily a marker of possession is even clearer in the rest of the examples in [4.39b] and [4.39c].
The farmer's story is a story told, not owned, by the farmer and
a day's journey is a journey that lasts a whole day – not one that
is owned by the day.

Thus the syntactic and semantic relationship of the genitive *'s*
with its host is variable. The syntactic role of this *'s* is to mark a
NP as being syntactically subordinated to another NP on its right,
which it modifies. The meaning of this *'s* clitic is difficult to pin
down. By contrast, affix morphemes tend to have a more readily
identifiable meaning: e.g. *-s* as in *trees* has a very predictable plural
meaning.

Furthermore, the relationship between a clitic and its host may
show schizophrenic tendencies. It may attach to one word phonologically but relate to another syntactically and semantically. Words
form cohesive units with their affixes. But CLITIC GROUPS (i.e.
forms containing clitics and their hosts) do not. The morphemes
belonging to a word are firmly bonded together and cannot be
separated by extraneous material.

Not so with a clitic group. Often we find, especially in casual
speech, clitics whose phonological host is different from their

syntactic/semantic host. The phonological host of *'s* is always the word that precedes the head. From a semantic angle, we can paraphrase *the farmer's tractor* as 'the tractor that is owned by the farmer'. The genitive *'s* is appended to the noun *farmer*, which is both the possessor from the semantic angle and the phonological host. However, in colloquial English the situation is more fluid. If we take a phrase like *the farmer next to our campsite's tractor*, we find that the semantic possessor and the phonological host are divorced. The *farmer* is still the owner of the *tractor*. But the genitive *'s* attaches to *campsite*, which is the phonological host. Suffixes cannot do that. For example, if semantically a noun is plural, it must receive the plural inflection itself. The plural suffix cannot turn up somewhere else in the sentence.

Whereas genitive *'s* is the only class 1 clitic, class 2 clitics, to which we now turn, are quite numerous. As already mentioned, class 2 clitics are forms capable of appearing either as independent words or as clitics appended to a host. Many auxiliary verbs appearing in unstressed position in a sentence can be free autonomous words as in [4.40a] or they may be reduced to a consonant which is appended as a clitic to a preceding host, as in [4.40b]:

[4.40] a *Full word*   b *Clitic*
          'I am 'cold.   'I'm 'cold.
          'He is 'cold.   'He's 'cold.

Note: ' marks secondary stress and ` marks primary stress.

The cognitive meaning of the sentences in each pair is the same. Cliticisation does not affect meaning. It only affects style. Use of class 2 clitics indicates greater informality than the use of full words. In formal written English cliticised forms are usually avoided – except where the writer is portraying spoken language.

All word-formation regardless of whether it is done by inflection or derivation takes place in the dictionary. But clitic group formation does not. Clitic groups are formed later when words are put together in syntactic phrases. The behaviour of genitive *'s* described above makes this very clear. Until you know what the words that form a genitive NP are, you are not in a position to identify the word immediately preceding the head of the construction to which you attach the *'s*. Clitics are appended after syntactic rules have grouped words together in phrases.

4.8 Summary

In this chapter we have explored the building blocks available for constructing words. We have established that roots are the core units to which different types of affixes can be attached. Affixes that precede the base are called prefixes and those that follow the base are called suffixes. Affixes may be neutral or non-neutral in their effect on the base.

Further, we have seen that word-formation involves two main processes: inflection and derivation. Inflection is motivated by syntax. Inflectional processes assign a stem certain grammatical properties so as to produce a grammatical word that can fit in a given syntactic slot. Derivation is not driven by syntax; its function is to create lexical items. There are three major classes of derivational processes: affixation, conversion and compounding. I have stressed the point that many words have internal structure and can be semantically analysed using compositionality. So the phrase structure rules used in syntax to generate innumerable permissible sentences can also be used to account for the productivity observed in compounding.

Next we observed that, although syntactic factors normally play a pivotal role in compounding, in the case of reduplicatives the situation is different: the phonological considerations of rhyme and ablaut have a central place.

A key difference between morphology and syntax is that normally morphemes and to a lesser extent words should be listed in the lexicon since their meaning is unpredictable; but sentences should not be as they are compositional. But this principle is relaxed in the case of compositional nonce words and idioms. Nonce words formed compositionally need not be listed as their meaning is predictable; idioms, though they are syntactic phrases, must be listed since they are non-compositional and their meaning cannot be inferred from the meaning of their parts.

Finally, we considered clitics. These constitute a class of bound morphemes which are attached at the periphery of words. Some of them are contracted forms of full words, while others are particles that always appear as bound morphemes and lack a fuller form. Both types are less fully integrated in words than true affixes.

Exercises

1 Illustrating your answer with fresh examples, explain the following:

    a morpheme and formative
    b root, stem, base
    c neutral vs. non-neutral suffix
    d inflectional morpheme vs. derivational morpheme
    e conversion
    f clitic

2 Draw labelled trees to show the structure of the following words:

motherhood	re-examining	unnaturalness	showmanship
shoemakers	shoplifted	dislocation	range-finder
unputdownable	underprivileged	unclassifiable	worm's eye view

3 State how the words *abstract*, *perfect* and *present* are stressed when they occur (a) as adjectives and (b) as verbs.

4 a Provide two fresh examples of different kinds of phonologically motivated word-formation.
    b Explain in detail the main phonological phenomenon that plays a role in the process you have chosen.

5 a Explain why the items *n't*, *'ve*, *'s*, and *'d* in the passage below should be treated as clitics rather than suffixes.
    b What type of clitic is each item an example of?

    '*Don't* you think *you've* got your bottom corner a bit far out?' came father'*s* voice from below. '*You'd* better be drawing in now, *hadn't* you?'
                           (Lawrence 1960: 13)

6 Study these idioms and answer the questions that follow:

a	stick-in-the-mud	f	to bury the hatchet
b	rule of thumb	g	to stick one's oar in
c	Hobson's choice	h	at each other's throat
d	tall order	i	to play to the gallery
e	by the skin of one's teeth	j	to change horses in midstream

i   Give a paraphrase of each idiom that clearly brings out its meaning.

ii Draw a phrase structure tree showing the syntactic structure of each idiom.

iii In the light of your answers to (i) and (ii) discuss the role of compositionality in the study of lexical items of this kind.

7   Using the criterion of compositionality determine which of the following words should be listed in the dictionary:

lifestyle	bigwig	foxtrot	sunshine	listing
roadside	grassroots	jaywalking	bandwagon	copycat
freelance	famous	autocue	environmental	laundrette
cockroach	sideburns	callous	supermarket	silhouette
desktop	whodunit	soundbite	exploit	ex-girlfriend
goalpost	footprint	sandbag	measurement	ornament
sandwich	bedside	tannery	happy	treetop
refinery	surgery	bootleg	removal	multinational
week-end	rooftop	hooligan	demonstration	
cupboard	campsite	savvy	postmodernism	

Part II

Words in a wider context

Words are put in the wider context in this section. In Chapter 5 you are introduced to lexical phonology and morphology, a theory of how phonology interacts with morphology. Chapter 6 presents approaches to lexical semantics.

Chapter 5

A lexicon with layers

5.1 The nature of the lexicon

This chapter is concerned with the lexicon from the perspective of the linguist constructing a model of language structure rather than the typical lexicographer's dictionary. We will address questions like: What should be included in the lexicon? In what form should it be included? How does the lexicon relate to the rest of the grammar? We will return to the lexicon in Part 4. Our concern there will be the MENTAL LEXICON to which language users must have access when constructing and interpreting sentences.

Our examination of the nature of the lexicon here will concentrate on the relationship between phonology and morphology in word-formation. But other matters will not be completely ignored. We will also deal more generally with the role of the lexicon in grammatical theory and how it relates to other modules (see section (1.1)).

Everyone agrees that the lexicon must contain a LIST of morphemes and simple words (in the sense of lexemes) because the relationship between their meaning and their form is arbitrary. Unless we are told what a word like *dew* means, we have no way of working out its meaning. All morphemes must also be listed in the lexicon since their meaning is unpredictable (there is no way of predicting what *dew*, *-ity* or *-ism* means).

But it is not necessary to list all the words (i.e. lexical items). As we saw in section (4.4.4) where we discussed compounds, many words have meanings that are COMPOSITIONAL. Compositionality means that the semantic interpretation of a complex semantic unit is predictable from the meaning of its parts. Morphology and the lexicon need to be equipped with rules that allow the creation and analysis of any word that is compositional. If that is done, it is not necessary to list the meanings of words like *smok-er*, *iron-ing*, *prearrang(e)-ed* and *farm-labour-er*, for the meanings of these words can be computed from the meanings of their parts. By the same token, it is not necessary for speakers to memorise the meanings of such words. They can just work them out.

In the theoretical framework that we are using, morphology is part of the lexicon. The lexicon is not a passive list of words and their meanings. It is not simply like an anatomy laboratory where existing words are dissected on a slab into their constituent morphemes and examined under a microscope. No, in this theory the lexicon is much more than that. It is also a place full of vitality where rules are used actively to create new words. To perform this function, the lexicon must include in dictionary entries these types of information about each simple word and each morpheme:

[5.1] 1 its meaning
2 its phonological properties
3 its syntactic properties
4 its morphological properties.

The reasons for including these kinds of information in dictionary entries will be made clear below.

5.2 Morphological information in the lexicon

The lexicon needs to contain various kinds of morphological information. Words behave differently in the language depending on the morphological subclasses they belong to. For instance, morphological rules often apply to words marked as belonging to specified subclasses. Thus, with regard to number, in English we need to know whether a particular word is a COUNT NOUN and has a plural form (e.g. *tables*, *voices*, *children* etc.) or a NON-COUNT NOUN that has no plural form (e.g. *furniture*, *gold*, *music* etc.). Further, we need to know whether a morpheme is native or of foreign origin as this may affect the range of morphemes that can co-occur with it in words. For example, some affixes borrowed from French (e.g. *-aire* as in *millionaire*, *communautaire*, *doctrinaire*, *solitaire*) only combine with roots adopted from that language.

5.3 Syntactic information in the lexicon

We cannot think of word-formation in total isolation from the rest of the grammar. The lexicon is not merely a list of the idiosyncratic syntactic properties of morphemes and lexical items. It has to be much more than that because much of the syntactic behaviour of words is predictable. For instance, normally if a TRANSITIVE VERB (i.e. a verb that takes a direct object) can occur in sentences like the ones in [5.2a], it can also occur in sentences like those in [5.2b]:

[5.2] a *Active voice*

SUBJECT	VERB	DIRECT OBJECT
The children	saw	the lions.
The thief	stole	his money.

   b *Passive voice*

SUBJECT	VERB	BY-NP (AGENT)
The lions	were seen	by the children.
His money	was stolen	by the thief.

It is not a peculiarity of the verbs *see* and *steal* that they appear in active and passive sentences. This is a general characteristic of transitive verbs (i.e. verbs that take a direct object like those in [5.2]). (Intransitive verbs like *smile* and *scowl* don't appear in passive sentences.) So, this fact should be captured by a general rule in the lexicon stating that corresponding to a passive sentence, there is normally an active sentence with a transitive verb preceded by the subject and followed by the direct object. In the passive sentence, the NP that would function as the direct object in the active version of the sentence functions as the subject and precedes the verb, while the NP that would be the subject if the sentence were in the active follows the verb and is part of an agent phrase introduced by the preposition *by* (Bresnan 1982). The verb itself also undergoes modification. A form of the verb *be* is put before it and the past participle *-en* or *-ed* is attached to it. In brief, the lexicon suffix must include the information needed to determine the syntactic behaviour of a word. Much of this information will be applicable to more than one word. So it can be captured by rules like the passive rule which we have just discussed.

5.4 Does it ring true? (phonological information)

Obviously, the lexical entry of a morpheme must include its pronunciation. The dictionary needs to say that *key* is pronounced /kiː/, as is *quay*; it needs to show that *victuals* is pronounced /vɪtlz/ and so on. But some phonological information is not specific to a particular entry. As we saw in section (2.2.1), in English certain combinations of sounds are permitted in certain positions in a word while others are not. Putative words like **tmiss*, **dnell* and **gnover* are forbidden by phonotactic rules. Any putative word must ring true. It must be a potentially well-formed phonological string. The lexicon only allows putative words that sound right. Word-formation rules are not allowed to concoct forms that are unpronounceable.

This applies not only to the rules that create new morphemes like (**tmiss*) but also to the rules that add affixes. For example, the rules that attach inflectional suffixes are not allowed to form a word like *twerd-s* **[twɜːds]* which has a voiceless [s] inflectional suffix that does not agree in voicing with [d], the final consonant of the stem which is voiced. *Twerd-s* must be pronounced [twɜːdz]. Similarly, the voice assimilation requirement would debar a putative noun plural form like *peeds* **[piːds]*.

The dictionary needs also to indicate any phonological peculiarities of derivational morphemes. For instance, the entry for the suffix morpheme *-al* needs to show that its *-al* allomorph is not added to bases ending in /l/. After a base ending in /l/, the right allomorph is *-ar*. If someone said something like **motoral* (instead of the correct *motorial*), meaning 'pertaining to motion', you might accept it as a possible word that you just happen not to know. But if they said **regular* (meaning *regular*) you would raise your eyebrows.

For literate speakers, the dictionary will obviously need to contain information about the orthographic form of lexical entries, especially in cases where the written forms are idiosyncratic or unpredictable. You need to have access to such lexical information as that /wɪmɪn/ is spelt *women* /baʊ/ is spelt *bough* etc. There is no way one would be able to work out these spellings unaided.

5.5 Rendezvous with lexical phonology and morphology

We have established that morphological rules are intimately coupled with phonological rules. In the rest of the chapter we will examine more closely the relationship between phonological and morphological rules in the lexicon. The theoretical framework in which the phonology–morphology interplay will be discussed is the theory of LEXICAL PHONOLOGY AND MORPHOLOGY developed by a number of generative linguists over the years (e.g. Allen 1978; Siegel 1974; Kiparsky 1982a, 1982b, 1983; Halle and Mohanan 1985; Mohanan 1986; Rubach 1984; Goldsmith 1990; Spencer 1991 and Katamba 1989, 1993). We will refer to it as lexical morphology (LP) for short.

5.5.1 Neutral and non-neutral affixes

The interaction of morphology and phonology is best approached from the perspective of the phonological properties of groups of affixes. As mentioned in section (4.4.1), there are two types of affixes in the English lexicon. One type is NEUTRAL in its effects on the stem to which it is attached and the other type is NON-NEUTRAL. The latter cause various changes in the vowels, consonants or stress of the bases to which they are affixed. The account presented here draws on the work of Kiparsky (1982a, 1982b).

In [5.3] I present some common neutral suffixes whose presence does not cause any phonological changes in the base to which they are attached:

[5.3] a *-ing*
decide	/dɪˈsaɪd/	deciding	/ˈdɪsaɪdɪŋ/
remind	/rɪˈmaɪnd/	reminding	/rɪˈmaɪndɪŋ/

    b *-ly*
expensive	/ɪkˈspensɪv/	expensively	/ɪkˈspensɪvlɪ/
sullen	/ˈsʌlən/	sullenly	/ˈsʌlənlɪ/

    c *-less*
joy	/ˈdʒɔɪ/	joyless	/ˈdʒɔɪləs/
penny	/ˈpenɪ/	penniless	/ˈpenɪləs/

    d *-er*
save	/ˈseɪv/	saver	/ˈseɪvə/
distil	/dɪˈstɪl/	distiller	/dɪˈstɪlə/

    e *-ness*
lively	/ˈlaɪvlɪ/	liveliness	/ˈlaɪvlɪnəs/
contagious	/kənˈteɪdʒəs/	contagiousness	/kənˈteɪdʒəsnəs/
steadfast	/ˈstedfɑːst/	steadfastness	/ˈstedfɑːstnəs/

By contrast, the presence of a non-neutral affix sets off phonological fireworks. Some or all of these things may happen: stress may shift from one syllable to another (as in *Canadian* in [5.4a]), some of the vowel segments may be modified (as in *mammalian* in [5.4a]) or the consonants may change as in *electricity* in [5.4b]. You can observe these changes in [5.4]:

[5.4] a *Input: Noun*   *Output*: [-*ian*]$_{Adj.}$
    Boston   /ˈbɒstən/   Bostonian   /bəˈstəʊnɪən/
    Canada   /ˈkænədə/   Canadian   /kəˈneɪdɪən/
    civil   /ˈsɪvəl/   civilian   /sɪˈvɪlɪən/
    mammal   /ˈmæməl/   mammalian   /məˈmeɪlɪən/
    Spenser   /ˈspensə/   Spenserian   /spenˈsɪərɪən/

   b *Input: Noun*   *Output*: [-*ic*]$_{Adj.}$
    fantasy   /ˈfæntəsɪ/   fantastic   /fənˈtæstɪk/
    hieroglyph   /ˈhɪərəʊglɪf/   hieroglyphic   /hɪərəʊˈglɪfɪk/
    idiosyncrasy /ɪdɪəˈsɪnkrəsɪ/ idiosyncratic /ɪdɪəsɪnˈkrætɪk/
    metal   /ˈmetəl/   metallic   /meˈtælɪk/
    system   /ˈsɪstəm/   systemic   /sɪˈstiːmɪk/
    electric   /ɪˈlektrɪk/   electricity   /ɪlekˈtrɪsətɪ/

   c *Input: Noun*   *Output*: [-*ify*]$_{Verb}$
    carbon   /ˈkɑːbən/   carbonify   /kɑːˈbɒnɪfaɪ/
    history   /ˈhistərɪ/   historify   /hɪˈstɒrɪfaɪ/
    object   /ˈɒbdʒekt/   objectify   /ɒbˈdʒektɪfaɪ/
    person   /ˈpɜːsən/   personify   /pəˈsɒnɪfaɪ/
    solid   /ˈsɒlɪd/   solidify   /səˈlɪdɪfaɪ/

Note: The suffix -*ian* (found in *Canadian*) can form both nouns and adjectives.

These suffixes attract stress like magnets attract iron. When any of the three suffixes is present, stress shifts from its original position and lands on the syllable immediately preceding the suffix. In this they are typical of many non-neutral affixes. As for the changes in the vowels, the broad generalisation is that vowels on which the stress falls are more prominent than they would be when they appear unstressed. For instance, a short vowel is replaced by a long vowel, e.g. like /ɪ/ → /iː/ (cf. /ˈsɪstəm/ → /sɪˈstiːmɪk/) and /ə/ by a diphthong (cf. /ˈbɒstən/ → /bəˈstəʊnɪən/).

For the most part neutral affixes are native, forming part of the Anglo-Saxon inheritance of English. But most non-neutral suffixes are LATINATE. They came in with words borrowed (as permanent, non-returnable loans) from Latin and its daughter, French (see Chapter 7). An example of a native non-neutral suffix is the derivational suffix -*th* used to form abstract nouns from adjectives. This suffix triggers a vowel change in the base, e.g. *long* → *length*; *broad* → *breadth*; *wide* → *width*.

5.5.2 The lexicon is like a layered cake

Kiparsky and the other writers on lexical morphology cited above have shown that it makes good sense to organise our lexicon in terms of HIERARCHICAL STRATA (or LEVELS) in order to characterise the differences between the effects of neutral and non-neutral affixes. A central plank of their argument is that the stratification of the lexicon is affix driven: affixes displaying particular types of behaviour and properties are grouped together and their attributes are used as the linguist's litmus paper to determine the strata of the lexicon. (This position is controversial. For an alternative account see section (5.8).)

Using the affix-driven stratification model, let us assume that all the non-neutral affixes are attached at one stratum in the lexicon, which we will call STRATUM 1. Let us further assume that all the neutral affixes are attached at another stratum, which we will call STRATUM 2. Stratum 1 (non-neutral) affixes are attached before the neutral affixes found at stratum 2. So, in a derivation, processes taking place at stratum 1 come before those that take place at stratum 2. The distinction between strata captures very broadly the distinction between native English affixes (stratum 2) and foreign affixes of French or Latin/Greek origin (stratum 1). Hence *metal* can give *metall-ic*$_{[stratum 1]}$ and perhaps *metal-ic*$_{[stratum 1]}$ -*ness*$_{[stratum 2]}$ but not *metal-ness$_{[stratum 2]}$-ic$_{[stratum 1]}$.

In the lexicon derivations start off with the UNDERIVED ROOT (i.e. the naked root without affixes) and work their way through relevant rules starting at stratum 1 and then progressing through stratum 2. The theory attempts to reflect the fact that at each stratum morphological rules are bonded together with phonological rules. The application of a morphological rule brings in its wake the application of a phonological rule. The reason for this is easy to see. When in the process of word-formation we put morphemes together using morphological rules, we need to know how the forms that we create are pronounced.

Look back to the tables of suffixes in [5.3] and [5.4]. See how different types of lexical information play a role in word-formation. As you can see, in order to attach an affix to a base, you need to know which kind of bases it can go with. For instance, *-ian* is attached to noun bases to yield adjectives. Given the noun *Canada* you can form the adjective *Canadian*. If your intention is to form a verb from a noun, then *-ian* is not a suitable suffix. You must try instead another suffix, e.g. *-ify* (as in *solidify*). Of course, in addition to knowing the grammatical characteristics of the word resulting from affixation, you need to know what it will mean. This point is obvious. We will not dwell on it.

Sample derivations of representative words listed in [5.3] and [5.4] are provided below. In [5.5] only stratum 1 rules apply, while in [5.6] only stratum 2 rules apply. But in [5.7] both stratum 1 and stratum 2 rules apply.

[5.5] Sample derivation no. 1 showing hierarchical strata
    Underived root

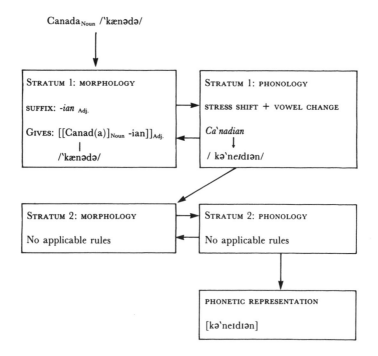

[5.6] Sample derivation no. 2 showing hierarchical strata
Underived root

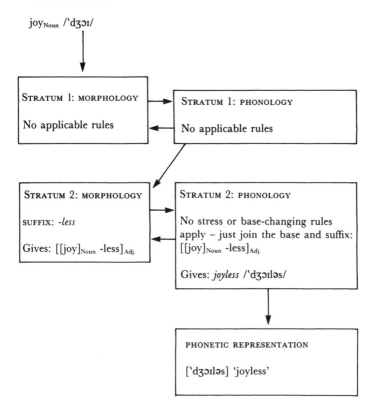

joy_{Noun} /ˈdʒɔɪ/

| STRATUM 1: MORPHOLOGY | STRATUM 1: PHONOLOGY |
| No applicable rules | No applicable rules |

STRATUM 2: MORPHOLOGY	STRATUM 2: PHONOLOGY
SUFFIX: *-less*	No stress or base-changing rules apply – just join the base and suffix: [[joy]_{Noun} -less]_{Adj.}
Gives: [[joy]_{Noun} -less]_{Adj.}	Gives: *joyless* /ˈdʒɔɪləs/

PHONETIC REPRESENTATION

[ˈdʒɔɪləs] 'joyless'

The claim that affixes are arranged on hierarchical strata has additional advantages. We will consider them briefly in turn.

First, as we saw in section (2.2.3), the order in which morphemes are arranged in words is rigidly fixed. Thus, *Canad-ian-ness* is the only permissible MORPHEME SEQUENCING in the word *Canadian-ness*. Any alternative arrangements of the same morphemes, such as *ian-Canada-ness*, *Canada-ness-ian* etc., are forbidden. Clearly, in order to be able to construct words as speakers and writers and to decode their meanings as hearers and readers we need to know what the morphemes they contain mean when put together, but that in itself is not enough. If a word contains affixes we need to know where they go. We need to know if they are prefixes or suffixes.

[5.7] Sample derivation no. 3 showing hierarchical strata
Underived root

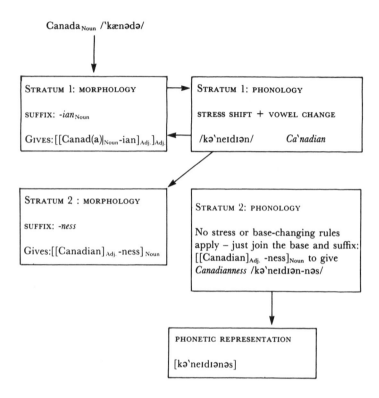

(It would not do to say *Is he ful-care?* if we want to mean *Is he care-ful?*)

Moreover, when several derivational affixes appear on the same side of a base as prefixes, or more likely in English as suffixes, there is a very general tendency for stratum 1 affixes to be closer to the root than stratum 2 ones. So, we have stratum 1 *-ian* right after the root and stratum 2 *-ness* on the outside as in *Canad(a)-ian-ness*. Further, as you will recall from section (4.4.1), derivational affixes usually go on the inside. They are nearer to the root than derivational suffixes, which are attached later and appear on the periphery of the word.

The second point concerns the way morphological rules interact in the lexicon. The organisation of strata in a hierarchical manner can be used to explain the phenomenon of BLOCKING, whereby one rule makes a pre-emptive strike, robbing another rule of its potential input. I will illustrate blocking with two sets of examples, one from inflectional morphology and the other from derivational morphology.

In derivational morphology it is not uncommon to find two or more affixes with virtually identical, or at any rate closely related, meanings. In such situations, usually only one of those affixes can be attached to a particular base. You can observe this if you consider the ways of deriving from verbs AGENTIVE NOUNS (with the meaning 'someone who does X') by suffixing *-er* or *-ant*:

[5.8] a *Agentive noun*   b *Agentive noun*
          -er   -ant
          sell-er   contest-ant
          send-er   defend-ant
          gaol-er   serv-ant

There is no doubt that *-er* is the more productive of the two suffixes. Most verbs can be turned into agentive nouns meaning 'the doer of X' by suffixing *-er*. More existing and potential nouns are formed by suffixing *-er* than are formed by suffixing *-ant*.

The *-ant* suffix is at stratum 1. It requires stress to fall two syllables before it, if it does not do so already:

[5.9] a *Stress-shifting*   b *Stress already 2 syllables before*
          'applicant (cf. a'pply)   'accountant (cf. 'account)
          'Protestant (cf. pro'test)   'occupant (cf. < 'occupy)

But *-er* is neutral and belongs to stratum 2 since it has no phonological special effects (cf. 'manage ~ 'manager; pro'duce; ~ pro-'ducer etc.).

The existence of a comparable stratum 1 affix attaching to the same class of bases and having a meaning that is very closely related to that of a stratum 2 affix usually deprives an otherwise general stratum 2 affix of its input. That is why, for example, the existence of *accountant*, formed at stratum 1, blocks the formation of **accounter*, and *applicant* blocks **applier*.

Observe, however, that blocking is only a strong tendency rather than an inviolable constraint. Sometimes closely related stratum 1 and stratum 2 affixes may be used with the same base on different occasions. Interestingly, this seldom results in synonymous words.

Rather, what we tend to get is one word which has a broad meaning and another which has a narrower, specialised meaning. For instance, a *Protestant* is a member of a Reformed Christian church while a *protester* is anyone who undertakes a protest action, usually of a political nature. So even the Pope could be a 'protester' against some cause while a Protestant Pope is just not on the cards.

Thus compositionality may work only partially with some stratum 1 affixes: we may be able to work out their morphological and phonological properties but their semantic contribution to a word may be idiosyncratic. Where that is the case (cf. *Protestant*), listing in the dictionary will be needed, despite the residual element of semantic predictability.

The third point concerns PRODUCTIVITY. The relative productivity of morphemes is reflected in the hierarchical organisation of strata. It is significant that, in our example, -*er*, which is a phonologically neutral, stratum 2 suffix, is more productive than -*ant*, the non-neutral stratum 1 suffix. This is typical. Stratum 2 affixes are typically more productive than their stratum 1 counterparts. Thus, the stratum on which a morpheme appears in the lexicon reflects its productivity (see Aronoff 1976: 35–45).

Turning to inflectional morphology we can make the same points. The hierarchical organisation of strata can be used to account for the fact that, in INFLECTIONAL ALLOMORPHY, a particular stem does not co-occur with all the available affixes. We shall illustrate this with plural formation. In addition to the regular plural with the phonologically conditioned allomorphs [-z, -ɪz, -s] (as in *birds*, *classes* and *bricks*: see section (3.3.3.1)), English has several other ways of forming the plural, including the following:

[5.10] a

Singular		*Plural*	b	*Singular*		*Plural*
foot	~	feet		deer	~	deer
tooth	~	teeth		sheep	~	sheep
goose	~	geese		salmon	~	salmon

[5.11] a

Singular		*Plural*	b	*Singular*		*Plural*
locus	~	loci		addendum	~	addenda
stimulus	~	stimuli		curriculum	~	curricula
fungus	~	fungi		stratum	~	strata

The use of internal root vowel change to signal plural as in [5.10a] is assumed to take place at stratum 1 since this is obviously a phonologically non-neutral, stem-changing process. This particular kind of plural formation, which is rare, cannot be successfully treated using normal suffixation rules. But it can be dealt with better if we assume a 'word-and-paradigm' analysis. In this approach, words are not segmented into individual morphemes each of which is said to represent a specific meaning and grammatical function; rather, words are taken in their entirety as constellations of forms belonging to paradigms. Entire words (and not individual word chunks) are associated with meanings and grammatical functions. In this account there would be a rule which simply says, for example, that the lexical item *foot*, when associated with the grammatical property *plural*, is realised by the word-form *feet*.

By contrast, the zero suffix causes no problems. There are no phonological upheavals in the stem; we place it at stratum 1 in order to reflect the fact that it is a very restricted and unproductive method of pluralising nouns. Unless a noun is expressly flagged in the lexicon as taking a zero plural suffix, we assume that it does not (see section (3.3.3.2)). The formation of the plural of the nouns in [5.10] at stratum 1 blocks regular plural formation by attaching the regular -*s* suffix at stratum 2. That way, the formation of disallowed plurals like **foots* and **gooses* or **deers* and **sheeps* is blocked.

Similarly, the plural suffixes -*i* and -*a* in the words in [5.11] which come from Latin also have to be at stratum 1. The suffixation of -*i* blocks the suffixation of -*s*. So, we get only *loci* not **locuses*. Thus, the notion of blocking enables us to explain why the formation of plural at stratum 1 hinders the formation of the plural using the regular [-z, -ɪz, -s] allomorphs. By the time they reach stratum 2, the words in [5.11] are already marked as plural and so are unavailable for the suffixation of regular [-z, -ɪz, -s].

However, because many speakers of English are unaware of the Latin origin of words with the -*i* plural, blocking is not any more successful in inflectional morphology than it is in derivational morphology. Commonly used words of Latin origin such as *virus* and *bonus* have been 'regularised' so that they only take the -*s* plural (i.e. *viruses*, *bonuses*). In other cases, such as *syllabuses* ~ *syllabi* and *aquariums* ~ *aquaria*, usage fluctuates between the Latin -*i* or -*a* and native -*s*. Some speakers use the stratum 2 suffix -*s*, bypassing the rule that attaches the stratum 1 Latinate one, while others use the rule that attaches the Latinate stratum 1 suffix and thereby pre-empt the suffixation of the regular -*s* suffix at stratum 2.

As mentioned with respect to the zero plural suffix, the placement of inflectional affixes on different strata reflects their relative productivity. The borrowed stratum 1 plural allomorphs *-i* and *-a* are not productive. If a new noun ending in *-us* or *-um* entered the language, its plural would be formed with the regular *-s* ending rather than *-i* or *-a*.

5.6 Productivity, the time-warp and cranberries

Let us begin by going back to the table of suffixes in [5.3] on p. 91. You will observe that the suffixes listed there are not all equally PRODUCTIVE. They do not all have the same likelihood of forming words. Some morphemes are more productive, more alive and more active than others which may be described as moribund, dormant or, at best, relatively inactive. The active morphemes are extensively used in contemporary English to form words while the inactive ones are used infrequently, if ever, to create new words (see Bauer 2001).

For examples of productive suffixes, take *-ly*, which can turn almost any adjective (e.g. *quiet, soft*) into an adverb (*quiet-ly, soft-ly*); the suffix *-er* which is used to derive agent nouns from verbs (e.g. *paint-er, teach-er*); and the suffix *-ing* which is used to form a gerundive noun meaning 'the act of doing X' from a verb (e.g. *wait-ing, sail-ing*). Such suffixes are attached almost exceptionlessly to virtually all eligible roots and the resulting word has a very predictable meaning. It is impossible to imagine a competent speaker of English who does not know how to construct words using these suffixes.

At the other end of the spectrum there are affixes which the erudite might be able to recognise but which have no active role in word-formation in the contemporary language. That is true of *-ery* (in *slav-ery, brav-ery* and *chican-ery*) which forms abstract nouns from nouns or adjectives. This suffix has the meaning 'having the property, state or behaviour indicated by the source noun or adjective'. I suspect some readers of this book may not have known that. But this is not surprising. This suffix ceased to be actively used several hundred years ago. It is not productive any more. It survives in only a few words as a fossil. At first sight, the case for isolating it as a morpheme in a purely synchronic analysis intended to reflect the knowledge of contemporary speakers of English is not altogether overwhelming. Arguably, *slavery, bravery, chicanery* and the like ought to be treated as root morphemes without affixes, whatever their history.

Treating the whole unit in the case of *chicanery* is unproblematic. But difficulties arise if we do the same with *slavery* and *bravery*. Both *slave* and *brave* are morphemes still on active service. They must be segregated from *-ery*. But doing that leaves behind a residual element whose credentials as a morpheme would be considered doubtful by many speakers. A morpheme that may have been active at some point in the past may cease to be so as time goes on. Also, the extent to which we can reliably associate meanings with some morphs that we isolate may diminish (see section (4.2.1)). One of the challenges that a morphologist faces is providing an analysis that distinguishes what is of purely arcane historical interest from what is relevant in an analysis of the contemporary language. The fact that linguists can see some morphological structure does not necessarily mean that Ms and Mr Average Native Speaker are aware of it too. What in principle should be compositional for some speakers may not be for all speakers.

The classic example of this is provided by the *cranberry* words (see Bloomfield 1933). These words highlight the problem of treating morph-like units that do not belong to any recognisable morpheme in the language as it is used today. A *cranberry* is a kind of *berry*. So, we can identify *berry* as a morpheme in that word. But that leaves us the problem of what to do with the apparently meaningless unit *cran-* that is left behind. The only loophole available is to treat *cranberry* as a compound word made up of the free root morpheme *berry* and the bound root morpheme *cran-* which has the peculiarity of only occurring as part of the word *cranberry*. Admittedly, the word *cran* does exist, meaning 'a measure of herrings (about 750 fish)', but that word is unrelated to the *cran-* in *cranberry*.

We are in a quandary. You might be willing to accept that *cran-* is a non-recurrent morpheme with a very restricted distribution – occurring only in *cranberry*. But you may still be wondering where that leaves the definition of the morpheme as a minimal meaningful unit. It seems that the definition has to be modified. It has to be weakened so that we make allowances for some morphemes which are not meaningful units on their own. All words have to mean something when they occur in isolation. However, morphemes are not absolutely required to have a clear, identifiable meaning on their own. They may be chameleon-like, with meanings that change somewhat in different words (see [4.2] on p. 51).

Cran- and similar words make a revision of the definition of the morpheme necessary. To overcome the problems some linguists have defined the morpheme in purely distributional terms: a linguistic entity 'uniquely identifiable in terms of phonemic elements, and occurring in stated environments of other morphemic segments (or in stated utterances)' (see Harris 1951: 171). This is a definition that highlights distribution. 'Cran-' can be isolated as a morpheme on distributional grounds, like the problematic Latinate root morphemes in [4.2]. For instance, in the case of *cran-* we can use the substitution test to show that *cran-* is a morpheme. In some other *berry* words such as *blueberry* and *blackberry* we have the morphemes *blue* and *black* occurring in the same slot as *cran-*. (See also Aronoff 1976: 15.)

In all this the difficulty is the fact that, between the productive morpheme used actively in the construction of words (e.g. agentive noun suffix *-er*) and dormant ones like *-ery* that are fossilised, there exists a myriad of possibilities. The difference between productive and unproductive morphemes is a gradient, not a dichotomy. There are numerous morphemes that are productive to different degrees for different speakers. For instance, *-aire* as in *doctrinaire* is found in only a few existing words and is unlikely to be used in the formation of new ones. Relatively few speakers recognise it as a suffix and its meaning is obscure. Nevertheless it is possible that it is moribund rather than dead. It could still be taken off the shelf and dusted down and used to form new words when the need arises. For instance, in the early 1990s those in British politics opposed to an ever closer union of the states that make up the European Union used the term *communautaire* (borrowed from French) to refer pejoratively to those firmly committed to greater European integration. Although it is unlikely that the man on the Clapham omnibus is aware of *-aire* being a suffix in *communautaire*, it is very likely the political pundits who use this term are able to identify *-aire* as a suffix here.

One of the intriguing phenomena in morphology is that across-the-board productivity in word-formation is very rare. Often an otherwise general word-formation process is blocked in some circumstances. This is particularly true in derivational morphology, which tends to be less predictable than inflectional morphology. Word-formation is often subject to various constraints which may be phonological, morphological or syntactic (cf. Aronoff 1976; Bauer 2001; Katamba 1993).

Here we will limit the discussion to some phonological constraints. We will see how the affixation of an otherwise productive affix may be inhibited for phonological reasons. We will illustrate this with the -al suffix, which derives action nouns from verbs. According to Siegel (1974), for a verb base to be eligible for the suffixation of -al, it must meet these phonological requirements:

1   The verb base must end in a stressed syllable.
2   The verb base must end phonologically in either a vowel, or a single consonant, or at most two consonants.
3   If the base does not end in a vowel, its final consonant must be made in the front of the mouth (i.e. it must be a labial or alveolar consonant).

These conditions are exemplified in [5.12]. (Consider the pronunciation, not the spelling):

[5.12] a   -al suffix after vowel-final bases
            trial   denial   betrayal   renewal

       b   -al after verb bases ending in a labial consonant
            revival   arrival   approval   removal

       c   -al after verb bases ending in a dental or alveolar consonant
            betrothal   appraisal   acquittal   recital   referral

       d   -al after verb bases ending in an (alveolar) consonant preceded by another underlying consonant
            rehearsal   dispersal   reversal   rental

However, if a verb ends in a palatal or velar consonant as in [5.13], suffixation of this -al is blocked:

[5.13] *judgeal   *attackal   *approachal   *rebukal   *encroachal

The stress on the final syllable is always a vital factor. A base that otherwise meets the conditions for -al suffixation will be ineligible if stress is not on the last syllable. Hence the ill-formedness of *`audital, *`combatal and *`limital.

As Siegel's analysis predicts, a base like *a'ttemptal*, which ends in a three-consonant cluster, cannot take the suffix either even though it has got stress in the right place, on the final syllable.

Even then there are inexplicable exceptions. Some seemingly well-formed potential words are disallowed although they appear to meet all the conditions. For instance, for no apparent reason, *con'testal*, *e'scortal* and *a'llowal* are not allowed through the net.

5.7 Peeping beyond the lexicon

After words have been formed in the lexicon, they are used in the syntax to form phrases and sentences. Even at this stage they are still subject to phonological rules. The phonological rules that affect words at this stage are called PHRASAL RULES (or POST-LEXICAL RULES). Post-lexical phonological rules differ from the phonological rules which operate in the lexicon in that they are not sensitive to the idiosyncratic lexical properties of words. They apply mechanically whenever the right phonetic circumstances are present, regardless of any special morphological or syntactic properties that words may have. We have seen that, in the lexicon, certain phonological processes apply only if certain morphemes are present. For example, STRESS SHIFT applies only when certain stratum 1 suffixes are attached. Unlike lexical rules, post-lexical rules do not take into account any of the peculiarities of the words they affect. They are general and exceptionless. They are automatically triggered by the presence of the appropriate phonological input.

An example of a post-lexical rule is the optional assimilation of an alveolar consonant at the end of one word to the place of articulation of the consonant at the beginning of the next word in fast casual speech. Thus, the word *mad* by itself is pronounced [mæd]. But in *mad guest* and *mad man* it may be uttered with a final [g] and [b] respectively so that we get [mæg gest] and [mæb mæn] when the /d/ assimilates to the place of articulation of the following velar /g/ and labial /b/. The phrasal, place of articulation assimilation rule applies in an environment that spans two phonological words. It is not a lexical rule confined to morphemes and single words. The assimilation can affect any word with the appropriate phonetic make-up if it appears in this phrasal context. However, since our concern in this book is morphology, the study of internal structure of words, we will not explore phrasal rules any further. We will stick to processes that affect morphemes and single words.

5.8 Base-driven stratification

The model of LP outlined so far has not been warmly embraced by all. There are some who, while seeing merit in a lexically stratified lexicon, reject the view that the behaviour of affixes should be used as the criterion for determining the strata. In this section we consider some of the objections as well as a possible remedy.

Gussmann (1988) in his review of Mohanan's 1986 book on LP had argued that this was a theory that took linguists on the road to nowhere and wanted to see it dead and buried. In response, Giegerich (1999) mounted a robust defence of LP and showed that any plans of a requiem for LP are premature. While conceding that there are problems with Mohanan's analysis, Giegerich demonstrates that in fact they are not endemic in all versions of the theory that existed in the 1980s (e.g. Kiparsky 1982a, 1982b). Moreover, those weaknesses that were present in the best versions of the 1980s model can be overcome without jettisoning its basic insight, namely the hypothesis that morphological and phonological rules apply in tandem in the lexicon, regulated by the principle of 'lexical stratification' (or 'level ordering').

Gussmann and other critics had pointed out that lexical stratification raises many problems for which so far there have been no satisfactory solutions, such as: How many strata are needed? What morphological and phonological properties belong to a particular stratum? On what basis is this determined? Are stratification principles part of Universal Grammar, the blueprint for human language which all infants are born with, or are they set up ad hoc for each language? The lack of both clarity and unanimity in the answers given to such questions by practitioners of LP had thrown the whole enterprise into disarray.

For instance, as seen in [5.14], there is neither agreement on the number of strata required in the lexicon of English nor on the stratum at which particular phenomena should be placed.

[5.14]	*Kiparsky (1982a)*	*Halle and Mohanan (1985) Mohanan (1986)*
Stratum 1	'+'-affixation: *-ity, -ic* irregular inflection: *cacti, oxen*	'+'-affixation: *-ity, -ic* irregular inflection: *cacti, oxen*
Stratum 2	'#'-affixation: -ness, -less, compounding	'#'-affixation: *-ness, -less*

Stratum 3	regular inflection	compounding
Stratum 4	–	regular inflection

In order to handle the interaction between '#'-affixation and compounding, Mohanan (1986) proposed what was to become a highly questionable device, namely a 'loop' that enables morphology to look back from stratum 3, where compounding takes place to form a word like the verb *aircondition*, to stratum 2 where regular '#'-affixation takes place to derive a word like *re-aircondition*. This loop totally undermines the insight of LP that morphological and phonological rules of the same stratum apply in tandem. Mohanan's use of the loop was not unprecedented. Earlier, Kiparsky (1982b) had also resorted to retracing his steps from stratum 3 back to stratum 2 in order to handle cases where regular inflection appears inside compounds (e.g. *systems analyst*). A more technical objection to Mohanan's model was that it allowed excessively abstract analyses.

Exploring this issue in depth is beyond the scope of an introductory text like this one. A major objective of Giegerich's book is to revert to a more constrained model where the Strict Cycle Condition is rigidly adhered to. According to Giegerich, LP got into trouble because it was based on a number of erroneous assumptions. Chief among these was AFFIX-DRIVEN STRATIFICATION (see [5.14]). The strata are defined on the basis of affixes that are attached at a particular stratum. But affixes are a very poor diagnostic test for lexical strata. The diagnostic inadequacy of affixes in determining lexical strata is shown to be due to the fact that many derivational affixes defy any attempt to pin them down to a single stratum. A good example of dual stratal membership of suffixes is *-able/-ible*. This is a suffix which is sometimes neutral in its phonological effect as in [5.15a] and has to be placed on stratum 2, but is also sometimes non-neutral as in [5.15b] and [5.15c] and has to be assigned to stratum 1:

[5.15]	a	manage	manage-able	
		accept	acceptable	
		deliver	deliverable	
		commend	commendable	
	b	tolerate	tolerable	(*tolerateble)
		navigate	navigable	(*navigateble)
	c	perceive	perceptible	(*perceivible)
		divide	divisible	(*dividible)

The case of *-able/-ible* is not at all unusual. There are numerous other well-known suffixes which belong to two strata. For example, the agentive *-er* (also spelt *-or*, e.g. *visit-or*), which is normally stratum 2 and attaches to words as in *singer* and *worker*, is also on stratum 1 in a few cases, e.g. *adulterer* and *presbyter*, and attaches to bound roots on stratum 1. The same is true of adjective forming *-y*. It is normally stratum 2 and attaches to fully formed words (e.g. *sunny, funny*) but can also occasionally be found on stratum 1 where it attaches to bound roots (e.g. *holy, dizzy, flimsy*). This evidence militates against using affixes as our litmus paper for determining strata since many affixes display dual stratal membership.

So, Giegerich proposes an alternative theory of BASE-DRIVEN STRATIFICATION, which maintains the insight of a stratified lexicon while at the same time avoiding the pitfalls of affix-driven stratification. In this model, the criteria used to define strata relate to the properties of affixation bases rather than affixes. In English stratum 1 is ROOT-BASED and stratum 2 WORD-BASED. This means that the input of stratum 2 must be a word; the input of stratum 1 is a root – which may or may not be a word.

The number of strata required in the grammar of any language is an empirical issue determined on the basis of the behaviour of its bases. Thus, for example, while two strata are sufficient for English, German requires three strata whose inputs are respectively the root, stem and word.

The hallmarks of stratum 1 are non-compositionality and non-productivity. It makes no sense from the point of view of present-day English to segment into separate meaningful units words such as:

[5.16] *maternity   fraternity   fraternize*

Hence, Giegerich proposes, no general word-formation rules are available at stratum 1. The linguist must list as lexical entries all stratum 1 roots (both simple and complex), as well as affixes.

Non-affix inputs to stratum 1 are all members of the category ROOT, which has a novel definition. While the traditional view is that the root is the core that remains when all affixes are stripped away (Lyons 1970: 325), Giegerich's root may be a morphologically simplex form (e.g. *lamp, gorm-, moll-*) or a complex one, where the complexity is the result of stratum 1 morphology yielding a base (e.g. *nation, fraction*) which can be expanded to form a word (e.g. *nation-al, fraction-al*).

Following Selkirk (1982), Giegerich assumes that, unlike words, roots are not members of lexical categories. Rather than arbitrarily characterise *moll-* as an adjective and *gorm-* as a noun, Giegerich proposes that the grammar should be assumed to have a root-to-word conversion rule which assigns word status and hence word-class labels to lexical category-free roots as they exit stratum 1 and enter stratum 2, thereby acquiring word status. The rule, which Giegerich refers to as RULE 1, takes this form:

[5.17] RULE 1

$$[\ ]_r \rightarrow [[\ ]_r]_L \qquad (L = N, V, A)$$

        Note: r = root,   L = lexical   item,   N = noun,   V = verb,
            A = adjective.

It is not possible to predict if a given root is subject to the root-to-word rule. A bound root like *matern-* is not, but a free root like *modern* is. So, each root must be marked with a diacritic (e.g. *modern* $_{[+fr]}$ (i.e. '+free root')) to indicate whether it can become a word at that point and what lexical category it will belong to. Unsatisfactory though it is from the point of view of capturing generalisation, Giegerich sees no way round the problem other than listing since no mechanism exists for predicting why *modern* is free but *matern-* is bound. Derivational affixes also carry diacritic marking to indicate the lexical category of words formed by attaching them. Thus, *-ity* is marked as forming nouns and *-ize* as yielding verbs.

Blocking plays the usual role in a stratified lexicon. While *lioness* is the female *lion*, *dogess is not what we call a female dog. The stratum 2 form ending in *-ess* is blocked in the latter case by the prior existence of *bitch*.

The stratal affiliation of affixes is handled thus: basic roots as well as affixes are treated as lexical entries. For each root the grammar indicates the affixes that are allowed to attach to it as in [5.18a]; for each affix the grammar lists the affixes it can have attached to it – or whether it yields a word as shown in [5.18b]:

[5.18] a matern $\begin{cases} \rightarrow \text{-al} \\ \rightarrow \text{-ity} \end{cases}$ b   -al $\begin{cases} \rightarrow \text{-ize} \\ \rightarrow \text{-ity} \\ \rightarrow \text{Adj (RULE (1))} \end{cases}$

           moll $\rightarrow$ -ity   -ade $\rightarrow$ Adj (RULE (1))
           gorm $\rightarrow$ -less   -ity $\rightarrow$ Adj (RULE (1))

This makes it unnecessary to mark each rule with a diacritic showing the level at which it applies, as was previously the case. The two strata of English are characterised by a clustering of interrelated properties. For instance, stratum 1 morphology displays phonological properties which are not shared with stratum 2, such as stress alternations (*átom~atómic*), syllabicity alternations (*rhythm* [rɪðəm] ~ *rhythmic* [rɪðmɪk]) and phonological rules restricted to this stratum such as trisyllabic laxing (*define*[dɪˈfaɪn] ~ *definition* [defɪˈnɪʃən]).

Base-driven LP does not completely succeed in banishing all overlap between strata. Giegerich subscribes to the CONTINUITY OF STRATA HYPOTHESIS (Mohanan 1986: 46) which envisages migration between two adjacent strata. For instance, the formation of abstract nouns using the suffix -*th* (as in *warmth*) is said to have moved from stratum 2 to stratum 1 when this mode of word formation ceased being productive.

5.9 Summary

In this chapter we have explored the kinds of lexical information that need to be included in the lexicon. We have established that the lexicon needs to contain semantic, phonological, morphological and syntactic properties. Word-formation interacts strongly with processes that apply in the other modules of the grammar since they all need access to various kinds of information about morphemes and words found in the lexicon.

Most of the chapter has been given over to characterising the relationship between morphological and phonological rules found in the lexicon using the multi-layered theory of lexical morphology. (For further exploration of this model see van der Hulst and Smith 1982a, 1982b, 1982c; Katamba 1989; Goldsmith 1990.)

We have seen that affix morphemes play a pivotal role since the division of the lexicon into strata is based on the phonological properties of affixes. Affixes are put on two strata depending on whether they are phonologically neutral or non-neutral. This enables us to handle simply several important morphological phenomena such as the sequencing of morphemes in words, the relative productivity of morphemes and blocking.

In the course of the discussion we re-examined the role of the morpheme as the minimal unit used to signal meaning. We saw that some morphemes have very elusive meanings and we considered a distributional approach as a possible way of characterising the morpheme.

Next we contrasted the idiosyncratic nature of lexical phonological rules with the predictable nature of phrasal rules that affect words after they have been processed through the syntax. The last section dealt with some of the criticism of the model of LP presented in this chapter. Many of the weaknesses stem from the standard assumption that the stratification of the lexicon is driven by affixes. Giegerich has shown that if affix-driven stratification is replaced with base-driven stratification, many of the objections are overcome and the basic insight of LP that certain morphological rules apply in tandem with certain phonological rules can be preserved.

Exercises

1   a   What kinds of information must the lexicon contain?

     b   Explain why the lexicon must be much more than a long list of words that are found in a language. What kinds of generalisations should be captured in the lexicon?

2   a   In the light of the discussion in this chapter and earlier discussion in Chapter 4, show how phonological rules interact with morphological rules in English.

     b   Show why a theory of language that insisted on keeping morphological rules segregated from phonological rules would miss some important generalisations about English. Back up your arguments with fresh examples.

3   a   What is the meaning of *pec-* and *mut-* in the following:

         pecunious   impecunious   pecuniary   peculate
         peculiar   commute   immutable   mutant
         permutation   mutate

     b   Should *pec-* and *mut-* be recognised as root morphemes in contemporary English? Justify your answer.

4   a   Use the data below to argue that the two distinct -*al* suffix morphemes must be recognised.

         acquittal   arrival   referral   betrayal
         refusal   residual   perusal   retrieval
         dispersal   reversal   committal   removal

architectural   medicinal   intellectual   instrumental
ancestral   universal   habitual   conceptual
presidential   commercial original   anecdotal

In your analysis, pay particular attention to the following:

i   the meaning of the suffix;
ii the word-class of the bases to which it attaches;
iii the word-class of the resulting word;
iv the effect, if any, that the -al suffix has on stress.

b   In the light of your analysis, at which lexical stratum or strata should -al be put?

5   Study these words and answer the questions that follow:

a	bagful	d	journalese	g	daily
	cupful		computerese		monthly
	jugful		officialese		quarterly
	plateful		telegraphese		weekly
b	childhood	e	friendship	h	arabesque
	knighthood		guardianship		grotesque
	parenthood		keepership		picturesque
	priesthood		membership		Turneresque
c	complimentary	f	absenteeism	i	decorative
	elementary		colonialism		generative
	evolutionary		expansionism		native
	inflationary		fatalism		productive
	revolutionary		imperialism		speculative

i   Segment each word into morphemes.
ii List the *suffixes* together with their meanings and their historical sources. As we have seen in this chapter, the distinction between native and borrowed morphemes is important in English although most speakers are not explicitly aware of it. This task is intended to make you examine this distinction consciously. (Looking up the suffixes in an etymological dictionary is recommended.)
iii Make a phonemic transcription of the first two words in each group. Indicate the syllable that receives the most prominent stress in the word.
iv What effect on stress, if any, does each suffix you have identified have?

v   At what stratum is each one of the suffixes you have identified found? What is your evidence?

vi Is there any correlation between the stratum at which a suffix is found and its historical origin?

6   Contrast the analysis of the words below that is available to a lexical phonologist using (a) affix-driven stratification and (b) base-driven stratification. In your view, which approach provides the better account of the facts?

a	painter	farmer	speaker	streaker
	cartographer	carpenter	almoner	doctor
	possessor	sailor	saviour	mentor
	creditor	janitor	juror	ancestor
b	glorify	beautify	terrify	pacify
	justify	satisfy	purify	gentrify
c	edification	eruption	caution	fiction
	nation	action	petition	edition
	nationalisation			
d	gormless	careless	handless	clueless
	armless	ruthless	priceless	fearless
e	disgruntled	dismayed	displeased	displaced
f	unkempt	unloved	unbiased	unprecedented

Chapter 6

Word meaning

6.1 Introducing meaning

The two sub-disciplines of linguistics that deal with meaning are known as SEMANTICS and PRAGMATICS. The former is concerned with the meaning of words in isolation and when they are put together in sentences, while the latter treats meanings that are assigned to utterances by speakers and hearers using language in particular contexts.

Word meaning has many facets. Normally, a basic distinction is drawn between the CONCEPTUAL meaning of words and sentences and their CONNOTATION. The conceptual meaning is the core, literal meaning that only includes the essential semantic characteristics. This is contrasted with connotation – the study of the vibes and associations that words have. Consider the following:

[6.1]		*Conceptual meaning*	*Connotations (associations)*
	a film star	a famous movie actor	celebrity, cool, very wealthy, probably good looking, part of glamorous Hollywood set, vain, has had many experiments in matrimony etc.
	b booze	alcoholic drinks	informal style, party, fun, overindulgence

Connotation is not treated as part of the conceptual meaning of a word or expression. For someone to be called a 'film star' they must be famous and must have acted in movies. But they need not have associations of glamour, being multiply married etc. The focus of semanticists and hence the focus of this chapter is conceptual meaning. That is not to say that associative meanings are unimportant. There are domains of language use, such as poetry and advertising, where associations are crucial, as in [6.2].

[6.2] **uk Fresh mobile phones**

No doubt the connotations of the word 'fresh' must have been paramount in its selection as part of the name of a mobile phone company.

The COLLOCATION of a word (i.e. the combination that a word enters into) plays a major role in determining its meaning in context. For instance, *red* is interpreted differently in *red rose*, where it is the flower that is red, as opposed to *red grapefruit*, where it is the flesh of the fruit that is red, and *red apple*, where it is the skin of the fruit that is red.

6.2 Word-meaning

In the western tradition, the most ancient theory of meaning is that proposed in Plato's dialogue, *Cratylus*, written in 360 BC. In this theory, words are labels for things and the name of each thing is only what people agree to call it. A key aspect of this theory is that convention plays a crucial role in assigning meaning to words. There is nothing about the nature of one of these animals 🐕 that makes it appropriate to refer to it using the word 'dog'. That is the word for it in English, but in German it is *Hund*, in French *chien* and in Swahili *mbwa*. Any of those words is quite adequate. In view of this, linguists have emphasised the importance of ARBITRARINESS in establishing a relationship between words and entities. Apart from instances of onomatopoeia where sound symbolism plays a role (e.g. the *cuckoo* is called a 'cuckoo' in English) (see pp. 44–7), the sounds that make up a word do not reflect aspects of its meaning.

So, what is the relation between words and the things that they name? In the case of proper names that pick out a unique individual, the naming is done directly. For instance, the sounds of the words in [6.3] do name a particular person or entity:

[6.3] a Britney Spears, Nelson Mandela, Shruti Patel
      b Mt Everest, Alice Springs, Barbados, Shanghai

The situation is less straightforward when we consider common nouns like those below:

[6.4] dog, house, boy, tree

The problem is that common nouns do not pick out a particular entity to name. One could argue that a word like *dog* names members of the set of quadruped mammals of genus *Canis*, such as the whippet, the chihuahua, the Labrador, the St Bernard etc. But which canine animals are included in the set of dogs? This is a question that cannot be answered simply by biology. *Canis lupus*, the wolf, is not normally considered a dog, though biologically he is grouped together with your domesticated Fido. (To muddy waters further, not every creature called a dog is a dog: the North American *prairie-dog* is in fact a rodent.)

To circumvent some of the difficulties, it has been suggested that the FORM of a common noun (e.g. the letters of the written word 'dog' or the phonological shape [dɒg] in speech) does not pick out a particular entity as its REFERENT out there in the world; rather, the form is associated with the referent indirectly via CONCEPTS in the minds of speakers that capture the essence of things. For instance, speakers have the general, abstract concept 'dog' (a (normally domesticated) carnivorous quadruped mammal of the genus Canis). This general concept is then associated with a concrete flesh and bone instantiation of a dog. On this view, to say what a word means entails identifying an entity outside language that it DENOTES (= REFERS TO or STANDS FOR). The relationship is represented in the semiotic triangle in [6.5].

[6.5]   concept

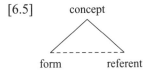

   form   referent

The theory runs into difficulties because of the elusiveness of concepts that was alluded to above and is further illustrated here by the everyday word, *tree*. We all know what trees are. We can speak of an oak tree and a bonsai tree and cypress tree – very different plants. What is the essence of being a tree? Do we all have the same mental picture of a tree? Where do we draw the line between a tree and a shrub? Find three willing volunteers and get them to provide you with their mental image of a tree. To what extent do their mental images coincide?

As seen, the naming theory assumes that for words to have meaning they have to denote entities outside language. That is perhaps true of concrete nouns like those we have considered up to now. But it is not true of abstract nouns such as those in [6.6a] and nouns that refer to imaginary entities that only inhabit the minds of speakers as in [6.6b]:

[6.6] a faith love wit trust courage fear wisdom sarcasm
         virtue negligence
      b Jack Frost unicorn goblin the bogey man dragon
         the Loch Ness Monster

Nor is it true of words that are not nouns:

[6.7] or not early fast at infer work thin but think

So, at best a naming theory of meaning would only be able to provide an account for a relatively small area of the language and have nothing to say about very large areas of the vocabulary. Reference (or 'denotation' or 'naming') is certainly an important aspect of the meaning of words. But all meaning cannot be reduced to reference.

Scholars have suggested a distinction between two aspects of word meaning to deal with some of the issues raised above. Although an expression like *unicorn* does not refer to a real living and kicking beast, it is far from nonsensical. A speaker of English can place it in the menagerie of imaginary creatures that populate the English lexicon. The word 'unicorn' has SENSE but no REFERENCE (denotation). Reference has to do with the entities outside language that a word picks out, whereas sense has to do with the inherent meaning – the notions that it evokes.

A simple way of showing the significance of this distinction is to consider sentences like the following:

[6.8] a My neighbour is my neighbour.
      b The Prime Minister is Mr Tony Blair.

What we have in [6.8a] is a tautologous sentence. It contains a repetition of 'my neighbour' that does not add any new information – it just refers twice to the same individual. By contrast, in [6.8b], although the expressions 'the Prime Minister' and 'Mr Tony Blair' do indeed refer to the same person, there is no tautology. This is because of a difference of sense between the expressions 'the Prime Minister' and 'Mr Tony Blair'. The sense of 'Prime Minister' is 'head of the UK government'. For now, a man called 'Mr Tony Blair' happens to have that role; there have been numerous holders of that position before him and there will be many more after him.

6.3 Sense and componential analysis

There is an intricate web of relations between the senses of words of a language. These relations can be captured by identifying the SEMANTIC COMPONENTS or SEMANTIC FEATURES that together characterise the meaning of a given word. Without knowing which individual is being referred to, for example, we know what words like *woman* and *girl*, *man* and *boy* mean. This is because we are aware of their relation to other words in the language.

The presence of a semantic feature as part of the semantic make-up of a word is signalled by linguists using a plus sign and its absence by a minus sign:

[6.9] Semantic features

woman

$$
\begin{pmatrix}
+ \text{HUMAN} \\
+ \text{FEMALE (or } -\text{MALE)} \\
+ \text{ADULT}
\end{pmatrix}
$$

girl

$$
\begin{pmatrix}
+ \text{HUMAN} \\
+ \text{FEMALE (or } -\text{MALE)} \\
- \text{ADULT}
\end{pmatrix}
$$

man

$$
\begin{pmatrix}
+ \text{HUMAN} \\
+ \text{MALE (or } -\text{FEMALE)} \\
+ \text{ADULT}
\end{pmatrix}
$$

boy

$$
\begin{pmatrix}
+ \text{HUMAN} \\
+ \text{MALE (or } -\text{FEMALE)} \\
- \text{ADULT}
\end{pmatrix}
$$

Componential analysis works well with groups of words that share certain fairly obvious semantic properties (as in [6.9]), but it is impossible to extend componential analysis to the entire vocabulary. There is no small set of universal semantic features that characterise all the words found in language. For instance, any attempt to decompose words like *home, mountain, visit, vague, rich, kind* and *love* is very unlikely to be successful. (See the discussion of prototypes in section (6.6).)

Furthermore, we need to be on our guard against the assumption that finding a technical label for a phenomenon in itself constitutes an advance in our understanding of the phenomenon. In some cases semantic features merely give us additional labels without advancing our understanding in any way. By saying that *colt, mare* and *stallion* are [+EQUINE] as opposed to *puppy, bitch* and *dog*, which are [+CANINE], what have we explained? Not much.

One of the main motivations for using componential analysis is to express semantic SELECTIONAL RESTRICTIONS on words occurring together in syntactic constructions. For instance, some verbs require human subjects. Compare the sentences in [6.10]:

[6.10] a Olga admires the teacher.
     b *Virtue admires Olga.
     c *The new door admires Olga.

In [6.10a] we have a well-formed sentence in every way. But in [6.10b] we have a sentence that is well formed as far as the syntax is concerned but clearly deviant in terms of its meaning. The verb 'admire' requires a subject noun phrase like 'the teacher', 'Olga', or 'our ex-milkman' whose head is a noun that has the semantic feature [+human]; it is incompatible with a subject noun phrase like 'virtue' which is an abstract and non-human noun, or 'the door' which is inanimate and non-human.

6.4 Semantic relations

As we have already noted, for many words it is not easy to come up with credible semantic features. There are no plausible semantic features that might distinguish [6.11]:

[6.11] petunia chrysanthemum rose crocus daffodil
       dahlia tulip

It seems in many cases that it makes more sense to talk of how one word relates to other words in the language rather than to attempt characterising its meaning using semantic features. If asked *What does daffodil mean?*, you might say it is a sort of flower which is yellow and blooms in early spring. The relationship between the words *daffodil* and *flower* is called a SENSE RELATION or SEMANTIC RELATION. There are many different types of semantic relation. We will now survey them in turn.

6.4.1 Hyponymy

The semantic relation which we have just illustrated is one where the meaning of one term is included in the meaning of another term. Technically, relationship of INCLUSION is called HYPONYMY. *Daffodil* is a HYPONYM of *flower*. Logically, if something is a daffodil it must be a flower: the meaning of flower is included in *daffodil*. Hence the oddity of a sentence like:

[6.12] Mrs McTavish had daffodils in her basket, but
      no flowers.

There is a hierarchical relation between words in this kind of relation. The term, such as *flower,* that is at the node that sits higher up in hierarchy is the SUPERORDINATE term. The terms such as *petunia, chrysanthemum, rose, crocus, dahlia, tulip* and *daffodil* that share the same superordinate term are said to be CO-HYPONYMS. As seen in [6.13] with the example of *rose,* a co-hyponym can be a superordinate term with respect to items lower down the hierarchy.

[6.13]

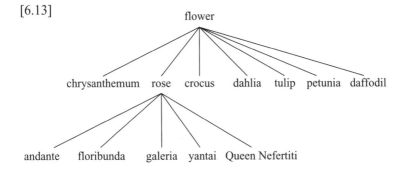

6.4.2 Synonymy

Synonyms normally have closely related, but not necessarily identical, meanings. Indeed, total identity of meaning in all contexts, as in the case of *pail* and *bucket*, is very rare. Typically, certain senses of words may be synonymous, without all senses being synonymous. So, the synonyms cannot be freely exchanged for each other in all contexts. For instance, synonyms of *cool* include *chilly* and *nippy*. The sentences in [6.14] mean more or less the same thing. If one of them is true, the other two are also true.

[6.14] a It is cool in my room.
     b It is chilly in my room.
     c It is nippy in my room.

Now consider [6.15]

[6.15] a Louisa remained cool under ferocious cross-examination.
     b Lee got a cool reception when he got home at midnight.
     c Fiona looked cool in her new Versace jeans.

Although *cool is* synonymous with *chilly* and *nippy*, substituting *cool* with either *chilly* or *nippy* in [6.15] would result in bizarre sentences because in none of these instances does *cool* have to do with low temperature. In [6.15a] the synonyms of *cool* are *calm*, *composed*; in [6.15b] the synonyms are *lukewarm*, *unfriendly*; and in [6.15c] *stylish*, *fashionable*.

6.4.3 Antonymy

Antonyms are words with OPPOSITE meanings.

[6.16] a good   bad
       large   small
       high   low
       clean   dirty
       short   tall
       rich   poor

     b alive   dead
       male   female
       front   behind

Two types of antonyms are recognised, namely GRADABLE ANTONYMS like those in [6.16a] and NON-GRADABLE ANTONYMS exemplified in [6.16b]. Gradable antonyms may be used in comparative constructions. For example, one person may be cleaner/ richer/shorter etc. than another. Furthermore, if one member of the pair is negated it does not necessarily imply that the other member is asserted. If I say to you that 'I am not rich', you should not necessarily infer that I am poor.

The situation is radically different with non-gradable antonyms. They cannot be used in comparative constructions. Something is either dead or alive; it cannot be 'deader' than something else. Also, the negation of one term implies the other. If my parrot is *not alive*, it is certainly *dead*.

Also, observe that in the case of gradable antonyms the two terms are not equal: one member of the pair is MARKED and the other UNMARKED. The unmarked member is the one that is normally expected. Compare:

[6.17] *Unmarked*   *Marked*

       How big is your house?   vs.   How small is your house.
       How well do you play   vs.   How badly do you play
          the guitar?   the guitar?

Where the unmarked member of the pair is used, the speaker is not prejudging anything. But where the marked member is used, the speaker presupposes that the house is small or that you play the guitar badly.

A further 'opposite' relationship is that of CONVERSENESS. The two meanings in question are like two sides of the same coin. The verb pairs *lend ~ borrow* and *sell ~ buy* are good examples of converseness. These verbs describe the same transaction, the difference being in the vantage point from which it is portrayed. If the transaction is seen from the point of view of the person who parts with the goods we speak of lending or selling; if it is seen from the point of view of the recipient we speak of borrowing and buying.

6.4.4 Homophones and homonyms

Words such as those in [6.18] that have unrelated meanings and different spellings but have the same pronunciation are called HOMOPHONES.

| [6.18] | ate | key | aural | Basque | board | leek |
| | eight | quay | oral | bask | bawd | leak |

HOMONYMY is a situation where one orthographic or spoken form represents more than one vocabulary item as in:

| [6.19] | mail | file | nail | fine | mine | bat |
| | nut | light | court | board | ruler | seed |

Homophones and homonyms result in LEXICAL AMBIGUITY. A sentence containing such words may be interpreted in more than one way depending on which lexeme is linked to the word-form it contains that can represent more than one lexeme. Without the help of context, it is not possible to determine the meaning of a homonym like *mail* in *Where is the mail?* (armour/post). It is equally impossible to assign a single meaning to homophones like *stair* and *stare* – both pronounced as [steə]; and *leak and leek* – both pronounced [liːk]. (See section (11.3.3).)

The family of tomatoes
A family of three tomatoes was walking downtown one day when the little baby tomato started lagging behind. The big father tomato walks back to the baby tomato, stomps on her, squashing her into a red paste, and says, "Ketchup!"
(http://www.ahajokes.com/foo006.html)

6.4.5 Polysemy

POLYSEMY is a relationship that holds between different senses of the same word. An identical form in both the spoken and written language has more than one meaning, and the meanings are related to each other. As a rule, polysemy is a result of one meaning being extended metaphorically over time to create new shades of meaning (i.e. new senses). Conventionally each of these senses is numbered and listed under the head word in a dictionary as seen in [6.20].

[6.20]   ○► **Leg** /leg/ *noun* [C] **1** PART OF BODY one of the parts of the
body of a human or animal that is used for standing and
walking *My legs are tired after so much walking.* • *He
broke his leg in the accident.* • *There were cuts on her
arms and legs.* • *She had bare legs and wore only a light
summer dress.* ⊃ *See colour picture* **The Body** *on
page Centre 2.* **2** FOOD the meat of an animal's leg
eaten as food *a chicken leg* **3** FURNITURE one of the
vertical parts of a chair, table, etc that is on the floor *a
chair/table leg* **4** CLOTHES the part of a pair of trousers
that covers one of your legs *He rolled up his trouser legs
and waded into the water.* **5** PART OF A JOURNEY one
part of a journey or competition the *first/ second/third leg
of the journey* **6 not have a leg to stand on** to have
no chance of proving that something is true *If you don't
have a witness you don't have a leg to stand on.* **7 be on
its last legs** *informal If a machine is on its last legs,* it

Source: *Cambridge Learner's Dictionary* (2001: 375).

For further examples of polysemy, look up the words *hand, net* and
seat in your dictionary.

Polysemy is another source of lexical ambiguity. Out of context
the sentences in [6.21] have more than one interpretation. I invite
you to supply the alternative interpretations:

[6.21] a The leg was broken.
      b The President said that lack of intelligence was the
         problem.

The distinction between homonymy and polysemy is not as categorical as the discussion so far suggests. In many cases it is far
from clear whether we have two different lexical items that happen
to be identical in form, or two different senses of the same lexical
item. Consider the entries for *plain* in a major dictionary of the
English language:

[6.22] **plain** ◁ P **Pronunciation Key** (plān)
       Adj. **plain·er, plain·est**

   1 Free from obstructions; open; clear: *in plain view.*
   2 Obvious to the mind; evident: *make one's intention plain.*
      See Synonyms at <u>apparent</u>.
   3 Not elaborate or complicated; simple: *plain food.*
   4 Straightforward; frank or candid: *plain talk.*
   5 Not mixed with other substances; pure: *plain water.*

6 Common in rank or station; average; ordinary: *a plain man.*
7 Not pretentious; unaffected.
8 Marked by little or no ornamentation or decoration.
9 Not dyed, twilled, or patterned: *a plain fabric.*
10 Lacking beauty or distinction: *a plain face.*
11 Sheer; utter; unqualified: *plain stupidity.*
12 *Archaic.* Having no visible elevation or depression; flat; level.

n.

1 a An extensive, level, usually treeless area of land.
   b A broad level expanse, as a part of the sea floor or a lunar mare.
2 Something free of ornamentation or extraneous matter.

Adv. Informal
Clearly; simply: *plain stubborn.*

[Middle English, from Old French, from Latin plānus. See pelə-² in Indo-European Roots.]

plain'ly *Adv.*
plain'ness *n.*
Synonyms: *plain, modest, simple, unostentatious, unpretentious*
These adjectives mean not ornate, ostentatious, or showy: *a plain hairstyle*; *a modest cottage*; *a simple dark suit*; *an unostentatious office*; *an unpretentious country church.*
Antonyms: *ornate*

Source: *The American Heritage® Dictionary of the English Language*, 4th edition. Copyright © 2000 by Houghton Mifflin Company. Published by Houghton Mifflin Company. All rights reserved.

It is debatable whether all the various meanings of *plain*, the adjective, should appear as different senses of the same head word. Is there not a case, perhaps, for considering the sense 'Not mixed with other substances; pure: *plain water*' a distinct word from the sense 'Lacking beauty or distinction: *a plain face*'? What it boils down to is a matter of judgement: how close must the different senses be for them to qualify as being close enough to justify the judgement that we have polysemy rather than homophony? There is no formula that guarantees the right answer to that question, if indeed there is a right answer.

6.5 Semantic fields

In the last section we saw that in a given language words are involved in a variety of semantic relationships with other words. In many cases, the meaning of a word is not characterised by the presence or absence of a particular semantic feature, but rather by the web of semantic relations which together help demarcate the scope of its meaning. A useful way of viewing semantic relations therefore is to assume that the lexicon is partitioned into SEMANTIC FIELDS, namely different zones of meaning. Words whose meanings are intimately related are put in the same semantic field; words that are in adjacent semantic fields have a closer semantic affinity than words found in distant semantic fields. For instance, the semantic fields of foods and beverages are closely related (and indeed overlap to some extent as in the case of *soup*) but neither is closely related to the semantic field of poetry. Consider the words in [6.23]:

[6.23]	*Semantic field*	*Words*
a	Beverages	drink, tea, cocktail, beer, lager, wine, whisky, coffee, (minestrone soup?)
	Food	eat, pudding, sausage, steak, fish and chips, rice, hamburger, noodles, pizza, (fish soup?)
b	Poetry	verse, stanza, iambic, troche, assonance, alliteration, sonnet, rhyme, enjambment
d	Kinship	mother, daughter, father, son, sister, brother, uncle, aunt, grandparent, cousin, mother-in-law
e	Colour terms	black, white, blue, orange, purple, green, yellow, brown orange, red

Various areas of meaning, notably colour and kinship terms, have been successfully studied in detail in this way.

We will exemplify the use of semantic fields to analyse colour terms drawing on the summary of the issues in Simpson (1979). As we all know, the colours of a rainbow do not have clear boundaries. This is to be expected since the spectrum of light is a continuum. However, the perception of colours is influenced by three key factors, namely hue (tint or colour type), luminosity (brightness) and saturation (intensity of the whiteness component). Although people with normal eyesight see pretty much the same range of colours, the actual colour terms used in different languages vary.

It has been suggested that the cross-linguistic differences are best interpreted in terms of the structure of the colour semantic field as shown in the figure in [6.24], where the horizontal axis indicates hue, and the vertical axis luminosity. As it is not a three-dimensional figure, there is no axis indicating saturation with white (shades of grey).

[6.24]

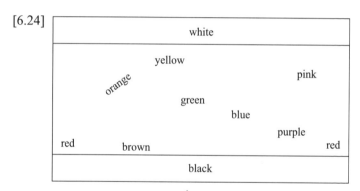

ENGLISH: eleven basic colour terms, including *grey*

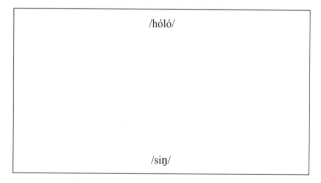

JALE (New Guinea Highlands): two basic colour terms

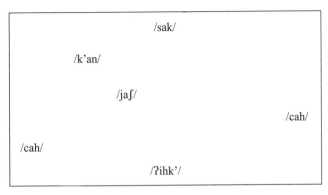

TZELTAL (Central America): five basic colour terms

Source: From J. M. Y. Simpson (1979) *A First Course in Linguistics*. Edinburgh: Edinburgh University Press, p. 189.

The way the spectrum is divided up linguistically is interesting. In English, hue, saturation and luminosity are all important. For instance, there is a continuum at the right edge of the diagram from pink to purple and red which reflects these three parameters.

The importance of the relationships between words belonging to the same semantic field can also be seen if you consider the colours yellow, green and blue. To know what *green* means one needs to be able to place it vis-à-vis *yellow* and *blue*. The 'value' or meaning of a term crucially depends on its place in the semantic field to which it belongs. English has eleven basic colour terms, Tzeltal five and Jale a mere two. Hence, the scope of the meaning of /hóló/ 'white' in Jale is very much broader than the meaning of 'white' in English.

6.6 Semantic prototypes: the birdiness rankings

In section (6.3) we saw that an approach to word meaning that is solely based on the decomposition of the meaning of words into their basic semantic components meets with very limited success. This is in large measure due to the VAGUENESS or FUZZINESS of a very large number of the concepts that underlie the lexical items of a language which makes them inappropriate for characterisation using a limited set of semantic features. Many semantic concepts do not belong to discrete categories. For example, there is no clear cut off point between a *hill* and a *mountain* or *big* and *small*. If I tell you that Geronimo is *big*, you will have a different idea of his size depending on whether I tell you that the Geronimo in question is a hamster, the toddler next door or an adult male African elephant.

To address these questions, Rosch (1973, 1978) and her colleagues proposed a psychological account of concepts and categorisation which was based on prototypes rather than discrete categories. In this approach, which is called PROTOTYPE THEORY, some members of a category are regarded as better examples or representatives of the category than others. At the core are the most representative members of the prototype and other members fan out from the core in concentric circles, with the worst exemplars of the prototype being found at the periphery and the rest occurring at various points in between.

This claim was supported by findings from an experiment eliciting the judgements of California undergraduates about the category 'bird'. It was established that the robin is a better example of a bird than the penguin or the ostrich and other birds fall somewhere in between as seen in [6.25].

[6.25] Birdiness rankings

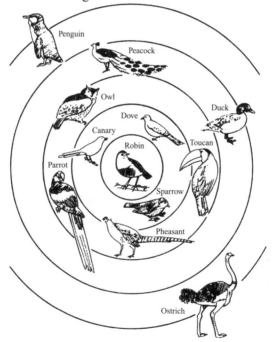

Source: From Jean Aitchison (2003) *Words in the Mind.* Blackwell: Oxford, p. 56.

It is easy to see how prototype theory applies to other concepts. If you consider wealth, for example, someone like Bill Gates will be a prototypical billionaire. So, he would be at the centre of the circle. A local restaurateur with assets worth a few thousand pounds will be at the periphery.

6.7 Beyond the lexicon

The focus of this chapter has been lexical semantics. However, a fuller treatment of meaning must also treat sentence meaning and pragmatics. The need to treat sentence meaning separately from word meaning is easy to see. Grammatical structures have a semantic role. Sentences that have identical words may express different meanings if the words are in different grammatical constructions. Consider [6.26]:

[6.26] a The dog frightened the burglar.
       b The burglar frightened the dog.

In [6.26a] it is the dog that is the subject and agent; it is responsible for scaring the burglar and the burglar is the object and patient. In [6.26b] the word order and grammatical roles are reversed and as a consequence the meaning is different.

Also, a single sentence may have more than one semantic interpretation that is not attributable to the polysemy of any of the words. Such a sentence is said to display SYNTACTIC AMBIGUITY (or STRUCTURAL AMBIGUITY):

[6.27] *1.40 a.m.* Donahue and guests discuss affairs with
       ex-spouses.

(Radio Times)

The syntactic ambiguity is due to the fact that the words in that sentence can be grouped syntactically in either of the two ways indicated in [6.27], with each grouping bringing with it a different interpretation.

[6.28] a Donahue and guests [discuss affairs] [with ex-spouses]
       b Donahue and guests [discuss] [affairs with ex-spouses]

In [6.28a] Donahue's guests discuss affairs, with ex-spouses as their interlocutors, whereas in [6.28b] Donahue and guests discuss some topic, and the topic they discuss is their affairs with former spouses.

Finally, the need to include pragmatics (namely meaning in contextualised interaction) is also easy to see. The interpretation of an UTTERANCE when language is used to communicate may vary with context and speaker intention. Consider [6.29]

[6.29]   Man huddled in shop doorway: Can you spare some change?
Man in suit: No (and walks on).

The intention of the beggar in asking the question is not really to establish whether the be-suited man has excess change in his wallet. Rather, his intention is to obtain some cash. But the be-suited man says 'no'. He appears to take the question at face value. He can think of uses for the coins in his wallet; they are not spare.

6.8 Summary

Word meaning has been the topic of this chapter. We started with the distinction between reference (denotation) and connotation. Then we focused on the former in an attempt to relate the words of a language to the extra-linguistic world out there. We noted that not all meaning can be reduced to reference. The core of the chapter contained a survey of approaches to sense, namely the semantic relations between words with related meanings. We explored the merits of four approaches to sense relations: sense relations, componential analysis, semantic fields and prototype theory.

The chapter ended with the observation that the study of meaning must go beyond word meaning. Grammar has a major role in the meaning of sentences and pragmatic considerations are also important for the interpretation of meaning when language is used in particular situations.

Exercises

1   What difficulties would be encountered by a naming theory of meaning in providing a characterisation of the meaning of *child*, *friend*, *book* and *home*?

2   What are the semantic components that recur in these words?

cow	bull	calf
ewe	ram	lamb

> sow boar piglet
> bitch dog puppy

3 What semantic features characterise the objects of the following verbs:

> *kill* *murder* *assassinate* *massacre*

4 a Where would you draw the semantic boundary between *tree* and *shrub*; *mountain* and *hill*; *blue* and *green*; *woman* and *girl*?

b Which approach to meaning provides us with the best representation of the meaning of the words in 4a?

5 Find synonyms for the following words, and then invent contexts where they would not be mutually substitutable:

> *shallow* *narrow* *wicked* *simple* *light*

6 What is the semantic relationship between these words:

> *bank* (a) financial institution; b) side of a river
> *page* (a) of a book; (b) servant
> *bark* (a) of a tree; (b) of a dog
> *steer* (a) guide; (b) young bull

7 Set up semantic fields for words in the fields of

a forest
b weather
c army ranks

8 Suggest a syntactic analysis that disambiguates each of the following:

a CALF BORN TO FARMER WITH TWO HEADS.
b The patient was referred to a psychiatrist with a severe emotional problem.
c She died in the home in which she was born at the age of 88.
d The judge sentenced the killer to die in the electric chair for the second time.

(From Lederer 1989: 102–3)

9   Referring to the discussion of meaning in this chapter, explain the basis of the humour in the picture [6.30].

[6.30]

On her Birthday Sarah felt like a nineteen year old, so she went out and got one.

Part III

A changing, expanding lexicon

The focus is on the change and expansion of the vocabulary. In Chapter 8 we discuss the effects of the massive infusion of words from other languages over the centuries and in Chapter 9 we investigate the ways in which the vocabulary has been expanded by using the internal resources of the language. In Chapter 10 we look at spelling and the development of the relationship between words in speech and in writing.

Chapter 7

A lexical mosaic

Sources of English vocabulary

7.1 The nature of borrowing

In the last chapter we saw the ways in which a language may use its internal resources to create new words. This chapter explores how, instead of building lexical items using its own resources, a language can add to the number of words in its lexicon by BORROW-ING vocabulary from other languages. English has borrowed so extensively from other languages that the English lexicon is like a large mosaic.

7.1.1 Direct and indirect borrowing

It is useful to distinguish between direct borrowing and indirect borrowing. If a language takes a word directly from another, as English got *omelette* from French, we call what happens DIRECT BORROWING. But in other cases a word may be passed indirectly like a relay baton from one language to another, and to another, e.g. *kahveh* (Turkish) > *kahva* (Arabic) > *koffie* > (Dutch) > *coffee* (English). This is called INDIRECT BORROWING. If a word is directly borrowed the chances of its undergoing drastic phonological modification are considerably less than those of a word that is indirectly borrowed. Anyone can see that French *omelette* and English *omelette* are evidently related. But I suspect many Turkish speakers would not recognise English *coffee* as a word originating from *kahveh*. For by the time *kahveh* had gone through Arabic and Dutch to reach English it had undergone considerable phonological changes, which are partly reflected in the spelling. Each time a word passes from one language to another, its pronunciation is adjusted to make it fit into the phonological system of the recipient language.

An even better example of phonological distortions arising in the course of indirect borrowing is *avocado*. The pear-shaped fruit produced by the Caribbean and Central American tree whose botanical name is *Persea gratissima* was called *ahuacatl* in Aztec. At the end of the seventeenth century the Spaniards borrowed this word as *aguacate*, which was a reasonably close approximation to the Aztec pronunciation. But in popular speech it was changed to *avigato* and then to *avocado* (like the Spanish word for *advocate*), from which we get English *avocado*. It was modified even more drastically in popular speech giving *alligator pear* from *avigato* in the eighteenth century.

This illustrates how often FALSE ETYMOLOGY plays a role in the phonological changes that take place when foreign words are nativised. People tend to rationalise; they want a reason for the imported word sounding the way it does. So they link it with a plausible real word in their language. Thus, they might have thought that, since the *ahuacatl* (avigato) fruit came from the Americas, the land of alligators, it 'made sense' to call it the *alligator pear*. Presumably because this fruit was exotic and expensive, it was something that only rich people, like advocates, would be able to afford. Hence the name *avocado* pear must also have seemed reasonable.

As an aside, note that in fact false etymology is not all that rare. There are quite a few words formed by joining pseudo-bases to affixes, e.g. *trimaran* 'a vessel with three hulls', which is formed from the *catamaran* 'a twin-hulled sailing boat' as though *-maran* were a base meaning 'hull'. Conversely, a form may be reanalysed as a pseudo-affix which is attached to bases. A famous example of this is *-holic*. By analogy to *alcoholic*, we get *work-a-holic*, *ice-cream-a-holic* etc. The form *-holic* is treated as a suffix meaning 'someone who overindulges in something', although that was not its original meaning.

As you would expect, meaning alterations may also occur as a word is handed from language to language. The more indirect the borrowing, the greater the alterations are likely to be. For instance, Luganda borrowed *pakitimane* from Swahili which in turn borrowed it from English *pocket money*. *Pakitimane* means 'wallet' rather than 'pocket money'. This is due to a misunderstanding of what the word denotes in English. The contents of a wallet may be someone's 'pocket money' but the wallet itself is not 'pocket money'. When borrowing words, there is always a danger of misunderstanding what exactly words denote – what aspect of an object they specifically pick out. A degree of drift is almost inevitable when a game of Chinese whispers is played. So it is with borrowing when meaning is handed on through several intermediaries. Thus, English *howitzer* 'light gun' comes from Dutch *houwitzer* which was itself borrowed from Czech *houfnice* 'catapult'.

7.1.2 Loanwords and loanshifts

We will recognise two kinds of borrowing: LOANWORDS and LOAN-SHIFTS (see Haugen 1950). A loanword is a word belonging to one language which is IMPORTED or ADOPTED by another, e.g. *catamaran* was imported into English from Tamil and *shopping* was imported into French as (*le*) *shopping*.

By contrast, a loanshift involves taking on board the meaning represented by a word in a foreign language, but not the word-form itself. Loanshifts are also called LOAN TRANSLATIONS or CALQUES. (The 'calque' metaphor comes from fine art where a calque is a tracing.) In a loanshift the borrowing is done by translating the meaning of the vocabulary item. Let us start with the English word *loanword* itself, which is a loan translation from German *Lehnwort*. Similarly, the name of *Superman*, that great popular culture hero made famous by Hollywood, is a loan translation of the German *Übermensch*. There are also a number of loan translations of Latin origin, especially in religious language, which is not surprising since for centuries Latin was the language of western Christendom. From *omnipotens* (*omni-* 'all' + *potens* 'power') have come the loan translations *almighty* and *all powerful*. Latin *Spiritus Sanctus* (*spiritus* 'spirit', *sanctus* 'holy') was rendered in English by the translation *Holy Spirit* or *Holy Ghost*.

However, it is from French that English gets most of its loan translations. Many English sayings are translations of the French:

[7.1] *French*   *English*
    ça va sans dire   it goes without saying
    d'un certain age   of a certain age (i.e. getting
                                        on in years)
    sans cérémonie   without ceremony
    dialogue de sourds   dialogue of the deaf
    en principe   in principle
    le commencement de la fin   the beginning of the end

Note in passing that the loan translation traffic is not all one way. English loans are also translated into other languages. Thus, *skyscraper* is translated and rendered as *le gratte-ciel (gratter* = 'to scratch' + *ciel* 'sky') in French. It is not simply borrowed as *(le) skyscraper*. (Italian too translates skyscraper as *gratta-cielo*.)

French is the most important source of imported vocabulary items by a very clear margin, so we will devote most of the space in this chapter to the discussion of borrowings from this language. Further, since loanwords are the dominant type of borrowed words, we concentrate on these rather than on loan translations.

7.1.3 Likely loans

In principle anything in language can be borrowed. In practice most of the words that are borrowed belong to the open lexical classes (i.e. nouns, verbs, adjectives and adverbs). And of these, nouns top the list, followed by verbs and adjectives. The reason why nouns are the commonest loanwords is not difficult to see. Normally, borrowing takes place because a word is needed to give a name to an unfamiliar animal, thing or cultural phenomenon.

It is rare (but not impossible) for a language to borrow words in the closed classes. In Old English, for example, the third person plural pronoun was *hī* (I am only considering the nominative and accusative cases for simplicity's sake). In the twelfth century Old English borrowed from Old Norse the third person plural pronoun *þeir* /θei/ from which *they* is descended.

For borrowing to take place, some degree of bilingualism or bi-dialectalism (knowledge of two dialects of the same language) is a prerequisite. Speakers need to know – or think they know – what the words that they import mean. (See the discussion of *pakitimane* in section (7.1.1).)

7.1.4 Why borrow?

As mentioned in previous chapters, in principle there is no limit to the number of words that can be formed in a language. There is no reason why a particular meaning should not be associated with any given form. So, there is really no purely linguistic reason for borrowing. Whenever the need for a word arises following contact with another culture, people could just make one up. But in most cases they do not. It is relatively rare for speakers to create completely new words. When a suitable word exists in another language, the easiest thing in the world to do is to adopt that word rather than to make up an original one from nothing. This is a reason for borrowing. But it is not the only one. There is a number of other good reasons for importing words. One of them is IDENTITY. Language is much more than simply a means of communication. It is also a badge that we wear to assert our identity. By using a particular language, bilingual speakers may be saying something about how they perceive themselves and how they wish to relate to their interlocutor. For instance, if a patient initiates an exchange with a doctor in the doctor's surgery in Yiddish, that may be a signal of solidarity, saying: you and I are members of the same sub-group. Alternatively, rather than choosing between languages, these two people may prefer CODE-SWITCHING. They may produce sentences which are partly in English and partly in Yiddish. If foreign words are used habitually in code-switching, they may pass from one language into another and eventually become fully integrated and cease being regarded as foreign. That is probably how words like *chutzpah* (brazen impudence), *schlemiel* (a very clumsy, bungling idiot who is always a victim), *schmaltz* (cloying, banal sentimentality) and *goyim* (gentile) passed from Yiddish into (American) English. The fact that there is no elegant English equivalent to these Yiddish words was no doubt also a factor in their adoption. (See p. 142 for further discussion.)

Sometimes the reason for code-switching is PRESTIGE, i.e. one-upmanship. People have always liked showing off. By using fashionable words from a fashionable foreign culture one shows that one is with it, one is modern, one is part of the crème de la crème and so on. Shakespeare's Mercutio, in his parody of the *pardonnez-moi* brigade, puts this point across succinctly:

[7.2] Why, is not this a lamentable thing, grandsire, that we should be thus afflicted with these strange flies, these fashion-mongers, these *pardonnez-mois*, who stand so much on the new form that they cannot sit at ease on the old bench? O, their *bons*, their *bons*!

(*Romeo and Juliet*, II, iv)

Another obvious reason for borrowing is to provide a word that meets a need for a word where no suitable English one exists. When new concepts, creatures, artefacts, institutions, religions etc.

are encountered or introduced through contact with speakers of another language, the words for them from the source language tend to be retained. At various periods in history different civilisations have been pre-eminent in one field or another. Normally, the language of the people who excel in a particular field of human endeavour becomes the international lingua franca of that field. Words belonging to the SEMANTIC FIELD (i.e. area of meaning (see section 6.5)) such as music, dance, religion, government and politics, architecture, science, clothes and fashion, are imported from the language of the pre-eminent civilisation during that period. Thus, the concentration of borrowed words in certain semantic fields reflects the nature of the contact between speech communities. It reflects the areas where new words had to be acquired in order to fill a perceived gap.

For instance, one reason for the intensive borrowing in the late medieval and early modern periods was the fact that the intelligentsia felt they were lumbered with a very inadequate language that was in need of improvement. In his poem 'Phillip Sparrow' the poet John Skelton complained about English being a rude language unsuitable for poetry. There were two problems. First, English was changing and deteriorating fast; and, second, English was inherently inadequate and prosaic, lacking the sophisticated metrical resources and poetic devices that the classical languages boasted of. An infusion of Latin and Greek (and a bit of French) was what was needed.

This concern was shared by many in the establishment. In 1531 Sir Thomas Elyot published a book entitled *The Governour*, which was intended to serve as a manual for training gentlemen who were going to be employed at court. He enthusiastically infiltrated words from the classical languages into the text in order to improve the English language. The words he introduced included *devulgate, describe, attempate, education, dedicate, esteme* etc. Elyot's zeal was matched by that of many others. The words flooded in: *commemorate, invidious, frequency, expectation, thermometer, affable* etc. (Baugh and Cable 2002: 214–15).

But still some remained sceptical about the merits of English even after it had been 'improved'. Sir Francis Bacon wrote his scientific work in both English and Latin to ensure that future generations would be able to read it – just in case English did not survive as a language of scholarship.

There were also many who disapproved of the 'improvement' that was being engineered. Some influential figures like Sir John

Cheke (1514–57) robustly resisted the influx of what came to be known pejoratively as INKHORN TERMS, i.e. words imported from Latin and Greek and anglicised in order to give gravitas to one's discourse. The objectors opposed the use of inkhorn terms because they alienated people who had not had the benefit of a good classical education.

Not all borrowing was from Latin and Greek. During the Middle Ages, when scientific knowledge was more advanced in the Arab world than in the west, a significant number of Arabic scientific terms were indirectly borrowed by English from French, which had acquired them from Spanish, a very important conduit of Arab science and culture to western Europe because Spain was occupied by the Moors. Examples of such scientific terms (many of which begin with *al* – the Arabic definite article) are listed in [7.3a]:

[7.3] a alchemy, alcohol, alembic, algebra, alkali, zenith, zero
       b Koran, imam, caliph, muezzin, mullah, Ramadan, etc.

Besides being the language of science in the Middle Ages, Arabic was, and still remains, the language of Islam. Virtually all the words used in English connected with Islam are borrowed from Arabic (see 7.3b).

For centuries, French was the language of government, politics, the military, diplomacy and protocol. Hence a large number of words in this semantic area are from French:

[7.4] a *Military*
          cordon sanitaire, barrage, hors de combat, matériel, RV
          (rendez-vous), reveille (in English pronounced /rɪvælɪ/)

       b *Diplomacy and protocol*
          corps diplomatique, chargé d'affaires, communiqué

       c *Government and politics*
          ancien régime, dirigiste, coup d'état, laissez-faire, l'état
          c'est moi, agent provocateur

We will return to French influence in more detail in section (7.3).

Names of animals, birds and plants from around the world have entered English from all kinds of languages spoken in different parts of the world, for example:

[7.5] *People*   Sherpa and Gurka (Nepal), pakeha (Maori)
      Animals   chimpanzee (Angola), panda (Nepal), koala
                      (Australia), kookaburra (Australia), kudu
                      (Xhosa, South Africa), zebra (Congo)
      Arts and culture samba (Brazil), rhumba (Cuba), tango
                      (Argentina), didgeridoo (Australia), batik
                      (Javanese)

Numerous words referring to food have been imported as the range of foreign foods eaten here has increased. Think of goulash (Hungarian), enchiladas (Mexican Spanish), moussaka (Greek) and tacos (Mexican Spanish).

The same point can be further illustrated with examples of words referring to dress. We could in principle coin a fresh word or just use a roundabout description of a

[7.6] sarong (Malay), parka (Aleutian), anorak (Greenlandic
      Eskimo), kimono (Japanese), shawl (Persian)

but it is simpler to import the object together with the name for it.

Sometimes borrowing occurs for a different reason – the need to acquire the *mot juste* which is available in another language. For instance, English does not have a native word or expression with the precise meaning conveyed by the French loanwords *chic*, *flair*, *esprit de corps*, *naïve*, *elegant* or *blasé*. Try to think of how you would convey these ideas without using the French imports. I suspect that almost any alternatives you come up with would appear somewhat clumsy. Or, think of a *ménage à trois*. You could use the loan translation 'a household with three partners', but it does not quite roll off the tongue.

In section (8.13), we will see how euphemism is used to avoid causing annoyance or embarrassment. The same motivation may also lie behind borrowing a word from another language. It seems that less embarrassment is caused when awkward things are said using words from a foreign language. So English borrowed *faeces* and *defecate* from Latin. Using them enables one to avoid distasteful four-letter words. Latin *faeces* meant 'dregs' and to *defecate* meant 'to clear from dregs or impurities'. This was metaphorically extended as a euphemism for 'to empty the bowels'. Propriety also lies behind the euphemistic use of the borrowed Latin words *genitalia* and *pudenda* as well as the importation of several words used to talk discreetly about shady sexual activities and participants therein, e.g. *maison de rendezvous, gigolo* and *madame* from French, and *bordello* from Italian.

7.1.5 The grass is ever greener on the other side

English has an extremely rich and varied vocabulary because it has enthusiastically borrowed foreign words in very large numbers. Each century the number of words adopted from foreign languages has increased. As we saw earlier, the main source of imports over the centuries has been French. This can be seen in [7.7], taken from Bliss (1966: 26), which shows the number of foreign words in use at various points in the history of English (c is short for 'century' in these tables):

[7.7]

	Medieval	16c	17c	18c	19c	20c
French	19	42	166	316	736	1103
Classical	89	237	371	173	328	250
Italian	–	26	48	100	90	153
German	–	2	2	4	58	240
Spanish	–	13	14	14	47	32
Other European	4	10	13	22	49	53
Non-European	2	12	56	35	97	55
Total	114	342	670	664	1405	1886

In another table on p. 27 of the same book (see [7.8]), Bliss presents figures showing the percentage of the total borrowing during each period, which is made up of words from each of these different languages:

[7.8]

	Medieval	16c	17c	18c	19c	20c
French	16.7	12.2	24.8	47.7	52.3	58.6
Classical	78	69.4	55.3	25.9	23.4	13.2
Italian		7.6	7.2	15.1	6.4	8.1
German		0.6	0.3	0.6	4.1	12.7
Spanish		3.8	2.1	2.1	3.4	1.7
Other European	3.5	2.9	1.9	3.3	3.5	2.8
Non-European	1.8	3.5	8.4	5.3	6.9	2.9

The preponderance of French loans becomes even clearer when they are seen as a percentage of the total number of words from other languages.

Making reliable estimates about the origins of words in present-day English is notoriously difficult. Probably more reliable than Bliss's findings are the results of a corpus study reported in *AskOxford*, where words of Old and Middle English (and Old Norse, and Dutch) stock account for a mere quarter of the vocabulary and French and Latin loans between them account for well over half of the items:

> the result of a computerized survey of roughly 80,000 words in the old *Shorter Oxford Dictionary* (3rd edition) was published in *Ordered Profusion* by Thomas Finkenstaedt and Dieter Wolff (1973). They reckoned the proportions as follows:
>
> - Latin, including modern scientific and technical Latin: 28.24%
> - French, including Old French and early Anglo-French: 28.3%
> - Old and Middle English, Old Norse, and Dutch: 25%
> - Greek: 5.32%
> - No etymology given: 4.03%
> - Derived from proper names: 3.28%
> - All other languages contributed less than 1%
>
> (From *AskOxford.com* 2002)

Although the classical languages, Greek and Latin, are major sources of roots and affixes we will not deal with them separately here, for two reasons. First, there was extensive borrowing by Latin from Greek and this sometimes makes it difficult to tell which words are Latin and which Greek. Second, French, the most important source of English loanwords, is descended from Latin. This muddies waters. It is not always clear whether a word is a direct Latin import or one that came in indirectly, via French. This does not mean that loans from the classical languages are ignored. We have dealt with them already in other contexts: see the earlier discussion in sections (4.2.1) and (5.5.1). (See also Bauer 1994: 29–49.)

7.1.6 Nativisation of loanwords

Many foreign words that are borrowed become fully NATIVISED. In the case of English, nativisation means ANGLICISATION. The words become assimilated and undistinguishable from indigenous English words, which raises the question: how do we distinguish between code-switching – the use of a foreign word as part of an English sentence – and borrowing – the use of a word that was once foreign but has become Anglicised? Evidently, there is no real problem in cases where the foreign import has been fully adopted and integrated into the English lexicon for so long that anyone who is not especially knowledgeable about etymology would be unable to sniff out its foreignness. Some, like *parent*, even take native English suffixes (e.g. *-hood* as in *parenthood*). Contrast this with the less well assimilated word *paternity*, which takes the Romance suffix *-ity* which has roughly the same meaning: 'the state of being X'. I suspect that very few readers of this book would have been aware before now that everyday words like these:

[7.9] animal   aunt   chair   change   colour   cost
      dinner   escape flower poor   table   uncle

and dozens more, are adopted French words. We cannot do without French loanwords in English. It would be extremely difficult to talk for even a few minutes without using any word of French origin (see Phythian 1982).

Equally unproblematic when considering nativisation are words and expressions that are very clearly French like those in [7.10a], which are typically used to add local colour, say, in a tourist brochure, or those in [7.10b], which are mostly used to impress the interlocutor, saying to them 'See me, I am sophisticated':

[7.10] a auberge   maître d'hôtel   château
          gendarme   mistral   midi

       b deraciné   façon de parler   soi-disant
          mauvais quatre d'heure   mauvais sujet   longueur

We would probably recognise this as code-switching.

The problem is that many words in the category of [7.10] are not totally foreign, although they are not fully Anglicised either. Words may resist nativisation to a greater or lesser degree. Even after a long period of use in English some words fail to become fully adopted. Instead, they remain on the fringes, as tolerated aliens with one foot in and the other foot out of the English lexicon. For the rest of this section we will consider in some detail 'les mots français' in English which, to different degrees, resist assimilation. Archetypical examples of such marginal entries in the English lexicon are the expressions *billet doux* and *esprit de corps*, which still feel foreign despite having been in use in English since the seventeenth and eighteenth centuries respectively.

A complicating factor in all this is that English speakers' judgements are not uniform. Some people may regard a word as foreign which others consider nativised. We will use a few rules of thumb to determine whether a foreign word is Anglicised or not. But always bear in mind that they are very crude rules. There is no set of exact, scientific principles that can enable us to infallibly separate foreign words used in code-switching from nativised borrowed words.

1   Foreign grammatical properties may be ignored when a borrowed word is assimilated into the grammatical system of English. Thus grammatical gender inflection gets ironed out since it is not relevant in English. Contrasts like *naïf* (masculine) as opposed to *naïve* (feminine) disappear. In English both men and women can be simply *naïve*. I have heard people say either in English. My impression is that conservative, older, highly educated speakers who are aware of the origin of this word are the most likely to treat this word in this fashion.

2   If a word is not perceived as foreign any more, writers stop giving it special treatment. Any foreign marks and diacritics used in its spelling disappear. They stop italicising it or putting it in inverted commas, or offering a gloss, or doing anything to draw attention to it any more than they would an indigenous word. Contrast the spelling of the fully Anglicised words in [7.11] with the spelling of those in [7.12]; the latter are not yet fully Anglicised, so normally retain their French spelling.

[7.11] *French*	*English*	*French*	*English*
théâtre	theatre	détour	detour
bâton	baton	débris	debris
bric à brac	bric-a-brac	dépôt	depot
café	cafe	élite	elite
châlet	chalet	rôle	role
décor	decor	simplicité	simplicity
détente	detente	naïve	naive

[7.12] *French*   *English*
      à la rigueur   à la rigueur
      démodé   démodé
      déshabillé   déshabillé
      engagé   engagé
      glacé   glacé, glace (cherries)

3   In the spoken language, the more nativised a borrowed word
    is, the more it is made to fit in with the standard rules that
    govern the pronunciation of words in the host language. If a
    French word containing sounds not found in English is
    Anglicised, such sounds are modified or replaced. If it contains
    sounds which do also occur in English, but has them in awkward
    combinations, changes are made to make the word conform to
    the phonotactic requirements of English. Stress is changed, if
    necessary, to fit in with the stress patterns of English. Thus,
    even the most pedantic person would not try to pronounce a
    French borrowing like *parent* [peərənt] in the French way as
    [paʁɑ̃], with the rolled guttural Parisian 'r' and nasalised vowel.
    Parent has been fully assimilated. It does not smell of any
    Frenchness at all.

However, when words are only partially assimilated there is
considerable scope for variation. Rarely is there unanimity in the
way such words are treated. Compare the English pronunciations
of the words in [7.13] with the French pronunciation. It is likely
that you will disagree with what I say:

[7.13] *French*   *English*
     a buffet   [byˈfɛ]   [byˈfɛ]   ~ [bʊˈfeɪ]
     b garage   [gaˈʁaʒ]   [gəˈrɑːʒ]   ~ [ˈgærɑːdʒ] ~
                                              [ˈgærɑːʒ] ~
                                              [ˈgærɪdʒ]
     c impasse [ɛ̃ˈpas]   [æmˈpɑːs]   ~ [ˈɪmpɑːs]
     d ensemble [ɑ̃ˈsɑ̃bl]]   [ɑ̃nˈsɑ̃mbl]   ~ [ɔːnˈsɔːmbl] ~
                                              [ɑːnˈsɑːmbl]
     e débâcle [deˈbakl]   [deˈbɑːkl]   ~ [deɪˈbɑːkl] ~
                                              [dɪˈbɑːkl]

Do you have any strong feelings about the 'correctness' of these
pronunciations? Do you believe that remaining as close as possible

to the original French pronunciation is highly desirable? Personally, I am agnostic. My opinion is that, whereas such questions might provide useful topics for the chattering classes to occupy themselves with on a dull day, they are not particularly important for most language users. As foreign words become fully integrated in a language, the pressure to make them conform to the standard rules is often irresistible. But, until they are fully assimilated, it is to be expected that speakers will treat them differently.

7.1.7 Effects of borrowing

Language is a system where all the pieces fit together (Saussure 1916). Borrowing has repercussions for the entire system. The introduction of words from other languages may affect the structure of the recipient language at the level of meaning, grammar (morphology and syntax) or pronunciation.

First, let us consider the PHONOLOGICAL EFFECTS OF BORROWING, which have not been drastic, using the history of *sk* as our illustration. Very early in its history, Old English underwent a phonological change which resulted in the consonant combination [sk] being pronounced as [ʃ]. Old English *scip* [skip] had become [ʃɪp] ('ship'), *sceap* [skæəp] had become [ʃæəp] ('sheep'), *scruncen* [skrunken] had become [ʃrunken] ('shrunken') etc. As a consonant cluster, [sk] became extinct although [s] and [k] continued to occur in other combinations.

After the arrival of the Norsemen on the scene at the end of the ninth century, who raided, and later settled in, many parts of the British Isles, English borrowed many Scandinavian words that contained [sk], e.g. *scatter*, *sky*, *skin*, *skill* and *skirt*. (The original Old English *scyrte*, the garment covering the upper part of the body, had become *shirt*.) As a consequence of borrowing, the [sk] cluster was reintroduced by the eleventh century.

Later on, borrowing from French during the Middle Ages also had some consequences for English phonology. It resulted in a PHONEME SPLIT. This is what happened. In Old English the fricatives [f v] and [s z] were not distinct phonemes. They were allophones of the phonemes /f/ and /s/ respectively. The voiced allophones occurred in heavily voiced environments. So they were found where these phonemes intervened between a stressed vowel and (i) another vowel (e.g. *lēōfost* (with *f* pronounced [v]) 'dearest'; or (ii) a nasal or a liquid that was followed by a vowel (e.g. *lēōfra* (with *f* pronounced [v]) 'dearer'. The voiceless fricative [f] occurred elsewhere: word-initially as in *feorr* 'far'; word-finally as in *lēōf* 'dear'; and when followed by a voiceless consonant as in *lufsum* 'amiable'. The same pattern of distribution was also shown by [s] and [z].

By contrast, Old French contrasted voiced and voiceless fricatives. So, as a consequence of borrowing French words like *vain, value, variable, veal, veil, zeal, zodiac* etc. it now became possible to contrast voiced fricatives with voiceless ones in the same environment as in *zeal* and *seal* (both borrowed from Old French). Hence these fricatives split into separate phonemes.

Borrowing may also have GRAMMATICAL EFFECTS, although these too have been quite modest in English. Adopting foreign nouns with their inflectional morphemes has resulted in the acquisition of a considerable number of allomorphs of the plural morpheme. In addition to the regular, native -*s* plural, English has other plural suffixes. Many Latin loans ending in -*um* (e.g. datum) take -*a* as their plural suffix (*data*); those ending in -*us* in the singular (e.g. *fungus*) take -*i* in the plural (*fungi*); and those ending in -*a* in the singular (e.g. *larva*) take -*ae* in the plural (*larvae*).

Some Greek loans also bring with them their plural endings. Nouns ending in -*is* in the singular take -*es* in the plural e.g. *thesis ~ theses*. Those ending in -*on* in the singular take -*a* as their plural suffix as in *ganglion ~ ganglia*.

Nouns borrowed from French which end in -*e(a)u* take -*x* in the plural, e.g. *bureau ~ bureaux* and *adieu ~ adieux*. And nouns borrowed from Hebrew take the plural -*im* as in *kibbutzim*.

Finally, the introduction of new borrowed items may have SEMANTIC EFFECTS. These are the most obvious and most important. Here I want to show that borrowing can affect the *structure* of the lexicon when the meanings of imported words are put side by side with the meanings of words which are already in the lexicon. This is because the lexicon is not just an unstructured list. Adding a new word may disturb the equilibrium of the words already in the language, causing semantic narrowing, for example. The new, borrowed word may take over part or most – but not all – of the meaning of the original word, and the original word may survive with a restricted meaning. An often cited example is the Old English noun *dēor*. This word originally meant any beast; but when the French word *animal* was borrowed, the original word *dēor* (which eventually became 'deer') was restricted to denoting the class of ruminant mammals with deciduous antlers. Similarly, the acquisition of the Norsemen's verb *cut* squeezed into a corner the original meaning of Old English *ceorfn* 'carve'. The meaning of *ceorfn* 'carve' was narrowed down to a special type of cutting.

The converse is also possible. Semantic narrowing may affect the borrowed word itself and not the words already found in the language. A word borrowed from a foreign language may have a more restricted meaning in the recipient language than it does in the source language. For instance, in Swahili *safari* means 'journey' – any kind of journey. However, when it is used in English, it normally has the meaning of a touristic, game-viewing African trip.

This concludes our survey of general issues in borrowing. In the remainder of this chapter we will look more closely at examples of loanwords that have come into English from various major sources.

7.2 Scandinavian loanwords

Very often language contact is through trade or colonial occupation. And so it was in the case of English during the Middle Ages. As a result of raids that started in the ninth century, which eventually led, by the eleventh century, to the settlement of large numbers of Norsemen in what came to be known as the Danelaw areas in the Midlands and the north of England, English acquired a substantial number of Scandinavian loanwords. Many of these words are still in use today, e.g.:

[7.14] *aloft* ME<ON: *á* = on + *lopt* = air

  anger ME<ON: *angr* = grief, sorrow. Whence Adj. angry

  bag ME: *bagge* < ON: *baggi*

  bang (to beat violently) ON: *banga*

  club ME: *clubbe, clobbe* = ON: *klubba*

  die ME: *deghen* < ON: *deyja*

  flat ME: *flat* = ON: *flatr*

  gift ME: *geten* < ON: *geta*

  husband Late OE: *hūsbōnda* < ON: *húsbóndi* = householder

  ill ME: *ille* < ON: *illr*

  ken ON: *kenna* (= know, discern as in 'beyond one's ken', obsolete except in Scotland)

  knife ME: *knif* < ON: *knifr*

  leg ME: *legge* < ON: *leggr*

outlaw   Late OE: *utlag* < ON: *útlagi* = one who is outside
           the law
sky   ME: *skie* = cloud < ON: *ský*
                                    (Based on Geipel 1971)

Note: ON = Old Norse; OE = Old English; ME = Middle
English.

7.3 The French influence

We have already emphasised the point that the most far-reaching
language contact that English has had through the ages has been
with French. In this section we will consider the French influence
in the English lexicon in two parts. First, we will deal with contact
with Norman French in the Middle Ages. The account of the effect
of medieval French on English draws on standard histories of the
language by Baugh and Cable (2002), Lass (1987) and Pyles and
Algeo (1982) as well as Trevelyan (1949) for a social history of
medieval England. In the second part of the section we will turn to
borrowing that has taken place in modern times.

7.3.1 The Norman French legacy

Following the Norman Conquest, England was taken over by the
French, who now controlled the church, the government and admin-
istration. Initially, the new masters did not take too much trouble
learning the language of their subjects and continued to speak
French. As time went on society came to be divided roughly between
those who spoke French, who might at a generous estimate have
numbered about 20 per cent of the population, and the rest who
spoke English, the ordinary people, who formed the overwhelming
majority (Lass 1987). At least 80 per cent of the population were
peasants, who never learned French. Outside the elite circle of the
court, nobility, higher clergy and assorted hangers on, English was
never totally eclipsed. It always remained a vibrant, albeit low-status
language.

Medieval England was a multilingual society. In addition to
English and French, in provincial Cornwall they spoke the now
extinct Celtic language, Cornish. Throughout the land, the most
urbane and erudite members of the intelligentsia, especially clergy-
men, used Latin (at least in official writings). The lower-level

officials of both church and state needed to speak to the people in order to try to save their souls, to exact taxes from them, to administer justice to them, to make them work in the fields of the monastery or in the lord of the manor's household and so on. This relatively small group of people had to be bilingual. The people who only used French in their daily lives were the exclusive and self-contained upper classes. The top echelons of the nobility and bishops could get by without knowing the language of the common people.

An example of the very routine use of Norman French is this extract from a contract in which Johan Lewyn undertook to build a wall round the keep of a castle:

[7.15] Ceste endent'e faite a Baumburgh le xxv iour doctobre lan &c. quart parentre Johan Roy de Castille &c. dune part et Johan Lewyn mason dautre part tesmoigne les couenances fatite parentre le dit Johan Roy et Duc par lauys de son conseil et le dit Johan Lewyn. Cestassauoir q'le dit Johan Lewyn ad empris p^r faire de nouell bien et couenablement un mantelett de freeston en certein lieu a lui diuise par le dit Johan Roy et Duc et son Conseil ento^r le grant tourre etc.

(Salzman 1952: 460)

Many of the nobles had estates in both Normandy and England and had split loyalties. In many cases they were more French than English. The Norman kings remained dukes of Normandy and some of them spent most of their time in France. This is understandable. Through marriage and conquest their French possessions had expanded to such an extent that, by the late twelfth century, Henry II (1154–89) was not only king of England but also ruler of almost two-thirds of France. But, gradually, through intermarriage and ever-closer contact, the Normans were integrated into English society. By the mid-twelfth century the integration was virtually complete.

For the small, but influential social group who were at the apex of society English was a second-class language in terms of status. And their competence in it was rather limited. They practised some code-switching, which contributed in a relatively small way to borrowing. But you should not get from this the impression that the use of French and code-switching between English and French was widespread throughout the population. The eclipsing of English only affected the upper classes.

Most of the borrowing took place after the middle of the thirteenth century after French had been knocked off its perch as the most prestigious language in everyday use in high places and had increasingly become a written language.

According to some estimates, about 10,000 French words entered English during the Middle Ages. Most of them came into the language after the mid-thirteenth century when the marginalisation of English in high places had been reversed and most came into English via the written language: many French (and Latin) words originally used only in writing eventually found their way into the spoken language (see Lass 1987).

In the period 1200–1500 a number of historical factors conspired to revive the fortunes of English. Not least among them was King John's loss of Normandy in 1204. Disaster on the battlefield saved the English language from obscurity. The bitter, protracted Hundred Years War with France, which began in 1337, put an end to French linguistic hegemony. Now the ruling classes had to put their mind to the task of becoming fully English and learning how to use the English language properly. The ties between the nobility in England and France were loosened. Understandably, the English aristocracy no longer had such warm feelings towards the French. And, in any event, those nobles who had estates in both countries were forced to make a choice: those who chose to be English had to renounce their French interests and learn to be truly English.

The following is the text of a letter written in 1440 by Robert Repps to John Paston, a member of one of the leading families of the gentry in Norfolk. Although this letter was written a long time after English had been re-established, it is richly spiced with French. You can see how French loanwords used in writing eventually became part of spoken English as well.

[7.16] 1440 Nov. 1

> Sir, I pray you, wyth all myn hert, hold me excusyd that I wryte thus homly and briefly on to you, for truly convenable space suffycyd me nowt.
>
> No more atte this tyme, butte the Trynyte have you in protection, &c.; and qwan your leysyr is, resorte ageyn on to your college, the Inner Temple, for ther ben many qwych sor desyr your presence, Welles and othyr, &c.
>
> Wretyn in le fest de touts Seynts, entre Messe et Mateyns, *calamo festinante*, &c. Yours,   ROB REPPES.

So what is the balance sheet of the linguistic effects of the Norman Conquest?

1 The Norman Conquest had a very far-reaching effect on the English lexicon. It started the habit of borrowing French words in large numbers which English has never been able to kick (see [7.7] and [7.8]).

2 Generally, the influx of French words into English had very little effect on the structure of English except in phonology, where it led to [f] ~ [v] and [s] ~ [z], which had been allophones of the same phoneme, splitting into separate phonemes, as we saw in section (7.1.7).

During the period of the French ascendancy following the Norman Conquest, a very large number of words were adopted from Norman French into English. Most of the vocabulary to do with the court and nobility, government and the law, war and diplomacy was borrowed from French:

[7.17] a *Government*:
       president, government, minister, territory, counsellor, council, people, power

   b *Nobility*:
       sovereign, royal, monarch, duke, prince, count, princess, principality, baron, baroness, noble

   c *Law*:
       assizes, judge, jurisdiction, puisne judge, advocate, jury, court, law, prison, crime, accuse

   d *War*:
       peace, battle, admiral, admiralty, captain, lieutenant

The adoption of French words that followed in the wake of the Norman Conquest has continued unabated.

7.3.2 French words in modern English

The discussion and examples in this section are based on Laure Chirol's (1973) book *Les 'mots français' et le mythe de la France en anglais contemporain*, which is an extensive survey of French words in contemporary English. We have already shown that English is hooked on French words. The number of French imports has risen steadily over the centuries. Chirol speculates on the reasons for this. She suggests that the use of French words in English serves to project the stereotyped, positive image of France on to the speakers themselves or the objects they speak about. And what is that image? It is an image of the French way of life, of high culture, sophistication in dress, food and social relations. This is reflected in the words and phrases habitually employed when an English speaker wraps herself or himself in the tricolour. (The fact that the real France and real French people might not live up to this idealised mythical image seems to be of no consequence.)

The French, who are not at all coy in these matters, would say that the appeal of the French language is probably due to the English-speakers' admiration of the French contribution to civilisation, which is well known. And, of course, the French never tire of reminding the world of it. France is perceived as the land of the arts in the broadest sense – encompassing literature, music, architecture, ballet, painting and sculpture. So, Chirol asks, what is more natural than that the nation which has given the world many of its greatest artists and artistic movements should be the leading supplier of critical terms for talking about the arts? Many English-speakers would concur. It is not that long since a sojourn in Paris by an American writer and a spell in Dieppe by an English painter were very useful ingredients of a successful career.

Many essential technical terms used in the arts are French. We will take literature and painting first. Examples are given below, together with the century in which they appeared in English:

[7.18] LITERATURE

17th century	*18th century*	*19th century*	*20th century*
ballade	comédie noire	enjambement	engagé
chef d'œuvre	brochure	genre	nouveau
précis	dénouement	nom de	roman
résumé	troubadour	plume	dada
		pastiche	faux amis

[7.19] PAINTING

17th century	*18th century*	*19th century*	*20th century*
critique	artiste	avant garde	art nouveau
chef-d'œuvre	baroque	expertise	calque
	embarras de	genre	collage
	richesses	renaissance	salon

Turning to music, we observe that Italian is the language which provides most musical terms (see section (7.4)). But here too French loans are by no means insignificant:

[7.20] MUSIC

17th century	18th century	19th century	20th century
aubade	ensemble	bâton	musique
rêverie	pot-pourri	conservatoire	concrète
		suite	

French is the international language of ballet. Virtually all ballet terms used in English are from French:

[7.21] BALLET

17th century	18th century	19th century	20th century	
ballet	pirouette	pas de deux	échappé	jeté
gavotte	terre à terre	chassé	plié	coupé
		(chassez)	tutu	
		danseur		

Society, refinement and fashionable living are also believed to be areas where the French excel. Hence the borrowing of words and expressions such as those below in order to enable English-speakers to bask in the reflected elegance of the French:

[7.22] SOCIETY

17th century	18th century	19th century	20th century
doyen	coterie	bête noire	chauffeur
finesse	élite	camaraderie	échelon
bizarre	clique	débutante	éminence
brusque	protégé(e)	divorcée,	grise,
tête-à-tête	esprit de corps	fiancé(e)	haut mode
rendez-vous	gauche	milieu	drôle
par excellence	savoire-vivre	prestige	facile
	tout court	rentier	gaffe
	en route	personnel	folie de
	nuance	nouveau	grandeur
		riche	R.S.V.P.
		élan	c'est la vie
		blasé	touché

Victorian values encourage the hypocritical 'No-sex-please-we're-British!' mentality. Figures in public life in Britain are hounded out of office and governments may collapse because of sexual peccadilloes. Probably this is why there is a secret admiration for the French who do not have such hang-ups about sex. The British admire the sexual prowess of the French – or, more precisely, the French attitude to sex. That may well be the reason for the large numbers of words to do with love and sexuality that have been adopted from French:

[7.23] LOVE AND SEXUALITY

17th century	18th century	19th century	20th century
amour	chaperon	liaison	cri du cœur
beau		affaire de	madame
belle		cœur	

The French have always been renowned for their cuisine. So, naturally, French words to do with food and cooking have been borrowed in substantial numbers down the ages (some French words have been fully Anglicised, and are therefore presented in English spellings). A few fancy French phrases on the menu always add to the quality of the gastronomic experience and are deemed to be worth an extra pound or two on the bill:

[7.24] CUISINE
14th–15th centuries
mustard, vinegar, beef, sauce, salad

16th–18th centuries
sirloin, gigot, carrot, cuisine, pastry, dessert, omelette, meringue, haricot, cognac, crème caramel, sage, pâtisserie, liqueur

19th–20th centuries
bombe, éclair, flan, gâteau, nougat, petit mousse, mille-feuilles, flambé, garni, en casserole, glacé, sauté, au gratin, brasserie, café, restaurant, à la carte, haute cuisine, rôtisserie, hors-d'œuvre, entrée

French fashion has also been held in high esteem for centuries. Hence the extensive list of borrowing in the area of clothes, hair, cosmetics etc.:

[7.25] FASHION

17th century	18th century	19th century	20th century
coiffure	lingerie	béret	après-ski
blonde	bouquet	chic	culottes
brunette		boutique	brassière
		haute couture	rouge
		crêpe	

Even fashionable car transport gets its terms from French, e.g. *marque, coupé, cabriolet.*

As we saw in section (7.1.2) when we discussed loan-translation, borrowing from French is not restricted to individual words. Whole phrases and sayings are also often borrowed, for example:

[7.26] à la rigueur   à propos   à la mode
       à la carte   au gratin au contraire

7.4 Words from other modern European languages

English has acquired many words from a number of other modern European languages in addition to French. We will focus on Italian and German and mention other languages very briefly.

Italian loanwords, though much fewer than the French ones, are nevertheless numerous. They are concentrated in the areas of the arts (in particular music) and food. Italian is the international language of classical music in the same way that French is the international language of ballet. So, the majority of musical terms are from Italian:

[7.27] adagio	allegro	allegretto	alto	andante
arpeggio	bravura	cantata	concerto	lento
finale	mezzo forte	noblimente	piano	pizzicato
rondo	scherzo	sonata	tempo	vivace

In the nineteenth and early twentieth centuries, Italians emigrated in large numbers to America. Many of the Italian immigrants went into the food business and popularised Italian food. Consequently many Italian food words entered American English and then spread to other dialects:

[7.28] pizza   pasta   spaghetti   macaroni ciabatta
        cannelloni   lasagne   zucchini   pesto   tagliatelle
                                (= courgette)

German has also been an important source of adopted words (see
[7.7] and [7.8]). Cultural stereotyping makes the loanwords (often
as loan translations) assimilated during the Nazi period especially
salient, though they are unrepresentative:

[7.29] swastika (= Nazi symbol)
        Nazi (< National socialist) (German *Nationalsozialist*)
        Gestapo (acronym formed from *Geheime Staats-Polizei*)
        (Secret State-Police)
        Blitzkrieg (shortened to Blitz)
        panzer (i.e. armoured) as in panzer division
        Luftwaffe (= air force)

In fact there are hundreds more German imports, especially in
the field of science. Some examples are listed in [7.30] which draws
on a large-scale statistical study of more than 200 million words
by Stubbs (1998):

[7.30] The arts   Bauhaus, leitmotif
        Food and drink   delicatessen, muesli, hamburger,
                          sauerkraut, schnitzel, frankfurter, lager,
                          riesling
        Science   Alzheimer's, Fahrenheit, gestalt, Geiger,
                          chromosome, gauss, ecology, enzyme,
                          formant, isogloss
        Politics   realpolitik, Ostpolitik, diktat
        General   abseil, rucksack, diesel, kindergarten,
                          hinterland, bivouac

7.5 Loanwords from non-European languages

At the close of the sixteenth century English was a rather unimportant language spoken by about seven million people in the British
Isles. Today, it is estimated to have over 350 million mother-tongue
speakers and at least as many second-language speakers found all
over the world. This massive expansion of English was mainly due
to the rise of the British Empire, which facilitated the spread of

English to every continent from the seventeenth to the twentieth century (see Bauer 2002: 13–29; Görlac 1991: 229–30). The decline and end of the British Empire shortly after the Second World War, was immediately followed by the ascendancy of America. In effect, the USA took over the baton of Empire (and indirectly the job of championing English). For the last half-century, American power and influence has been projected across the planet with ever growing intensity. This situation has further promoted the global spread of English and the consolidation of its role as the world's dominant lingua franca.

Our focus here will be on the consequences for the English language of its spread. English has had an impact on many of the languages that it has come in contact with all over the world. But it has not been one-way traffic. Other languages have also left their mark on English, especially on its lexicon (see [7.5] on p. 142).

In North America, English borrowed from Native American languages many words in the semantic fields of artefacts (e.g. *wampum* and *toboggan*) and animals (e.g. *caribou* and *coyote*). But an even more important group of loans was the place names (e.g. mountains like the *Appalachians* and the *Alleghenies*; the Great Lakes: *Erie, Ontario, Huron, Michigan* and *Superior* (Ojibwa *Gitchi* via French *Supérieur*); and states, such as Massachusetts and Oklahoma) (based on *The American Heritage(r) Dictionary of the English Language*, 4th edn, 2000).

On the other side of the world, the languages of the Indian subcontinent in what is now India, Pakistan and Bangladesh, have been an especially important source of verbal imports. India has been in contact with Britain since the seventeenth century, and these centuries of contact have left their mark on English. There are many words borrowed from Indian languages in various areas of the English lexicon. The account below of Indian loanwords in English is based on Rao (1954).

Rao points out that the nature of the borrowed words changed as time went on, reflecting developments outside language. There are a few loanwords for trade goods which pre-date the Raj, e.g. *copra, coir, pepper, sugar, indigo, ginger* and *sandal*. These were indirect borrowings which came into English via Latin, Greek, French and so on.

In the early years of the British colonisation of India, loans reflected the commerce between India and Britain – not surprisingly, since that is what colonising India was all about. Words for various kinds of Indian textiles, e.g. *calico, chintz, dungaree* (extended in the nineteenth century to trousers made from this material), came into English with the goods. With the passage of time, the range of Indian loanwords widened. As they became more involved with the Indians, the British realised that the subcontinent had more to it than *calico* and *chintz*. Words for mundane trade goods still figured in the verbal imports, but they were joined by words in diverse areas of meaning such as religion, philology, food, cooking and so on. The table in [7.31] (from Rao 1954) gives some idea of the wealth and diversity of the Indian borrowings:

[7.31] a *Hinduism*:
Buddha, Brahmin, karma, pundit, yoga, yogi, mantra, nirvana, sutra

b *Food*:
chutney, chapati, curry, poppadom

c *Clothing*:
cashmere, pyjamas, khaki (= brown), mufti, saree (sari)

d *Philology (19th century)*:
sandhi, bahuvrihi (compounds), dvandva (compounds)

e *People and society*:
Aryan (Sanskrit), pariah, mem-sahib, sahib, coolie

f *Animals and plants*:
mongoose, zebu, bhang, paddy, teak

g *Buildings and domestic*:
bungalow, pagoda, cot

h *Assorted*:
catamaran, cash (= small coin), chit, lilac, tattoo, loot, polo, swastika (Sanskrit), cushy, juggernaut, tom-tom

A smaller number of loanwords have come from farther east, from languages such as Japanese and Chinese. The stereotype of the warlike, militaristic Japanese addicted to martial arts may have both encouraged and been encouraged by loanwords like *samurai, karate, hara-kiri* and *kamikaze*. Fortunately, the image of Japan as reflected through borrowings is not all negative. The militaristic words are balanced by the artistic *origami*, the elegant *kimono*, the poetic *haiku* and, in popular entertainment, the *kabuki* and *karaoke*. With the passage of time English has become a diverse tongue. Many international varieties of English have evolved, not only first-language varieties like American English and Australian English, but also second-language varieties such as Singaporean English and Indian English as well as creole varieties like Jamaican English. These varieties have lexical, phonological and grammatical peculiarities of their own. They may have words borrowed from various local languages, or common English words that are used in a way unique to a particular country. Consider this sample of Indian English vocabulary:

[7.32] IndEng   EngEng
almirah   'a chest of drawers' (from Portuguese)
co-brother   'wife's sister's husband'
colony   'residential area'
cousin-sister   'female cousin'
jawan   'soldier'
ryot   'farmer'
                   (From Trudgill and Hannah 1994: 134)

7.6 The Germanic inheritance

Borrowing is the main external cause of LANGUAGE CHANGE. As we have seen, borrowing has had a big impact on the English lexicon: a high proportion of English words and affix morphemes are of foreign origin. Does that make English a hybrid language? In this section we will see that, in spite of the very large number of foreign acquisitions, much has remained of the original language.

English belongs to the GERMANIC branch of the INDO-EUROPEAN FAMILY, which includes these languages:

[7.33] HELLENIC, the mother of Ancient Greek;
GERMANIC languages (e.g. German, English, Dutch, Flemish, Afrikaans, Danish, Norwegian, Swedish, Icelandic);
ROMANCE languages (e.g. French, Italian, Spanish), which are descendants of Latin, itself a daughter of Italic;
CELTIC languages (e.g. Breton, Welsh, Scottish, Irish Gaelic);
SLAVIC languages (e.g. Russian, Ukrainian, Serbo-Croat, Czech);

INDO-IRANIAN languages (e.g. Sanskrit, Hindi, Punjabi, Kurdish, Persian).

Historical linguists have shown that much of the core vocabulary of Indo-European languages is COGNATE, i.e. it developed from the same historical source. You can verify this for yourself by examining the table below:

[7.34] Indo-European cognates

	heart	*lung*	*night*	*sun*
Old English	heorte	lungen	niht	sunne
German	Herz	Lungen	Nacht	Sonne
Old Norse	hjarta	lunga	nátt	sól, sunna
Gothic	hairto	leihts 'light'	nahts	sauil, sunno
Latin	cordis	levis 'light'	noctis	sōl
Greek	kardia	elachus 'little'	nuktos	hēlios
Russian	serdtse	legkoe	noch'	solntse
Lithuanian	Sirdis	lengvas 'light'	naktis	saule
Irish	cridhe	laigiu 'less'	nocht	heol
				(Breton)
Sanskrit	hrd-	laghus 'light'	naktam	surya
Proto-Indo-European	*kerd-	*le(n)gwh-	*nokwt-	sāwel-/sun-

(Based on Algeo 1972: 90–1)

Languages belonging to the same family inherit from the parent language many structural features (of phonology, morphology and syntax) as well as CORE VOCABULARY items (i.e. basic words, such as words for parts of the body, kinship terms, numbers and basic bodily functions like eating and sleeping). The more closely related languages are, the more shared vocabulary items they have.

Borrowing does not alter the genetic inheritance of a language. The acquisition of foreign words has led to diversification in the English lexicon, but it has not destroyed the Germanic and Old English inheritance. Words of Anglo-Saxon origin are still the words people use most frequently in everyday conversation (e.g. *I*, *the*, *am*, *a*, *are*, *on*, *child*, *see*, *sun* etc.).

However, extensive borrowing has had very important stylistic consequences. Often there are near synonyms, one of which is an everyday word of Anglo-Saxon origin and the other a foreign (usually Latinate) word which is used in formal situations – or just by people 'talking posh':

[7.35] *Old or Middle English*	*Latinate*
house, home	habitation, domicile
limb	member
walk	promenade
food	victuals
dying	expiring
leave	depart
get	obtain
give	donate
sweat	perspiration
gushy	sentimental
put out (a fire)	extinguish (a fire)

7.7 Summary

Over the centuries, English has expanded its vocabulary by extensively borrowing lexical items from other languages. Of all sources of loanwords French is by far the most important. But there is a significant number of words borrowed from other languages, which reflects the contacts English-speaking people have had with other peoples and their cultures.

Normally, a loanword (i.e. a word-form plus meaning) is imported, but sometimes loan translation takes place – the meaning of a foreign lexical item is simply translated into English. For borrowing to take place it is obviously necessary to have some bilingual speakers who regularly code-switch or use foreign words in English. This may result in words seeping into English from another language.

Foreign words are borrowed for a number of reasons, e.g. to meet the need for a way of expressing a particular meaning, to court admiration etc. Borrowed words from a particular language tend to reflect the nature of the contact, e.g. cultural contact, colonisation, religion, trade and so on.

The likelihood of being borrowed is not the same for all words. Content words are more likely to be borrowed than function words and among content words nouns are the most likely candidates for borrowing, but words in other word-classes are not exempt. Once borrowed, words may get Anglicised to different degrees. Borrowing words from foreign languages may affect the phonological, grammatical and semantic structure of the recipient language.

Borrowing has enriched the English lexicon. But at the core English remains a Germanic language. Most of the commonest and most basic words used today are descended from Anglo-Saxon. Often there are near synonyms, one of which is native and the other borrowed, which differ stylistically.

Exercises

1 Why do languages borrow words?

2 Explain how different types of borrowing can be classified.

3 What is meant by the 'nativisation of loanwords'? Give two fresh examples of foreign words that have become nativised using different techniques.

4 a Give two fresh examples of affixes and bound roots borrowed from Latin.
  b With the help of a good dictionary, explain the meanings of each of the morphemes that you have selected.

5 A large number of Latin words, phrases and abbreviations are used in English such as:

AD	de jure	homo sapiens	Moratorium
ad hoc	e.g.	honorarium	non sequitur
ad infinitum	ego	i.e.	prima facie
ad nauseam	et al.	in loco parentis	primus inter
alma mater	et cetera (etc.)	magnum opus	pares
bona fide	exeunt	malefactor	referendum
caveat	exit	modus operandi	sine die
de facto	ex gratia	modus vivendi	status quo
			subpoena

  a State in plain English what each of these abbreviations, words and phrases means. Where appropriate, indicate whether there is a standard loan translation of the Latin phrase.
  b In what area of the vocabulary (i.e. semantic field) is each phrase found? Is there any reason for this? Can any generalisation(s) be made?

6   Many words in the scientific, technical and learned vocabulary
     are borrowed from Greek. Study the words below and, using a
     good etymological dictionary, find out the meanings of the
     morphemes in each word:

chemotherapy	laryngoscope	physiology	stethoscope
econometrics	microbiology	physiotherapy	telescope
economics	microscope	psychology	theology
kilometre	morphology	psychotherapy	thermometer

7   Look up the words below in a good etymological dictionary
     and answer the questions that follow:

banana	female	mosquito	serve
bandit	fjord	sincerity	shampoo
banquet	flamenco	ombudsman	shinto
beauty	fruit	opossum	ski
pariah	shebeen	orange	skunk
bog	goulash	ganja	sugar
boil	taboo	pecan	sumo
booze	igloo	philharmonic	Talmud
boss	inhabitant	piano	tea
buffalo	judo	plaza	theory
caftan/kaftan	jungle	pleasure	thermometer
chihuahua	junta	pneumonia	tobacco
chop suey	kangaroo	poach	tomato
church	kirk	potato	tulip
clan	landscape	pound	virgin
coffee	maize	pray	virtue
cosher/kosher	mardi-gras	propaganda	wigwam
cotton	mayonnaise	ptarmigan	wildebeest
courage	mazurka	regal	wine
crag	menu	religion	yoga
culture	mercy	roast	yoghurt
deck	military	robot	zany
delicatessen	model	scene	zen
falcon	moose	school	zenith
glycine	bongo	gestalt	urbane
seminar	psychology	graphite	league
self-portrait	Neanderthal	semester	futon

a   Find out when and from which language the above words
     came into English.

b   Where appropriate, attempt to make generalisations about
    the observed patterns of borrowing (e.g. are words from
    certain languages concentrated in certain semantic fields?
    If the answer is yes, is there a plausible reason for this?).

Chapter 8

Words galore
Innovation and change

8.1 A verbal bonanza

We saw in the last chapter the strategy of expanding the vocabulary through the importation of words from other languages. In this chapter we consider those methods of manufacturing LEXICAL ITEMS using the internal resources of the language which do not fall within the scope of affixation, compounding, conversion etc. discussed earlier. The processes we will explore in this chapter generally involve some sort of recycling of existing words.

8.2 Jargon

There are speech sub-varieties that are associated with particular occupations. These sub-varieties are primarily distinguished by their JARGON (i.e. their peculiar words and word-like expressions). Today the manufacture of jargon is one of the richest sources of new words.

Jargon serves a very useful purpose. It provides members of a social sub-group with the lexical items they need in order to talk about the subject matter that their field deals with. As a student beginning the study of linguistics you have had the experience of being immersed in a world of bewildering jargon. You have had to come to grips with terms like *morphemes*, *alveolar* and *phrase structure tree*. You can add to this list your own favourite bits of linguistic terminology.

Sometimes the jargon of a specialist group seeps into the common language of the wider community. This is particularly likely to happen where the activities of that sub-group are fashionable or impinge directly on the life of the wider community. So, for example, non-astronomers know about *black holes*; even those of us who know little, or nothing, about chemistry do talk about *catalysts* and *percolation*. In many cases the metaphorical nature of such expressions largely goes unnoticed when they become entrenched in the general lexicon. The discussion of computer jargon in later sections of this chapter provides further illustration of this.

8.3 Slang

SLANG is the term used to describe a variety of language with informal, often faddy, non-standard vocabulary. Slang is a major source of new words (typically with a very limited life expectancy). In many cases it involves the use of standard forms in a new and non-standard way. Slang displays great creativity as we will see presently.

According to Partridge (1933), there are at least 15 good reasons for using slang. They include the desire to experiment with using language 'poetically' or creatively for pleasure; the desire to be secretive; the desire to be expressive; the desire to use language as a badge of group membership so as to express intimacy with those inside the group and to exclude those who are not (technical jargon also does this job); to indicate that one is casual and relaxed etc. In the next few paragraphs we will consider examples of these uses of slang.

Let us start with the language of insults, which is very rich in expressive slang. An idiot may be called any one of these colourful names:

[8.1] oaf, balloon, jerk, plonker, plodger, flake (USA), wally, nerd, dope, goof, gwot (USA), bampot (Glasgow)

The language of marginal and marginalised communities is particularly rich in slang, which serves to create a feeling of solidarity. EBONICS (or BLACK TALK – also called AAE (African American English)), the everyday language of African Americans, uses very colourful slang, some of which has crossed over into other varieties of English, mainly through music, e.g. *bad* (meaning 'good, excellent') and *funk* (the sound of African American music, e.g. jazz, blues, soul etc.) But, as seen in [8.2], many other expressions have not crossed over:

[8.2] applause   gonorrhoea (play on the older term 'the clap')
     coal   intensifier indicating that something is being done intensely or strenuously, e.g. 'we just coal chillin',

meaning 'We are really relaxing.' (*Stone* is an earlier intensifier with the same meaning as *coal*.)

gangsta   meaning 'rebellious nonconformist'

frog   a promiscuous person; one who hops and jumps – like a frog – into anybody's bed

(Based on Smitherman 1994)

Prison is another environment where slang thrives. American prison slang is also characterised by creative word-play. Some of the slang, e.g. 'attitude' and 'inside', has crossed into the mainstream language. But much has not, e.g.:

[8.3] all day   a life sentence, as in 'He's doin' all day ...'

big jab   lethal injection – also referred to as 'stainless steel ride' 'doctorate in applied chemistry', or the 'needle'

deuce   a two-year sentence

8.4 Rhyming slang

No less full of invention is the tradition of RHYMING SLANG that exists in some working-class communities. It serves both the poetic function and the solidarity-with-the-in-group function. COCKNEY RHYMING SLANG (also known as COCKNEY RABBIT) is probably the best-known example. The underlying principle is that the speaker decides what he or she wants to say using the words of standard English and replaces the key lexical items with words that rhyme with it.

Rhyming slang evolved as a secret language used by shady street traders in London's East End in the nineteenth century to conceal their business dealings from the authorities. Some rhyming slang words such as *pork pies* meaning 'lies', *pigs* or *pork chops* meaning 'police' and *bread* (short for *bread and honey*) meaning 'money' have passed into the general lexicon of English. But many others are restricted to Cockney in the main, though they may be more widely understood thanks to the considerable media exposure that Cockney gets.

The rhyming slang lexicon is quite fluid. There are some words like *joy of my life* and *storm of my life*, meaning 'wife', which are of long standing. But there are also many ephemeral rhymes, e.g. those that involve the name of a celebrity who is still in the limelight (e.g. *Germaine Greer* 'beer', *Al Pacino* 'cappuccino' etc.). Others fall somewhere in between:

[8.4] dancing bears   stairs
dancing fleas   keys
dog and bone   phone
Douglas Hurd   turd
drum and fife   knife
Duke of Kent   rent
Dwight Yorke   pork
(From *Web's Greatest Dictionary of Cockney Rhyming Slang* © Gordon Daniel Smith 1998–2002, http://www.cockneyrhymingslang.co.uk/)

Rhyming slang is not solely a working-class based variety of the language. As Baker (2002) observes, POLARI, the language of gay men, is enriched by creative use of rhyming slang which draws on Cockney:

[8.5] *Rhyming word*	*Derived from*	*Meaning*
Barnet	Barnet Fair	hair
Hampsteads	Hampstead Heath	teeth
Irish	Irish jig	wig
Minces	mince pies	eyes
Plates	plates of meat	feet
Scotches	Scotch peg	legs
Two and eight	two and eight	state
Steamer	steam tug	mug (prostitute's client)

Source: From Paul Baker (2002) *Polari: The Lost Language of Gay Men.* London: Routledge, p. 30.

At one time the orthodoxy was that language change was initiated from above: 'a speaker will imitate those whom he believes to have the highest "social" standing' (Bloomfield 1933: 476). Our data show that this is not always the case. Much innovation comes from below, nowadays especially through popular youth culture. MTV is a more powerful influence on the language than the Queen's Christmas speech (see Labov 1972).

8.5 Clichés and catch-phrases

A CLICHÉ is a hackneyed expression that has become trite, insipid and banal due to overexposure. Of course, before it became worn out by overuse, it may have had a freshness, sharpness and precision that made it memorable. As Zijderveld (1979: 11) puts it, 'clichés contain the stale wisdom of past generations – elements of the "collective consciousness" of yester-year'. This is most obviously true of proverbs and sayings like *spare the rod and spoil the child*, *out of the frying pan into the fire* and *a storm in a teacup*.

Memorable expressions from literary language also tend to turn into clichés. From Shakespeare we get *a rose by any other name* (*Romeo and Juliet*). The bard's *Hamlet* is also the source of *I must be cruel only to be kind* as well as *to be or not to be*. Even titles of books may become clichés, e.g. Dostoevsky's *Crime and Punishment*.

Like memorable titles, good political slogans are effective because they are easy to remember and to reuse again and again. Overexposure may eventually turn a political slogan into a cliché. That has been the fate of political slogans like *better dead than red*, *la lutta continua*, *power to the people*, *black is beautiful*, *for Queen and country*, *the free world*, *give peace a chance*, *no surrender*, *the new world order* and so forth.

The same is true of religious sayings and advertising slogans. Religious sayings may become hackneyed, e.g. *to fall on stony ground*, said of ideas that fail to win acceptance (an allusion to the parable of the sower in Matthew 13:5–6), or *to turn the other cheek* (Matthew 5:39). Successful advertising campaigns can suffer the same fate, e.g. there are numerous hackneyed variations on the theme of Heineken's brilliant 1980s' advertising campaign: [*the lager that*] *refreshes the parts other beers cannot reach*.

Many clichés contain words that almost invariably occur in each other's company. Although they contain several distinct words, these are often used as though they were single lexical items, e.g. *blissful ignorance, a bouncing baby, grim death* and *a raving loony*.

Some clichés are called CATCH-PHRASES. Catch-phrases are popular expressions which virtually function as lexical items. Often such expressions are associated with a well-known song, film, show, book or personality. For instance, Sherlock Holmes's '*elementary, my dear Watson*' (i.e. 'obvious') is now part of the standard language, as is '*make my day*' – a catchphrase of Clint Eastwood as Dirty Harry in the 1983 film *Sudden Impact*, where the saying means 'do something that provides me with an excuse for whacking you'.

8.6 A rose by any other name

The relationship between the meaning and the physical pronunciation or spelling of a word is normally ARBITRARY. (We are excluding the marginal cases of onomatopoeic words like *cuckoo* where the name of the bird imitates its song; see section (3.5).)

The nature of entities and individuals is in no way affected by the words used to refer to them. As Shakespeare's Juliet says:

[8.6] O! be some other name:
    What's in a name? that which we call a rose
    By any other name would smell as sweet;
    So Romeo would, were he not Romeo call'd,
    Retain that dear perfection which he owes
    Without that title.
                              (*Romeo and Juliet*, II, ii)

This ARBITRARINESS OF THE LINGUISTIC SIGN (see Saussure 1916) has far-reaching implications. Any meaning can be associated with any word-form. A word-form already associated with one meaning can be associated with additional meanings. This is especially clear when you consider the aspects of word meaning discussed earlier in section (6.2):

(1) *Homonymy*, the use of the same form in speech and writing to convey different unrelated meanings is common in word coinage. Thus, more and more meanings may be added to the language, without more word-forms being added, e.g. originally you had the *chips* that you ate. When the new word *microchips* was shortened to *chips*, the language acquired a new homonym (see section 6.4.4).

(2) *Homophony*, the use of the same sounds (but not spelling) to represent different words also occurs frequently in word coinage. A new word may be given a new and distinct orthographic form, but in the spoken language it might be represented by an old phonological word-form, e.g. *bite* and *byte* are both pronounced as [baɪt] (see section 6.4.4).

(3) *Polysemy*, the use of the same form to represent different but related senses, is also common, e.g. *high* was slang for drunk; in the 1930s it acquired the additional sense of being intoxicated by drugs (see section 6.4.5).

In principle it should be easy to coin a new word-form any time the need to represent a particular lexical meaning arises. Any sound or sound combination is as arbitrary as any other that can be used in its place to represent a given meaning. In practice it is rare that completely fresh words are made up. Most of the time an existing word-form is recycled to represent a new meaning. Metaphorically speaking, a word-form is a vessel in which different measures of meaning can be poured without necessarily changing the vessel itself. There are no scientific laws that govern how this is done. Nonetheless, as we will see in the next few subsections, there are some observable recurrent patterns in the ways in which the associations of sounds with meanings change (see also Bauer 1994; Copley 1961; Jackson 1988).

8.6.1 Semantic widening

Semantic change often involves the WIDENING (i.e. increasing the number of lexemes with distinct meanings associated with a word-form). Widening may result either in more homonymy or in more polysemy. Examples of widening are listed in [8.7]:

[8.7] a *Manage*   (originally spelt *menage*) means 'to handle anything successfully' but originally it meant 'handle a horse'.

b *Manufacture*   'the process of making products'. Manufacture comes from Latin *manu factum* 'make by hand'. In early modern times its meaning was extended so as to include 'to make by hand or by machinery'. Subsequently, in the industrial and post-industrial age it came to mean to make by machinery rather than by hand. The original link with manual work was eventually lost.

Personal names often undergo widening. Many commercial products are named after the principal people who were instrumental in bringing them to the market-place. We vacuum floors with *Hoovers* and drive *Ford* cars on *macadamised* roads. In so doing we are (unknowingly) paying tribute to Hoover, Henry Ford and John Loudon McAdam.

Many scientific principles and instruments are also named after their inventors. Thus the instrument for measuring radiation is called the Geiger (-Müller) counter after its inventor. In the centigrade system, temperatures are measured in degrees *Celsius*. Anders Celsius was an eighteenth-century Swedish astronomer. Mathematical concepts deriving from the work of the nineteenth-century British mathematician George Boole are described as *Boolean*. The ratio of the speed of an aircraft in a fluid to that of the speed of sound at the same point is referred to as *mach one, mach two* etc. after the Austrian physicist Ernst Mach who died in 1916.

8.6.2 Semantic narrowing

The converse of widening is narrowing. The range of meanings associated with word-forms may become more restricted. This is called SEMANTIC NARROWING. The discussion and exemplification of narrowing draws on the *OED* and Room (1986).

[8.8] *Accident*   means an unintended injurious or disastrous event. Its original meaning was just any event, especially one that was unforeseen. Thus, in the final act of *The Tempest* Prospero speaks of what has happened to him since his arrival on the island as:

> . . . *the particular accidents gone by*
> *Since I came to this isle.*

Adder   in Old English meant any serpent. Later the meaning of this word was restricted to vipers.

Deer   originally referred to any four-legged beast. Later the meaning of *deer* was narrowed to a family of ruminant mammals with deciduous antlers that includes the reindeer, red deer etc. The imported French word *animal*, meaning beast, supplanted deer around the middle of the sixteenth century.

Fowl   in Old English referred to any bird. Subsequently, the meaning of this word was narrowed to a bird raised for food, or a wild bird hunted for 'sport'.

Ledger   was originally a word that referred to any book, e.g. a register, or large bible that lay permanently in the same place, but by the seventeenth century its meaning had narrowed to an accounts book.

8.6.3 Going up and down in the world

The associations and connotations of a word may change. If a word acquires a more positive meaning, we speak of AMELIORATION; if it acquires a more negative meaning we speak of PEJORATION.

Take the meaning of the word *villain* (originally spelt *villein*). It has gone downhill. In the age of feudalism a villein was just a type of humble serf who cultivated the lord's land. (The feudal *vill* was a farm). Today a *villain* is not a peasant, but a person of doubtful virtue, a scoundrel. Note also how *peasant* has acquired negative connotations. I think you would be insulted if someone called you a peasant. When it was first adopted from French, this word simply meant a country person who worked the land. Current French *paysan* comes from Old French *païsant*. Old French *païs* became Modern French *pays* 'country'. The *-ant* suffix indicated origin in Old French. So, a *peasant* was someone from a country district. That meaning is not lost in the modern English *peasant*. But the word has acquired the additional negative connotations of 'boorish, very low-status person'.

While the words *villain* and *peasant* have gone down the scale, the opposite has happened to *knight*. Originally it meant 'servant'. (In modern German the related word *Knecht* still means 'servant'.) But in the age of chivalry the *knight* went up in public esteem. Being knighted is still considered a great honour.

Amelioration and pejoration of meaning have a lot to do with social values. Nowhere is this clearer than in the attitude to different occupations. For instance, at one time the *surgeon* enjoyed no more prestige than the butcher. Both were seen as tradesmen very skilled in cutting and chopping flesh and bones with sharp knives. However, with the professionalisation of surgery and the establishment of the Royal College of Surgeons, practitioners of surgery enjoyed ever increasing public esteem. Today nobody would contemplate lumping them with butchers. (Would butchers too have enjoyed improved status had they established a Royal College of Butchers?)

8.6.4 Loss account

Words get lost. This may happen for a number of reasons. For instance, a new word may come into the language and supplant the old. The new word may be created using the internal resources of the language, or it may be imported from another language. For instance, in the late Middle Ages the adjectives *wæstmbærce* and *wynnfæst*, which had been handed down from Old English, became obsolete. They were replaced by 'fertile' and 'pleasant', which came from French. The Old English nouns *greed* 'voice' and *læcedom* 'medicine' suffered the same fate. These were not isolated changes. The replacement of Old English words by French ones was particularly widespread in the language of religion and government (see Chapter 7). You can see this if you compare the two columns in [8.9]:

[8.9]   *Obsolete Old English word*   *Current word*
     a *Religion*
        hǣlend or nergend   saviour
        scyppend   creator
        gesceaft   creation

     b *Government*
        healdend   chief
        rǣdend   ruler
        æðeling   prince
        dēmend   judge

Loss does not always occur across the board. Words that have become obsolete in standard English may survive in some dialects. Thus, according to the *OED*, late Middle English *tonguey*, meaning 'loquacious', is still used in some dialects in America, but is lost elsewhere. The word *gigot*, meaning 'a leg of veal, mutton etc.', was borrowed from French in the sixteenth century. It is now generally obsolete – except in Scotland where a butcher will still sell you a *gigot*.

Change, be it in fashion, cultural, social or political institutions, values, science or technology, is a factor in the loss of words. For example, because hardly any men (except a tiny minority of monks who are out of the public eye) shave their heads to create a bald patch as part of a religious rite, the word *tonsure*, which describes such a bald patch, is no longer in current everyday use. In medieval times, when the practice of shaving such bald patches was common, *tonsure* was a useful word to have.

Similarly, *breeches*, a word of Norse origin, gradually fell into disuse when fashion changed and *trousers* replaced *breeches* in the seventeenth century as the garment that covers the loins and legs.

But *breeches* was retained for a longer time in the dialects of the North of England and in Scotland (where in some dialects it survives as *breeks*, meaning 'trousers').

The same points can be made about changes in social institutions. With the end of feudalism, a great many words associated with it disappeared from common use and remain only in historical textbooks. Outside books on medieval history, you are not going to find words like *bondsman, serf, steelbow* and *vassal*. These words are defined by the *OED* as follows:

[8.10] *bondsman* 'one who becomes surety by bond'
     serf   'a slave, bondman'
     steelbow (Scottish Law) 'a quantity of farming stock, which a tenant received from his landlord on entering, and which he was bound to render up undiminished at the close of his tenancy'
     vassal 'in the feudal system, one holding lands from a superior on conditions of homage and allegiance'

Scientific and technological terms too may become archaic when the technology to which they refer is superseded. With the demise of alchemy and the rise of chemistry, the need for the term *alkahest* ('the universal solvent' used in experiments seeking to transmute base metals into gold) disappeared. In technology similar cases also abound. For instance, in the 1780s the *spinning-jenny* was state-of-the-art technology. Now it is a museum piece. We only encounter the word 'spinning-jenny' in books on the history of the Industrial Revolution.

The discussion here has concentrated on the loss of words. In fact, it is not just words that can be lost. Languages also lose morphemes. For instance, in Old English, from the verb *dēman* 'judge' one could form the noun *dēmend* 'judge'; from the verb *hælen* 'save' one could form the noun *hælend* 'saviour' and so on. Today, we cannot form a noun like **kepend* meaning *keeper* from the verb *keep*. The suffix *-end* which was used in English to derive masculine, agentive nouns is now extinct.

8.6.5 Lexical revivals

The reverse can also happen. Sometimes a word that had become a museum piece is dusted down and put back in circulation, albeit with a changed meaning. Barber (1964) cites *frigate*, *corvette* and *armour* as examples of LEXICAL REVIVALS. *Frigate* and *corvette* had become moribund words only used technically in historical books to describe types of obsolete, small, fast sixteenth- and seventeenth-century fighting ships. The word *armour* had also become obsolete after the end of the age of chivalry and the disappearance of medieval knights in shining armour.

All three words were revived early in the twentieth century and came back into general use – with new meanings. The two naval terms were pressed back into service to refer to modern fighting ships which were very different from the *frigates* and *corvettes* of early modern times. Similarly, when the word *armour* was revived, it referred to tanks and other mechanised fighting vehicles rather than to knights' suits of mail.

8.6.6 Metaphors

Figurative language is yet another source of lexical terms. Worn-out figures of speech often end up becoming conventional lexical items. We speak of 'the *legs* of tables and chairs' because *leg*, meaning 'limb', was metaphorically extended to furniture. We speak of 'the *tongue* of a shoe' by analogy to the tongue of an animal. For the same reason we speak of 'the *eye* of a needle' and 'an *ear* of corn', 'the *foot* of a mountain' and 'the *brow* of a hill'.

As seen, many DEAD METAPHORS are based on body parts. However, metaphors and metaphorical extensions of meaning from other sources are not difficult to find. In recent years, British political pundits have talked about the *banana skin*, meaning 'a political misadventure that causes a politician to metaphorically skid and suffer a humiliating fall'. Continuing in the fruity vein, a concoction of narcotics is colloquially referred to as a *fruit salad*. The comparison with the legal and innocuous fruit salad served as a dessert is obvious. There is also an alcoholic beverage metaphor: a marijuana joint smoked by putting the drug in the butt of a legal tobacco cigarette is called a *cocktail* in Ebonics. This term has crossed over and is part of wider slang.

In the late 1980s, in popular speech, if a person received shocking news that left them totally devastated, they could say that they were *gutted* or *kippered* or *filleted*. The analogy between the effect of the shock that goes to the very core and what a fishmonger does to fish is plain to see.

The metaphorical dimension of such expressions is obvious if you stand back and think about their structure and likely source. But normally people use such expressions without thinking about their metaphorical basis. They simply treat them as plain, ordinary lexical terms.

8.7 Clipping

CLIPPING is the term for the formation of a new word-form, with the same meaning as the original lexical term, by lopping off a portion and reducing it to a monosyllabic or disyllabic rump. This phenomenon has been around for a long time. Eighteenth-century purists like Swift and Campbell fought a determined, but in the end unsuccessful, campaign against it. George Campbell, writing in 1776, objected to what he saw as the barbarism of shortening poly-syllabic words and retaining just the first syllable or just the first and second syllables, as in:

[8.11] *hyp* for *hypochondriac*   *rep* for *reputation*
      ult for *ultimate*   *penult* for *penultimate*
      incog for *incognito*   *hyper* for *hypercritic*
      extra for *extraordinary*   *mob* for *mobile crowd*
                    (from Baugh and Cable 2002: 259–60)

Despite eloquent protests against it, clipping did survive as a fairly productive word-formation process. In contemporary English, very occasionally, the middle of a word is dropped. That is how *vegan* was formed from *veg(etari)an*. More commonly we have FORE-CLIPPING, where the front of the word is trimmed, as in [8.12]:

[8.12] *Fore-clipping*
      plane   aeroplane
      bus   omnibus
      van   caravan
      hood   hoodlum

However, BACK-CLIPPING, where the end of the word is trimmed, is by far the commonest:

[8.13] *Back-clipping*
      disco   discotheque
      mike   microphone

bike	bicycle
lab	laboratory

In colloquial speech, clippings tend to end in a familiar suffix pronounced [ɪ] (and spelled *-ie* or *-y*) as in [8.14]:

[8.14]	Gerry	<	Gerald
	Monty	<	Montgomery
	Lizzie	<	Elizabeth
	loony	<	lunatic
	telly	<	television
	poly	<	polytechnic

Clipping accompanied by [ɪ] (*-ie/-y*) suffixation is especially common in nicknames and familiar versions of names. It is not easy to predict what part of a name is going to be retained because the principles that determine the version of the clipping process that applies in a particular instance are not clear. Back-clipping may take place, as in *Gerald > Gerry*, *Montgomery > Monty* etc. Or it can be fore-clipping, as in *Antoinette > Netty*, *Patricia > Trish* and *Alexander > Sandy*. Or again, occasionally, it may be a combination of the two as in *Lizzie* from (*E*)*liz*(*abeth*).

We shall now take a closer look at Australian English because it uses clipping and diminutives more frequently and in more varied ways than any other variety of the language. Some typical uses are listed in [8.15]:

[8.15] a ***-ie/-y***

fierie	fire officer
cuey	cucumber
u-ey	u-turn
Aussie	(Pronounced 'Ozzie'): Australian.
barbie	barbecue
bikies	motorcyclists
divvy van	police divisional van
esky	large insulated box for keeping beer etc. cold (short for Eskimo box)
postie	postman
mozzie	mosquito

b ***-o***

ambo	ambulance officer
metho	methylated spirits

compo	worker's compensation
evo	evening
aggro	aggressive
milko	milkman
rego	registration, as in car rego

c **-s**
(Take the first syllable and add -s)

turps	turpentine
Slats	Michael Slater

d **last syllable(s)**
(Keep only the last two syllables if the word ends in a vowel, or the last syllable if the word ends in a consonant)

Gabba	wooloongabba
Weal	Camooweal

e **first syllable**

Shep	Shepparton, Vic.
cuec	cucumber

There is also a process whereby the definite article is placed before proper names as in *the Alice*. This is functionally similar though structurally different from clipping.

The semantics and pragmatics of clipping and diminutives is complex. These processes are typically used to express one or more of these notions:

[8.16] a   small size
 b   close emotion – positive
 c   close emotion – negative
 d   familiarity (with the entity referred to, and/or with the addressee)

The actual interpretation is largely context-dependent. For example, normally *horsey* has positive emotional connotations when used to refer to a horse when talking to a child. But when *postie* is used to refer to a postman it probably indicates warmth towards the letter carrier and not an allusion to his being small; and when a mosquito is referred to as a *mozzie* probably neither affection nor warmth should be inferred. Likewise, when the diminutive *dero* is used to refer to a derelict person it is almost certain to be disparaging.[1]

8.8 Acronyms and abbreviations

The shortening of words is taken to its logical conclusion in
ACRONYMS and ABBREVIATIONS. Words forming a complex expression referring to the name of an organisation, company or a scientific
concept may be reduced to their initial letters alone which together
represent sounds that form perfectly acceptable syllables and hence
can be pronounced as words. Words formed in this way are called
ACRONYMS.

[8.17] HALO   high altitude large optics
       NASA   National Aeronautics and Space Administration
       RAM   random-access memory

As we will see in section (9.6), this type of word-formation is an
interesting example of a role reversal: spoken word-forms are
derived from words in the written language.

Usually, to begin with acronyms are spelt with capital letters as
shown in [8.17], when people are conscious of their special status.
But, with the passage of time, some commonly used acronyms end
up being transmogrified into simple root morphemes and are treated
as common or garden words. Then they tend to be spelt like any
other word. This is happening to *NATO* (North Atlantic Treaty
Organisation) which is now sometimes spelt as *Nato*. Farther down
the road is AIDS, which is very frequently written as *Aids*. Indeed,
many people do not know that *Aids* is an abbreviation of 'acquired
immune deficiency syndrome'.

In the twentieth century an increasingly large number of acronyms
became established, institutionalised words. Few people have the
slightest inkling that these are acronyms:

[8.18] basic   Beginner's All-purpose Symbolic Instruction Code
       nimby   not in my back yard
       midi   musical instrument digital interface
       pin   personal identification number

Sometimes shortened forms are created using the initial letters of
words which do not give permissible syllables. They fail the phonological test. In such cases, each letter is sounded separately. We
call such forms ABBREVIATIONS rather than acronyms. The term
acronym is restricted to forms that obey the phonotactic constraints
of the language and are pronounceable as normal words.

In the last few decades there has been an explosion in the growth of abbreviations. As seen in the examples in [8.19], names of organisations, academic institutions, businesses and scientific jargon are frequent candidates for this treatment, though it is not restricted to them:

[8.19] *Organisations*

| UN | United Nations |
| WTO | World Trade Organisation |

Places

| LA | Los Angeles |
| NSW | New South Wales |

Scientific jargon

| DNA | deoxyribonucleic acid |
| CJD | Creutzfeldt-Jakob disease |

Media companies

| BBC | British Broadcasting Corporation |
| CNN | Cable News Network |

Academic institutions

| UCL | University College London |
| UCLA | University of California, Los Angeles |

Miscellaneous

| TLC | tender loving care |
| DJ | disc jockey |

8.9 Fads and copycat formations

Word-formation is subject to fashion. A word in vogue often gives rise to copycat formations which are fashionable for a time and then quickly become dated. Let us take the 1980s' in-word *yuppie* (see p. 74). It spawned a number of words formed by analogy, such as:

[8.20]	woppies	wealthy older professional persons
	yummies	young upwardly mobile marxists
	dinkies	double-income-no-kids
	nilkies	no-income-lots-of-kids

Yuppie will probably survive. But it is unlikely that the other faddy words will still be in use in another 10 years. They already sound dated.

It is not just faddy words referring to social trends that tend to be short-lived. Words referring to technologies also fade out if the technology finds few long-term devotees. For instance, in 1929 futurologists, having witnessed the success of the 'talkies', speculated about future film technologies that would yield *smellies*, i.e. films where the sounds and moving pictures were synchronised with appropriate odours pumped into the cinema auditorium. This technology did materialise in the form of *smell-o-vision* in 1958. But, alas, audiences were unimpressed and smell-o-vision technology was stillborn. Hence the word *smell-o-vision* had a short life (Ayto 1999: 366).

8.10 Back-formation

Normally words are formed by adding affixes. Less commonly the reverse happens and a word is formed by removing affixes from a base. This is called BACK-FORMATION. Typically this happens when there is an apparent gap in the lexicon, i.e. there 'ought to be' a word from which an apparently affixed word is derived, but there is not.

According to Marchand (1969), on whose work this account of back-formation is based, the verb *peddle* was formed from the noun *pedlar*, and the verb *juggle* was formed from the noun *juggler* by a series of deductive steps. If a noun meaning 'someone who does X' ends in [ə] (spelled variously as *-er/-or/-ar*), there exists a corresponding verb which is minus the suffix, e.g. keep ~ keeper, ride ~ rider etc. But in fact, the verbs did not exist in the case of *pedlar* and *juggler*. So speakers formed them by dropping the suffixes from the nouns.

Likewise, *typewrite*$_{Verb}$ was formed from *typewriter*$_{Noun}$ at the end of the nineteenth century by analogy to *write*$_{Verb}$ → *writer*$_{Noun}$ and the verb *edit* was derived in the eighteenth century from the noun *editor* using the same analogical formation. And when the age of television dawned in the early twentieth century, the language got the noun *television* first. There was a perceived need for a verb. So, the verb *televise* was created from the noun *television* following the pattern of *revise*$_{Verb}$ → *revision*$_{Noun}$.

Back-formation applies equally to compounds. The verb *stage-manage* is a back-formation from the noun *stage-manager*. So is the computer-age verb *word-process* which comes from the noun *word-processor*.

8.11 Blends

BLENDS are hybrid words. They are compounds made in an unorthodox way by joining chunks of word-forms belonging to two distinct lexemes. This word-formation method has grown in popularity in recent decades. Many ordinary words are blends. Like acronyms, some of them are so well installed in the lexicon that most speakers are unaware of the fact that they are hybrid words rather than simple roots. Which of the following words did you know were hybrids?

[8.21]	smog	smoke + fog
	brunch	breakfast + lunch
	splurgundy	sparkling burgundy (Australian sparkling red wine)
	bit	binary + digit
	chunnel	channel + tunnel
	Oxbridge	Oxford + Cambridge
	guestimate	guess + estimate
	selectric	select + electric
	heliport	helicopter + airport
	Franglais	Français + Anglais
	Konglish	Korean English

8.12 Geek-speak: internet slang and jargon

As couch potatoes become 'mouse potatoes', as teenagers become 'screenagers', the once lowly geek has become a cultural icon, studied by the fashionistas of Seventh Avenue and the Nasdaq watchers of Wall Street alike. And as geek chic takes hold of the technology-obsessed culture, geek-speak seeps into everyday language.

So wrote the *New York Times* lead book critic, Michiko Kakutani, in 2000.

Kakutani went on to observe that the strong impact of technology on the lexicon is not new. Over the last two centuries technology has been an important driver of lexical innovation. Earlier technological revolutions also spawned their lingoes: the railway age generated metaphorical expressions like 'going off the rails' and 'getting sidetracked'; the steam engine produced 'working up a head of steam' and 'full steam ahead'; and the automobile left us with 'pedal to the metal', 'firing on all cylinders' etc. What is novel is the assuredness with which the computer geek has colonised an ever growing sector of the lexicon of contemporary English. In the last few decades, computer jargon has spread into the linguistic mainstream as the use of computers has spread (Green 1987). People who are not computer wizards now use words like *web, internet, email, database* and *broadband* as part of their everyday vocabulary.

In this section I will examine the principal ways of forming words in cyberspeak, focusing on slang and jargon.[2] Computer slang is often used for solidarity. There are many words that are used to indicate who is in, and who is out of the group. For instance, in chat rooms on the internet *pona* [pɔːna], an acronym derived from 'person of no account' (i.e. 'a person who is not, or never has been online') is a derogatory term for referring to people who are not denizens of the net. A related snide term is *muggle*. This was originally a slang expression for marijuana. It was fading out of the language when it was given a new lease of life by J. K. Rowling in her *Harry Potter* magical children's novels. In Harry Potter's world, a *muggle* is a non-magical person. By extension, *muggle* can be used by group members to refer to outsiders. In cyberspeak, a *pona* is a *muggle*. By further extension, *muggle* also refers to a *saddo*, i.e. a *sad person* – someone who is simply boring.

We will take a close look at abbreviations and acronyms as both these methods of word-formation are used extensively in cyberspeak:

[8.22] a *Abbreviations*

ISP	internet service provider	
HTH	hope this helps	internet slang, often used in newsgroup postings
http	Hypertext Transfer Protocol	
WDYMBT	what do you mean by that?	used in online chat, email, and newsgroup postings
IMO (or IMHO)	in my (honest) opinion	internet slang
IANAL	I am not a lawyer	internet slang

b *Acronyms*

WAM	wait a minute	used in online chat, email, and newsgroup postings
RAM	random-access memory	
GIF	graphic interchange format	
HAND	have a nice day	internet slang, often used ironically
SIR	*Serial InfraRed*	wireless communication system for PCs and peripherals, especially laptops

Another interesting innovation in cyberspeak is a tendency to combine letter abbreviations with numbers like 2 [tuː], 4 [fɔː] and 8 [eɪt] whose phonological properties are then exploited so that the abbreviations become pronounceable as though they were normal words or acronyms. What is going on here with the numbers is reminiscent of the emergence of the REBUS PRINCIPLE in Sumerian writing in about 3000 BC, which represented a big step towards alphabetic writing. Till then the Sumerians had used pictograms to represent whole words. Now, pictograms worked well for words referring to concrete nouns like 'tree', but were not much use when one wanted to write words referring to abstract nouns like 'life'. The rebus principle enabled the Sumerians to write any word if they already had a pictogram for another word that sounded like it. Thus, *ti* 'arrow' was written as →— and so the word *ti* 'life' that sounded the same was also written as →— (O'Grady *et al.* 1997: 596).

This development is exemplified in [8.23]. It is something that cyberspeak shares with the language of texting that is used on mobile phones (see section (9.7)):

[8.23]	2B or not 2B	to be or not to be	used in online chat
	B2E	business-to-employee	
	L8R	later	Used in online chat, email and newsgroup postings
	M8	mate	Used in online chat, email and newsgroup postings

| B2B | business-to-business | |
| talk21 | Talk-to-one | A free web-based email service from British Telecom |

Wit and invention are especially evident in the creation of blends as seen in [8.24]:

[8.24]	netizen	citizen of the net, formed by analogy to 'citizen' and 'denizen'
	triority	the three most important (cf. pri-ority)
	tradigital	adjective formed by blending 'traditional' with 'digital'; hence, 'tradition' but in the digital sense, as in the 'combinations of word of mouth, practice and binary code'
	newbie	new beginner, i.e. internet novice; here we have both blending and clipping
	emoticon	blend of 'emotion' and 'icon'; refers to a group of symbols (e.g. *smileys*) used to indicate emotions in email or newsgroups

Coinage of entirely new words is not unknown. *Pentium*, the name of the leading PC processor manufactured by Intel, is a new coinage, as is *Athlon*, its rival, which is produced by AMD. At the start of this section we encountered the neologism *muggle*, which now refers to a person who does not spend time on the net.

Rather than coin new words, cyberspeak sometimes assigns existing words a new meaning, e.g. as in the following:

[8.25]	monitor	computer screen
	mouse	device used to move a pointer around on the computer screen
	notebook	miniature all-in-one portable with computer system unit, screen and keyboard
	portal	virtual gateway between computer systems

Compounding, especially noun plus noun compounding is another word-formation technique that is favoured in this variety of English. Some examples are given in [8.26].

[8.26]	*Noun + Noun compounds*	*Adjective + Noun*
	desktop	software
	notebook	hardware

hairball   firmware
wallpaper   blue tooth

Far from being all dry and stuffy, word-formation in computer language is often idiomatic or metaphorical. The words *daisychain* (i.e. a device that links a number of devices to a single controller) and *handshake* (i.e. communication between two parts of a system, e.g. computer and printer) are interesting metaphorical extensions of meaning. Wealthy individuals who invest their own money in a start-up dotcom company are referred to as *business angels*, or simply *angels*. The *lasagne syndrome* aptly describes badly written code with overlapping dialogue boxes that make the completion of a task difficult. Finally, a situation where the management of a computer business changes and the old guard who have been in place for a long time are replaced is referred to by the idiomatic expression *the farmer died*.

8.13 Euphemism

People normally try to avoid topics or words that they or their interlocutor might find distasteful, unpleasant or embarrassing. So they use EUPHEMISMS to replace an unpleasant word with a more pleasant one (see Holder 1987; Green 1987).

There are cases of euphemisms leading to lexical change in the past. For instance, *imbecile* originally meant 'weak' and *idiot* meant 'non-expert, layperson'. When these words had their meanings extended to soften the blow of saying that someone had very limited intellectual powers, the original meanings were obscured and eventually got lost. Unfortunately, when we use euphemisms, the unpleasant associations eventually catch up with the new word. Then it is time to find another one. (Surely, a more effective solution to the problem of reducing the hurt caused by using pejorative language is to change the attitudes of people who consciously or unconsciously use such language. Not an easy task.)

Euphemisms are often motivated by TABOO rather than the desire not to hurt people's feelings. Every culture has its forbidden subjects which are normally not referred to directly because of decency or respect or fear. Let us take respect first. At one time *God* could not be referred to by name, for using his name in vain was blasphemous. So, instead of saying God, people spoke of *the Lord, the Lord of Lords, the King of Kings, the King of Glory, the Omnipotent, the All-Powerful* and so on.

There are many euphemisms for the *devil* too, but these are motivated by fear rather than respect. As the saying goes, 'Speak of the devil . . .'. So, euphemisms were used in more superstitious times. Many of these are immortalised in the poem 'Address to the De'il' (Devil) by Robert Burns (in Beattie and Meikle (1972)) which opens with the lines:

[8.27] O thou! whatever title suit thee,
  Auld Hornie, Satan, Nick or Clootie,
  Wha in yon cavern grim an' sootie,
   Clos'd under hatches
  Spairges about the brunstane cootie,
   To scaud poor wretches!
  Hear me, auld Hangie, for a wee,
  An' let poor damnèd bodies be;
  I'm sure sma' pleasure it can gie,
   E'en to a de'il,
  To skelp an' scaud poor dogs like me,
   An' hear us squeel!

Taboo may also be due to decency. As the philosopher and essayist Bertrand Russell observed, 'It is permissible with certain

[8.28]

WE'VE HAD A LOT OF THESE 'QUIDDITCH' INJURIES SINCE "HARRY POTTER" WAS RELEASED!

Source: From http://www.cartoonstock.com/newscartoons/buyers.asp.

precautions to speak in print of coitus, but it is not permissible to employ the monosyllabic synonym for this word.'

Sexually explicit language is often avoided. Use of four-letter words is disapproved of in many situations. Thus, the Victorians spoke of a lady's *limb*, not her *leg* because that was deemed too suggestive. (This was even extended to pianos. They would refer to a piano's limbs rather than its legs.) And today in North America a *rooster* is called a *rooster* in order to avoid saying the embarrassing *cock* word.

There is a particular kind of euphemism that involves using language in a perverse way to conceal thought. This is called DOUBLESPEAK. It is an indispensable weapon in the armoury of totalitarian regimes. It endeavours to make acts of unspeakable brutality look tolerable, or even humane and civilised. When political opponents are incarcerated without even a semblance of a trial, they are said to be in *preventive detention*. Extra-judicial killings are referred to as mere *disappearances*. Torture colonies are called *protected villages* or *re-education centres*. The state agency responsible for the assassination of political opponents during the apartheid regime in the Republic of South Africa was called the *Civil Co-operation Bureau*. Population purges, pogroms and forced migrations are referred to as *ethnic cleansing* in Bosnia. Hitler called the genocide of the Jewish people in death factories the *final solution*.

A perverse use can be found for almost any word in doublespeak. Let us illustrate this with the word *friendly*. In the carve-up of Europe at Yalta, Stalin insisted on the governments of Eastern Europe being 'friendly'. A reasonable demand? We all know what he meant. He wanted Eastern Europe to be part of the Soviet empire, which he ruled with an iron fist.

Doublespeak is very common in the language of the military of all colours – even the good guys. Many a militaristic regime which regularly terrorises its neighbours will refer to its war machine as a *defence force*. An unprovoked attack is often referred to as a *preventive war*. If a campaign goes badly wrong and the troops are forced by enemy fire to retreat, the official report that goes out describes the disaster as a *strategic withdrawal*. If things go disastrously wrong and you kill soldiers on your own side, you tell the world that they were killed by *friendly fire*.

[8.29]

'Just an idea, but we could do these at once if we had an electric sofa.'

Source: From http://www.cartoonstock.com/newscartoons/buyers.asp.

Killing people is something that shocks even the hardened professional soldier or the executioner. The shock is usually dampened by using euphemisms like:

[8.30]
neutralise	kill
take out	kill
stretch the hemp	to kill by hanging
the (electric) chair	electrocution
neck-tie party	lynching

Thus language is used not to reveal thought or represent reality, but to obscure both. The false images created using doublespeak replace the inconvenient reality one would rather not confront.

8.14 Summary

This chapter has dealt with ways of changing and enriching the vocabulary. We have seen that jargon created for a specialised linguistic field may seep into the mainstream vocabulary. We have also seen that the vocabulary may be enlarged by associating new meanings with existing word-forms. This may involve metaphorical extensions of meaning, widening, narrowing, amelioration or pejoration. Slang too is an important source of lexical innovation: non-standard meanings may come to be associated with word-forms of the mainstream language.

Conversely, the same meaning may be kept but the word-form representing it may be changed, usually by shortening it. This takes a variety of forms such as clipping, back-formation and blending. In all this, lexical changes coming in the wake of social and technological change play a major role.

The words of a language are used by speakers to convey meanings in a social context. So, inevitably social factors impinge on the lexicon. Sayings and slogans encapsulating a shared value system are turned into clichés which trigger socially conditioned reflexes. Technological innovation has a major role in lexical change. Euphemisms are used to smooth over reality where its jagged edges as expressed by the normal non-euphemistic terms are too disconcerting. This may be done for the best of reasons or for sinister purposes.

Exercises

1 With the help of a good dictionary, find out the methods by which the following words were formed:

con	leotard	radar	pre-buttal
temp	laser	sonar	UB40
deli	e-commerce	epos	VATman
porn	eco-tourism	disco	GI
pram	kissogram	nappy	no-go area
scuba	Rambogram	pre-teen	Dimania
cred	prequel	screenager	gotcha

Find one more word formed using each of the methods that you have identified.

2 Comment on the meaning of the words below in current English and the word-formation technique used to form them:

ladette	new lad	Pop Idol	waif
acid house	luvvie	E	Britpop
handbag (music)	crack	boyband	Generation X

3   a   What is political correctness?

    b   Is political correctness desirable?

    c   Referring to at least two specific examples involving euphemism, show how political correctness has been a factor behind some changes in the English lexicon in recent years.

4   Like words, affixes can have both referential and cognitive meaning:

    a   Find at least six words with the suffix *-ess* as in *baroness*, *manageress*, *priestess* and *mistress*.

    b   Comment on both the cognitive and connotative meaning of words formed with this suffix. Bear in mind the fact that the connotations of a morpheme can change over time as social values change.

5   Look up in a good etymological dictionary the entries for the words below and comment on the semantic changes which they have undergone:

    a   *villa, village, villain* and *-ville* (as in Hopkinsville, Madisonville, Louisville in Kentucky, Nashville in Tennessee and Jacksonville in Florida); and *-ville* (as in airheadville and boneheadville).

    b   *ace, boor* (Boer), *meat, garbage, kill* and *lavatory.*

6   a   Determine the meaning of the computer jargon below:

    b   Describe in detail the technique used to create each item.

firewall	weblog	LAN
spam	toggle	P2P
B4N	FAT	screen saver

7   a   Provide one example of semantic narrowing and one of semantic widening.

    b   Give one fresh example of a lexical item whose use is motivated by taboo. What kind of taboo is involved?

    c   If possible, find out from a person from another culture the kinds of taboo that influence lexical choices in their culture.

8   Comment on the techniques used to form the following words
    and say whether they need to be listed in the dictionary:

   a   sexploitation   blaxploitation
   b   four-letter word   liquorice all-sorts
   c   blackout   adventure playground

Chapter 9

Should English be spelt as she is spoke?

9.1 Writing systems

In earlier chapters we examined the representation of words in speech – the way in which morphological representations interface with phonological representations of words. What is the relationship between the orthographic word and the phonological word which both represent the same lexeme? That is the question we are going to tackle in this chapter.

English is written using an ALPHABETIC writing system. In an ideal alphabetic system there should always be just one letter corresponding to one PHONEME (i.e. distinctive sound of the language). Probably no such system exists, but Italian and Swahili come fairly close to it. For instance, in Italian *impepare* 'to season with pepper' is pronounced /impepare/ and in Swahili *kupika* 'to cook' is pronounced /kupika/. As Sampson observes, that was true of English as well. 'Once, at some remote time in the historical past, English had a "phonemic" orthography in which words were spelt as they were pronounced' (Sampson 1985: 94). That is not the case any more. What happened?

9.2 Is the English orthography mad?

The English orthography is still basically phonemic and reasonably regular, although it does have irregularities. I realise that the suggestion that English spelling is at all regular may come as a surprise, because for almost 800 years it is the absurdly irregular aspects of English spelling that have been in the limelight in most discussions of the English orthography. Those aspects that are regular have for the most part tended to go unnoticed; the regularities are just taken for granted.

[9.1]

You can test for yourself the claim that English spelling is to some degree regular and phonemic by considering the relationship between the letters and sounds in words like *nap* and *pan*; *nip* and *pin*; *keel* and *leek*. It is clear that the match of sounds with letters is quite systematic. The consonant letters have the same values that they have in the phonetic alphabet; the letter *a* corresponds to phoneme /æ/, *i* corresponds to /ɪ/ and *ee* corresponds to /iː/.

With this in mind, examine the relationship between spelling and pronunciation in the following extract from *The History of an Apple Pie Written by Z*:

[9.2] A Apple Pie,
        B Bit it,
        C Cried for it,
        D Danced for it,
        E Eyed it,
        F Fiddled for it,
        G Gobbled it,
        H Hid it.

(From Opie and Opie 1980: 20–1)

In this rhyme, which is not at all unrepresentative of the language as a whole, spelling is reasonably phonemic. This is intentionally put in the limelight since the point of the rhyme is to teach children the alphabet. In almost every line, the first letter corresponds predictably to the appropriate sound. *A* is pronounced as /æ/, *b* is pronounced as /b/ etc. Internally in words, the letter *i* corresponds to the sound /ɪ/ (in *bit*, *it*, *fiddled* and *hid*), while the DIGRAPH (i.e. the letter combination) *ie* represents the sound /aɪ/ (as in *pie* and *cried*).

Rumours of English spelling being absolutely chaotic are grossly exaggerated, if not totally baseless. Nevertheless, these rumours have persisted since the beginning of the thirteenth century, when the first spelling reformer, a monk named Orm, proposed innovations intended to ensure a one-to-one correspondence between sound and letter (Scragg 1973).

Accusations that English spelling is on the whole arbitrary are based on quick impressionistic surveys of a relatively small number of problem words like *through*, *though*, *enough*, *thigh*, *this*, *write*, *rite* and *right*. Many careful, thorough studies give a totally different picture. I will quote Crystal:

> A major American study, published in the early 1970s, carried out a computer analysis of 17,000 words and showed that no less than 84 per cent of the words were spelt according to a regular pattern, and that only 3 per cent were so unpredictable that they would have to be learned by heart. Several other projects have reported comparable results of 75 per cent regularity or more.
>
> (1988: 69–70)

9.2.1 The apparent madness in the English spelling system

The English orthography is still reasonably phonemic, but not entirely so. Over the centuries, a combination of factors has undermined the phonemic nature of English spelling. Unfortunately for the person trying to become literate, although English spelling is mostly rule-governed, the rules are extremely complex and riddled with exceptions. The aim of this chapter is to outline some of the principles that lie behind English spelling and to give you a flavour of how the system works. But it is not my intention to provide an exhaustive survey of the relationship between English spelling and pronunciation. For that turn to books like Scragg (1973), Sampson (1985), Stubbs (1980) and Vachek (1973).

I will start as every critic or reformer of English spelling starts – by listing (in [9.3]) some of the glaring examples of the irregularities, inconsistencies and arbitrariness of English spelling that have led some to proclaim that the relationship between spelling and pronunciation is simply mad.

[9.3] aisle	could	isle	quay
are	debt	key	rough
although	do	knight	son
aunt	does	knock	sugar
autumn	dough	laugh	trough
blood	eye	listen	two
bough	fought	move	victuals
climb	fraught	of	water
colour	friend	once	where
come	ghoul	people	who
cough	hour	psalm	you

(Based on Crystal 1988: 68)

In fact, the list in [9.3] does not contain the worst examples. The pronunciation of unfamiliar place names and personal names provides even worse horrors. It is the equivalent of negotiating a verbal minefield. All too often the spelling has only a tenuous link with the pronunciation. For instance, there is a hamlet near Lancaster in Lancashire called *Quernmore* – you probably expect it to be called /kwɜːnmɔː/ or /kwɜːnmɔə/, but in fact it is called /kwɔːmə/; the Yorkshire town of *Keighley* is pronounced /kiːθlɪ/ not */kiːflɪ/; *Hawick* in Scotland is pronounced /hɔːɪk/ not */hæwɪk/ and so on.

Frequently, the relationship between the spelling and pronunciation of personal names is equally unpredictable. For instance, *Beauchamp* is pronounced /biːtʃəm/; *Cockburn* is pronounced /kəʊbən/; *Maugham* is pronounced /mɔːm/ or /mɒfəm/; *Mainwaring* is pronounced as /mænərɪŋ/, *Clowes* may be pronounced /klaʊz/ or /kluːz/ and so on.

9.2.2 There is a method in the madness: spelling rules and pronunciation

Despite the existence of a very sizeable minority of words like those we have just surveyed whose spelling is to varying degrees arbitrary, English spelling is not totally unpredictable. Take your own experience as a reader. How often do you stumble when you come across an unfamiliar word? Let us imagine you are encountering for the first time the biochemical term *thiamine*: would you know how to pronounce it? I suspect you would. You would not hesitate to read it as /θaɪəmaɪn/. When you see a novel orthographic word like *stroople* (which I have made up and which I invite you to assign a meaning to), you will have no trouble reading it aloud.

Part of the reason why we know how to pronounce unfamiliar words is that spelling is reasonably phonemic. Another factor that helps is that, as we saw in section (5.4), the phonological word is subject to various phonotactic constraints. Thus, for example, no word spelt as **dmell*, **tsip* or **ftalation* can be found in English because the consonant sequences *dn*, *ts* and *ft* are disallowed at the beginning of a word in English (though of course they all occur in other positions in a word as in *admire*, *cats* and *lift*). If you saw a 'word' with any one of the impermissible word-initial consonant combinations I have just described, you would know it was not English. Furthermore, as we shall see later in this section, there are rules that predict – fairly reliably in many cases – how a given letter or digraph is to be pronounced in different contexts. In sum, English spelling is not chaotic. There are strict restrictions on letter combinations that are allowed to represent speech sounds in different positions.

The problem is that, although the system is essentially phonemic, regular correspondences between letters and speech sounds are sometimes subverted. A stock example of the irregularity of English spelling is the variety of spellings corresponding to the /f/ phoneme. But Carney (1994: 104–5) claims the overwhelming dominance of the use of 'f' to represent the /f/ phoneme. This claim is based on a statistical analysis of letter–sound correspondences in multimillion-word databases of English. Only in a small minority of cases is the spelling not transparent. The odd 'gh' spelling of the phoneme is shown to be extremely infrequent both in the lexicon and in running texts.

[9.4] Text and lexical frequencies for the spelling of /f/

<f>	TF 83.5%	LF 77.0%
<ff>	TF 3.9%	LF 13.9%
<ph>	TF 10.7%	LF 8.4%
<gh>	TF 1.9%	LF 0.7%

Notes: TF = Text frequency; LF = Lexical frequency

There are about 400 very common, everyday words (in the sense of lexemes or separate vocabulary items) whose spelling is irregular. The fact that these frequently used words are irregularly spelt gives the erroneous impression that matching sound with pronunciation in a totally unsystematic fashion is the norm. The situation is made to look bleaker than it is because in discussions of spelling the distinction between words as vocabulary items and words as orthographic forms is seldom recognised. All too often each occurrence of an orthographic word-form is counted as a separate word without this being explicitly stated. As a great many of the common lexical items have irregular spelling, they skew the figures.

If, however, you distinguish between words in the sense of orthographic words that have distinct written forms on the page, and distinct vocabulary items that are listable in a dictionary, the number of words with irregular spelling is considerably reduced. For example, if you count *plough*, *ploughs*, *ploughing* and *ploughed* as different words, you get five orthographic words whose spelling is irregular. By contrast, if you only recognise that the spelling *plough* which is always associated with this particular vocabulary item is always pronounced /plaʊ/, the irregularity need be noted only once, since *plough*, *ploughs*, *ploughing* and *ploughed* are all forms of the same word. If you can pronounce *plough*, the other orthographic forms present no difficulties. Similarly, while the pronunciation of *quay* as /kiː/ is arbitrary, that arbitrariness needs to be noted only once. Anyone who knows how to read or spell *quay* in the singular need not be troubled by *quays* /kiːz/ in the plural.

While recognising the substantial irregularity in the system, I will still argue in the following paragraphs that English spelling is neither whimsical nor crazy. English spelling normally follows some discernible pattern. Many of the irregularities can be accounted for. First, we will see that there are usually historical reasons for the non-phonemic spelling, although, unfortunately, knowing this is not of much practical use to the average speaker of English who is unacquainted with the history of the language and has spelling problems.

We will start with the spelling that represents the sound /g/. At the beginning of *get* it is spelt with the letter g while the same sound at the beginning of *ghost* is spelt with the digraph gh. At the same time, word-initially the sound /f/ as in *fit* is spelt with the letter f whereas in *rough* /f/ is spelt with the digraph gh. It is obvious that the same sound may be represented by different letters. On what basis is a particular spelling selected? Is the choice random?

The answer is a clear 'No'. There is a general pattern here. Although the use of the spelling *gh* is not phonemic in these examples (since only the *g* is sounded and the *h* is silent), there is a regularity which can be captured by the following pair of statements:

[9.5] within syllables,   gh = /g/ before a vowel
  e.g.   *ghost, ghoul, ghetto, aghast*
                                          gh = /f/ after a vowel
  e.g.   *enough, tough, rough, cough*
                                                      (Based on Stubbs 1980: 51)

But these rules are not inviolable. For instance, in a small number of words *gh* following a vowel is not pronounced at all:

[9.6] caught   taught   bought   sought
  light   right   tight   night
  plough   bough   though   through

Historical studies of English spelling hold the key to how these spelling patterns involving *gh* arose. Students of the history of English spelling have shown that the use of *gh* for *g* at the beginning of a word is the result of a historical accident (see Scragg 1973; Stubbs 1980). Caxton, the person who introduced printing to England in 1476, though an Englishman, had spent much of his life on the continent, in Holland in particular. He was not fully conversant with the conventions of English spelling and he brought back with him many European compositors and setters, most of whom were Dutch. Their control of English spelling was also far from perfect and their Dutch spelling habits interfered with the spelling norms of English. They used *gh*, as was the norm in Dutch, where English would have used *g*. That is how *gost* became *ghost* and how similar words came to be spelt with word-initial *gh*. In some cases this tendency was reversed. For instance, *girl* and *goose* temporarily acquired a letter *h* after the arrival of printing and were written as *gherle* and *ghoos*. But later they reverted to their original *g* spelling (Stubbs 1980: 51).

There is also a good historical explanation for the unpronounced *gh* following a vowel. English pronunciation has changed over the centuries, but the spelling has not been revised to bring it up to date. At one time the letters *gh* after a vowel represented a sound like that guttural fricative /x/ heard in the Scottish pronunciation of *och* and *loch*. Various changes in the pronunciation took place and words like *night* and *light* became pronounced as /naɪt/ and /laɪt/, but the spelling was not revised to reflect these changes. In sum, what might look like arbitrary spelling conventions may have some organising principle behind them buried deep in the history of the language. We will return to the historical dimension in more detail in the next section.

Let us turn to the present. I shall now show that, even where spelling is not phonemic, normally it is subject to rules. But the rules tend to be leaky. We will use the doubling of consonants as our case study. Although the use of a single or double consonant makes no difference to the consonant itself, it is a useful clue as to whether the vowel preceding it is long or short. By spotting the single or double consonant following a vowel you can tell that the vowel in the first of the two nonsense words in each pair is short and the second is long.

[9.7] *Short*   *Long*
    ditter   deater
    hodder   hooder
    tusser   tuser

The interplay of vowel length in the pronunciation and consonant doubling in the orthography is important in English spelling. We will illustrate this with the example of doubling consonant letters in the spelling of monosyllabic verbs ending in a consonant when the suffix *-ing* is attached. This discussion draws on Crystal (1988).

The data in [9.8] illustrate the fact that, whether the consonant following a vowel in this context is doubled as in *wetting* (**weting*), or not as in *waiting* (**waitting*), depends crucially on whether the vowel in the verb stem is short or long; for this purpose a diphthong counts as a long vowel. (See the key to symbols used on pp. xviii–xix.)

[9.8] a *Short*   b *Long*
    hit   hitting   heat   heating
    rid   ridding   read   reading
    chat   chatting   chart   charting

If *-ing* is added to a monosyllabic word ending in a consonant the final consonant of the base is doubled as in [9.8a]. However, no doubling takes place if the base has a long vowel as in [9.8b]. Should you encounter verbs like *fip* and *spleed* (which I have made up) you would instinctively know that, since the former has a short vowel, its final consonant must be doubled when the suffix *-ing* is attached to give *fipping*. But not so *spleed*, which has a long vowel. It must be written as *spleeding*.

The doubling of the last consonant of a monosyllabic verb when a suffix is attached is more general than I have indiated so far. It is not uniqely triggered by the presence of *-ing*. Other suffixes, e.g. *-er* and *-en* also induce consonant doubling, as seen in [9.9]:

[9.9] *Short*

knit ~ knitter
wet ~ wetter
shut ~ shutter

Long

neat ~ neater
wait ~ waiter
shoot ~ shooter

Doubling is not influenced by phonology alone. Consonant doubling rules may be sensitive to how vowels are spelt. Thus, a consonant following two vowel letters, regardless of whether they represent a short or long vowel, is not doubled:

[9.10] *Short*

spread ~ spreading
head ~ heading
sweat ~ sweating

Long

plead ~ pleading
read ~ reading
leaf ~ leafing

In addition, where the suffix starts with a consonant no doubling occurs. Hence we have *bagful*, *madly* and *fitment*, rather than **baggful*, **maddly* and **fittment*.

In disyllabic words, the doubling of final consonant letters in the orthography is subject to a variety of constraints. Normally, if a word ends in a consonant other than 'l' the final letter is only doubled if the primary stress is on the second syllable. No doubling takes place if primary stress is on the first syllable. This is shown in [9.11a]. However, if a word ends in 'l', when a suffix is added that letter may be doubled regardless of where the main stress of the word falls. This is illustrated in [9.11b].

[9.11] *Initial stress*

a cushion ~ cushioning
enter ~ entered
fashion ~ fashioned

Stress on second syllable

refer ~ referred
defer ~ deferring
occur ~ occurrence

profit ~ profiting	admit ~ admitting
ballot ~ balloted	patrol ~ patroller
pilot ~ piloting	upset ~ upsetting
b travel ~ traveller	compel ~ compelling
marvel ~ marvellous	expel ~ expelling
revel ~ reveller	rebel ~ rebellion
label ~ labelling	appal ~ appalled

It should be noted that these rules are not without exceptions. At best they indicate significant tendencies. For instance, though 'l' is normally doubled in disyllabic words, regardless of where stress falls, there are words like *appealing* and *revealed* in which 'l' is not doubled when a suffix is added. Moreover, in a few cases there are differences between British and American English: the rule responsible for doubling 'l' is applied less rigorously in American English, and as a result, words like *traveling* and *labeling* are spelt with one 'l'.

Finally, doubling is used to underline the distinction between content words and function words. There is an orthographic requirement that content words (i.e. verbs, nouns, adjectives and adverbs) must be spelt with at least three letters if they contain a short vowel. But there is no such minimality requirement applicable to function words. So, one-letter function words like *a* and *I*, as well as two-letter ones like *if*, *it*, *on* etc., are allowed. By contrast, putative nouns, adjectives or verbs with a short vowel like **ad*, **od*, **as*, **eg*, **bo* and **se* are ruled out of court. In each case, to obtain a properly formed content word you need to double the last letter. This gives you *add*, *odd*, *ass*, *egg*, *boo* and *see* (cf. Albrow 1972; Sampson 1985). Of course, content words, e.g. the verbs *be*, *do*, and *go*, exist. But they are not counter-examples since each one of them contains either a long vowel or a diphthong.

9.2.3 Is A for apple? Why vowel letters pinch like ill-fitting shoes

In this section we will continue exploring the main reasons for the inconsistencies in English spelling, paying special though not exclusive attention to vowels. The correspondence between the spelling and pronunciation of vowel sounds is much less systematic than that of consonants. We shall see the reasons why this is so.

1 The main source of the inconsistency between the spelling and pronunciation of vowels is that the roman alphabet, with a mere five vowel letters, does not have sufficient symbols to represent all the 20 or so distinct vowel sounds of English. In many cases the representation of vowel sounds in the spelling is not phonemic: there is not a one-to-one match between letters and vowel phonemes. Often the same vowel letter represents different sounds, e.g. *a* represents /æ/ in /bæd/ *bad*, /ɑː/ in /pɑːs/ *pass*, /eɪ/ in /leɪt/ *late*, /ɔː/ in /fɔːn/ *fawn* etc. (Refer to the Key on pp. xviii–xix.) But still certain generalisations can be made, as we will see later in this section.

2 After the Norman Conquest, Norman scribes introduced some of the spelling conventions of French into English, e.g. /kw/, which had been spelt as *cw* (as in *cwic(u)*) before the Conquest, was now spelt as *qu* (as in *quick*). But this was not done across the board: for example *call* (from OE *ceallian*) was not changed to *quall; nor was *come* (from OE *cuman*) changed to *quome.

The French scribes were also unhappy with the letter *u* when next to the letters *m*, *v*, or *n*, because the handwriting strokes used to form these letters were very similar and often this made them difficult to read. So they decided that the original *u* should be replaced by *o* in words like *son*, *love* and *come*. For the same reason, the earlier spelling of 'woman' as *wimman* was changed to *woman*.

3 English spelling is extremely conservative, as we saw in connection with [9.6]. While pronunciation has continued to change, spelling has remained more or less fixed since the fifteenth century. Nowhere is this more evident than in the case of vowels. Their pronunciation underwent a tremendous upheaval called the GREAT VOWEL SHIFT, which started around 1400 and finished around 1600. As you can see in [9.12], something akin to a game of musical chairs was played in the phonology of vowels, but scribes, and later printers, took no notice of these changes and went on spelling words as they had always done. The examples, in which the Modern English forms are written in parenthesis, illustrate how Old English vowels have evolved.

[9.12] *a* as in *habban* (have)   *ī* as in *rīdan* (ride)
ā as in *hām* (home)   *o* as in *moððe* (moth)
æ as in *þæt* (that)   *ō* as in *fōda* (food)
ǣ as in *dǣl* (deal)   *u* as in *sundor* (sunder)
e as in *settan* (set)   *ū* as in *mūs* (mouse)

$\bar{e}$ as in *fēdan* (feed)   *y* as in *fyllan* (fill)
i as in *sittan* (sit)   *ȳ* as in *mȳs* (mice)

(From Pyles and Algeo 1982: 106)

Note: In the Middle Ages there was a convention of using
a macron (little line) over a vowel to indicate its
length. Later, doubling of vowel letters was used for
this purpose. The vowel letters had phonetic values
similar to those they have in Italian or Spanish. The
letter *y* represented a front rounded vowel – a sound
similar to that found in French *tu* 'you' (Sing.) or
German *Güte* 'goodness'.

Observe that, while the short vowels have remained mostly
unchanged and are represented reasonably phonemically in current
spelling, the long vowels have generally changed. Retention of
the pre-Great Vowel Shift spelling of long vowels means that,
typically, long vowels are not written phonemically in present-day
English. Long $\bar{e}$ (*ee*) now represents long /iː/ (as in *feed*); and long
oo (*oo*) now represents long /uː/ (as in *soon*).[1] In each case the
double letters represent a vowel that came to be pronounced higher
than it had been before the Great Vowel Shift. The highest vowels
$\bar{\imath}$ (as in *rīdan* (ride)) and $\bar{u}$ (as in *mūs* (mouse)) became diphthongs,
yielding [raɪd] and [maʊs].

To illustrate the conservatism of the English orthography, let us
take a closer look at the vowel in the word *mouse*, which most
speakers of English pronounce as /maʊs/. How did the pronunciation come to diverge so much from the spelling? This is how. In
the early Middle Ages this word had the orthographic form *mūs*.
This spelling is reflected in the pronunciation in conservative
non-standard Scottish dialects where this word is still pronounced
mus. Two things happened which explain the divergence of the
pronunciation from the spelling.

First came 1066 and its aftermath. As already mentioned, after
the Norman Conquest, French scribes arrived. They did not always
respect Anglo-Saxon spelling conventions for English – not an
untypical attitude for a conquering power. They just spelt the /u/
sound as *ou* (as they did and still do in French in words like *vous*,
mousse, fou, coup etc. If this spelling was good enough for French,
it was also good enough for English.). So, /u/ of *mus* came to be
spelt with the digraph *ou*. Later, in the fifteenth century, the vowel

u changed to /əʊ/ and so they said /məʊs/ (which sounded quite similar to the modern Canadian pronunciation of this vowel). Later still, the /əʊ/ pronunciation was changed to /aʊ/, the pronunciation that is used in most varieties of Modern English. But because the spelling had atrophied in the late Middle Ages, none of these changes in pronunciation is reflected in the spelling.

[9.13]

Questions, Quistions & Quoshtions

Daddy how does an elephant feel
When he swallows a piece of steel?
Does he get drunk
And fall on his trunk
Or roll down the road like a wheel?

Daddy what would a pelican do
If he swallowed a bottle of glue?
Would his beak get stuck
Would he run out of luck
And lose his job at the zoo?

Son tell me tell me true,
If I belted you with a shoe,
Would you fall down dead?
Would you go up to bed?
– Either of those would do.

Spike Milligan

Conservatism is also to blame for the silent word-initial letters *k* and *g* before *n* as in *knee, knock, knife, knight, gnaw, gnat* etc. Neither /k/ nor /g/ can be combined with /n/ at the beginning of a syllable, but at one time these consonants would have been sounded in that position. The /k/ in such clusters was lost by the early seventeenth century. (We can infer this from evidence of puns on words like *knight* and *night* in Shakespeare.) Today, pronouncing *knock-kneed* as *[knɒk kniːd] rather than [nɒk niːd] sounds very strange.

4 Vowel pronunciation may vary depending on whether a vowel is stressed or unstressed. Compare the pronunciation of stressed and unstressed o and e in the following:

[9.14] a allergy /ˈælədʒɪ/   aˈll*er*gic /əˈlɜːdʒɪk/
      b education /edjʊˈkeɪʃn/   educative /ˈedjʊkətɪv/

Vowels get their full, clear value when stressed but are muffled and pronounced as /ə/ (schwa) when unstressed. There is no letter in the orthography to represent schwa. This is unfortunate since it is the commonest vowel in English speech.

5 We noted above that the same vowel letter may represent different sounds. This is not to say that it is all chaotic. Often, the vowel has predictable phonetic values if it occurs in the vicinity of certain consonants. For instance, the data in [9.15] exemplify the pronunciation of *a* in a variety of phonological contexts:

[9.15] /ɔː/   /ɑː/   /æ/

pawn	part	bat
spawn	calm	sat
dawn	palm	mat
walk	past	hat
swart	cast	grand

As the rules in [9.16], which reflect historical changes, show, the pronunciation that is appropriate for the vowel *a* is normally predictable:

[9.16] Pronounce *a* as:
    1 /ɔː/ before or after *w*;
    2 /ɑː/ before *r* or *l*, or before a fricative sound like /s/ or /f/;
    3 /æ/ normally elsewhere.

Some of the rules interact. For example, the rule that gives /ɔː/ if *a* is adjacent to *w* pre-empts the rule that says 'pronounce *a* as /ɑː/ if it is followed by *r* or *l*. That is why *walk* is pronounced as /wɔːk/ and not */wɑː(l)k/ or */wæː(l)k/ – except in some very conservative Northumbrian dialects such as Pitmatic, spoken in Ashington, where [æː] survives in [wæːlk], [tæːlk] etc. (BBC Radio 4 2003).

6 Many words end in a silent letter *e*. This is not entirely haphazard. Although there are words like *come* whose final *-e* has no function, in many other cases word-final *e* is used as a special orthographic mark indicating that the preceding vowel is either long or a diphthong. That is the case in *nice, rose, fate* etc., where the final silent *e* indicates that the vowel letter before it stands for a diphthong and in *lute, rude, scene* etc., where it signals length.

Caveat: it would be rash to assume that a word-final *-e* is an infallible clue to the status of the preceding vowel. For instance, in *love* and *dove* the vowel is short. The *e* is there simply to ensure that the words do not end in *v* as the presence of this letter at the end of a word is not permitted (see p. 213).

9.3 Morphological signposts in the spelling

In some cases, the orthographic form of a word may not attempt to indicate pronunciation but instead may serve the function of showing visually connections between words and allomorphs that are related in terms of grammar or meaning. Let us take grammar first. English spelling typically ignores alternations in the realisation of morphemes. Normally it uses the same letters to represent allomorphs of the same morpheme even though there may be significant differences in the pronunciation of those allomorphs. For example, the regular noun plural ending is spelt as *-s* but is pronounced as /-s/, /-z/ or /-ɪz/ in different contexts. The spelling thus fails to indicate the exact pronunciation but succeeds in showing the grammatical identity of the ending (see Chomsky and Halle (1968) and the discussion of allomorphs in section (3.3.3.1)).

The morphological signposting role of spelling can be further illustrated by the alternation between the letters *i* and *y* at the end of nouns with the plural suffix *-s*. If in the singular a noun ends in a consonant followed by *y* (e.g. *berry, doggy, pony*), the *y* is replaced by *i* in the plural (e.g. *berries, doggies, ponies*). But if in the spelling the letter *y* is preceded by a vowel, it remains unchanged, even where it is followed by the plural suffix spelt as *-s* (as in *two donkeys*). Note, however, that, if the *-s* does not represent the plural morpheme, *y* remains (cf. *the pony's tail, doggy's bone* etc., where *s* represents the genitive).

Spelling may also do another morphological job: it may help to distinguish native from imported words by restricting certain spelling conventions to borrowed words. Certain letters or sequences of letters are only found in words that have come into English from other languages and retain a degree of foreignness. For example, native English words (excluding names and trade names) do not end in the letters *i*, *u* or *v*. Instead of *i*, the letter *y* is used in word-final position as in [9.17a]. Where a word would otherwise end in *u* or *v*, the letter *e* is added, as in [9.17b] and [9.17c]. (Words ending in *v* like the slang word *spiv*, whose origin is uncertain, are very rare.)

[9.17] a pity   nutty   naughty
      b true   blue   glue
      c shove   live   glove

No such restriction applies to words of foreign origin like those in [9.18] which are not totally assimilated:

[9.18] a okapi   ski   yeti   kiwi
      b tutu   gnu   guru   emu

Similarly, any word beginning with *kh* (e.g. *khaki, khalifa, khalsa* etc.) is marked as being of foreign extraction by its spelling. No native word begins with those letters. All these words come from Indian languages.

Other examples are not difficult to find. There are words of Greek origin, which came into English second-hand from Latin, whose initial consonant sound is not pronounced in English because it would give an impermissible consonant combination, for example *g* in *gnome* and *gnostic*; and *p* in *psychology, psalm, pneumonia, pterosaur, pneumatic* etc.

In addition, of course, there are words which are overtly marked as foreign by the use of diacritic marks not found in English, e.g. *crèche, façade, débâcle* and *cliché* which come from French. (See also section (7.3.2.))

9.4 Lexical signposting in the spelling

Spelling may also serve the function of signposting semantic relationships between orthographic words. This is quite useful where the orthographic words in question have significantly different pronunciations:

[9.19] a	sign	/saɪn/	b	sane	/seɪn/
	signify	/sɪgnɪfaɪ/		sanity	/sænɪtɪ/
	significant	/sɪgnɪfɪkənt/		sanitise	/sænɪtaɪz/

If you were reading and came across the word *signification*, which you had not encountered before, by looking at its spelling you would probably be able to relate it to the words in [9.19a] and to work out its meaning.

Conversely, spelling may serve to distinguish homophonous word-forms which realise totally different lexemes, such as these:

[9.20]	reed	read		
	stationary	stationery		
	born	borne		
	weak	week		
	sea	see		
	site	cite	sight	
	right	rite	write	wright

Such words are like traps set to catch the unwary. They give English spelling a bad name.

But there is another way of looking at it. When the spelling does not reflect pronunciation, it is not necessarily crazy. After all, most of the time we do not read aloud. So, the lack of fit between sounds and letters need not cause problems if non-phonemic spelling conveys useful information by representing the same grammatical suffix (e.g. plural noun -*s*) consistently or by representing word-forms of related lexemes consistently, as in [9.19]. Nor is it unhelpful when, by not being phonemic, it distinguishes homophones, as in [9.20].

9.5 Spelling reform

I have argued that English spelling is not as arbitrary and chaotic as its critics often proclaim. It is essentially phonemic with many non-phonemic quirks. But even the quirky parts are often not totally crazy. Nevertheless, I must concede that there is a prima facie case for some spelling reform to remove or reduce the extent to which the system is not transparent. First, there is the educational argument. An ideal alphabet should consistently ensure that there is a one-to-one correspondence between letter and symbol. English does not quite live up to that ideal. If English were spelt like Italian, the pronunciation could almost always be inferred from the spelling. As a result, learning to read and write would be a piece of cake. Many a child would have a happier and less stressful life at school. Fewer people would leave school illiterate and feeling inadequate.

[9.21]

Beg Parding

'Beg parding, Mrs Harding,
Is my kitting in your garding?'
'Is *your* kitting in *my* garding?
Yes she is, and all alone,
Chewing of a mutting bone.'

ENGLISH CHILDREN'S RHYME

Second, there is the economic argument. Most people spend a lot of their time at work reading or writing. The standard orthography contains a considerable number of superfluous letters (e.g. *plough* uses six letters to represent three distinct sounds – it could be simplified to *plow* as indeed it has been in North America). This makes the process of writing slow and laborious. It costs money. Reform would save money and improve efficiency. (The discussion here draws on Stubbs 1980 and Crystal 1988.)

While in theory spelling reform to make English phonemic looks like a very sensible idea, in practice it is simply a non-starter. There are too many practical considerations that militate against it. Most of them revolve round the fact that literacy is a social phenomenon: it is not merely a matter of representing language using the medium of writing. Unless spelling reformers can persuade the users of English that the upheaval of implementing spelling reform is worth the great expense that would be involved and the attendant hassle, no movement towards reform can take place.

For a variety of reasons outlined below, the seeds of reform have fallen on stony ground and withered away.

1 English is a world language. It is the mother tongue of over 350 million language users and is used as a second language or lingua franca by 1,000–1,500 million people. There are many standard Englishes and they all have a variety of dialects and accents. If each speaker spelt words in a way that reflected their pronunciation, the possibility of easy communication on paper by users of (standard) English would be diminished. Today, no matter how they pronounce words, speakers of standard English spell words identically in the vast majority of cases. There are only a few minor differences between British and American English, e.g. British *plough* corresponds to American *plow*, British *travelling* corresponds to American *traveling*. Otherwise, in virtually all cases, spelling is the same regardless of pronunciation. The written standard language is nearly the same in all parts of the world. This facilitates the use of written English for communication with literate speakers, regardless of where they come from (see Crystal 1997).

Assuming, as most of us do, that using a common standard language is useful for communication among people whose pronunciation is significantly different, if a reformed phonemic spelling system were adopted, there would be fierce arguments about the right dialect to provide the basis for the reformed orthography. It is much easier to agree, more or less, on a written standard language; it is well nigh impossible to agree on a spoken standard variety.

In Britain, many of the speakers of RP would no doubt insist on an orthography that reflected the pronunciation of the Queen's English. But, from the English regions, Wales, Scotland and Ireland, one would no doubt hear other voices arguing for other dialects and accents. Of course, the situation would become even more complex once speakers of English from other countries joined the debate. Given the fact that there are more native speakers of American English than of any other dialect, and given the prestige and power of the United States, an obvious case could and would be made for spoken American English forming the basis of the standard written language. But it is unlikely that this would appeal to speakers of other major dialects, e.g. Australian English, Canadian English and Indian English. Certainly most British people would not be willing to replace the Queen's English with a transatlantic standard. But, even if they were persuaded, since American English is not a mono-lith, the question of which variety should be represented in the new phonemic alphabet would rear its ugly head again – should it be Appalachian, Ebonics, the Chicago dialect or the dialect of New York? A single phonemic spelling system for all speakers of English is unattainable since different dialects have different phonemic systems, e.g. some dialects have an 'r' sound in *car* and *cart* and others do not. No single transcription can represent all dialects accurately.

Obviously there would be little point in introducing several competing alternative systems. That is the biggest obstacle that faces spelling reformers. This is probably the main reason why both the British Simplified Spelling Society and the Spelling Reform Association in America have made no headway, although they have been campaigning for change for almost a century.

2 Persuading those who had acquired the present orthography to give it up for the sake of making life easier for novice readers and writers would be an uphill struggle.

3 While it is difficult to learn English spelling because it is not always phonemic, once you have acquired it, some of its weak-nesses turn out to be strengths. For instance, as we have seen, some grammatical forms remain invariant and hence easy to recognise on the page no matter how they are actually pronounced. For example, the plural of nouns is normally marked by the letter -*s* (or -*es*) even though it is pronounced in three different ways (as /s/ as in *cups*, as /z/ as in *mugs* and as /ɪz/ as in *glasses*). Also, the phonetically unhelpful differentiation between words like *weather* and *whether* is quite useful since these word-forms represent different lexemes. So, there would be resistance to a transparently phonemic alphabet on the grounds that it would not be capable of conveying grammatical and lexical distinctions like these.

4 The transition from the old to the new spelling would take some time. In that period could we live tolerably with the confusion that would inevitably occur as old readers/writers learned the new system?

5 Millions of books and other materials have been produced over the last 500 or so years using the current writing system. It is inconceivable that future generations could just turn their backs on the accumulated culture, scholarship and scientific knowledge that these contain. Even after the reform, many people would still need to be able to cope with the present orthography. The alternative of reprinting all existing books using the reformed orthography is just impracticable.

6 What would be the attitude of the English speech community? Test your own attitude to the proposed revised spellings in [9.22].

[9.22]

He pauzd for a moement and a wield feeling ov piti kaem oever him.
(New Spelling)

He pauzed for a moment and a wilde feeling ov pity came over him.
(Regularized English)

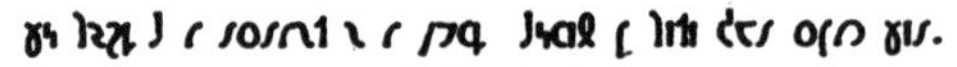

𝔶𝔥 ℞𝔶 𝕁 𝔯 𝔧𝔬𝔯𝔫𝟙 𝔵 𝔯 𝔯𝔮 𝕁𝔶𝔞� 𝔠 𝔩𝔯𝔥 𝔮𝔯𝔯 𝔬𝔯𝔯 𝔶𝔩𝔯.
(Shavian)

hee pausd for a moement and a wield feeliŋ ov pity cæm œver him.
(i.t.a.)

Reformed English Spelling
(From Sampson 1985: 195)

Notes:
1 New Spelling was jointly proposed by the Simplified Spelling Society of Great Britain and the Simpler Spelling Society of the USA in 1956.
2 Regularized English was proposed by Axel Wijk in 1959.
3 Shavian was the brainchild of George Bernard Shaw, who left instructions in his will that a regularised alphabet of at least 40 letters, representing systematically the distinctive sounds of English, should be produced. The winning design was by Kingsley Reed (Crystal 1988: 81).
4 i.t.a. = Initial Teaching Alphabet, proposed by Pitman in 1960.

In addition to the very reasonable intellectual objections outlined above, the present spelling system is something which many people are sentimentally attached to. They would resist drastic change that made the written language they know and love look strange. Sampson points out that if New Spelling was adopted, for example, it would result in the spelling of about 90 per cent of existing words being changed to varying degrees. Change on this scale would not be embraced and celebrated, with street parties and universal rejoicing all over the English-speaking world.

For all these reasons, the present orthography is unlikely to be drastically reformed. But this is not to say that tinkering at the margins should not take place. In the past various changes have been made and I expect that more could be profitably made without adverse side effects. For example, words that came into English from Latin or French had silent consonants introduced in their spelling by scribes who wanted to be clever and reveal the etymology of words, but in fact were wrong about the etymology. Omitting such consonants should simplify matters without causing problems. A typical example of what I have in mind is the word *island* which has an *s* in it because someone imagined that it came from the same root as the word *isle* which originally had an *s* in it (because it is descended from French *île* which comes from Latin *insula*). In fact, though *isle* and *island* are related in meaning, they do not have a common ancestry. *Island* never had an *s* in it to begin with: its source was the Old English form *iegland*, where *ieg* is the earlier Old English word for 'island'.

A more general case in which etymological considerations are relevant and which is ripe for reform is the spelling of the verb-forming suffix *-ise/-ize*. There are two spellings of this suffix, found in a verb such as *civilize/civilise*. Both *-ise/-ize* spellings are pronounced /aɪz/. In general Americans tend to prefer *-ize* and the British *-ise* (so, I have used *-ise* spellings in this book because that is the norm in British English), but life would be simpler if we all used *-ize*:

> but a queer conservatism, mainly on the part of printers, supported by the *OED*, forces us back on an etymological distinction which few of us are capable of making, offhand at any rate. The pundits say that words derived from those containing the Greek suffix *-izein* should be spelt with the *-ize* ending; the others *-ise*. But for ordinary people this rule conveys nothing at all.
>
> (Scragg 1973: 35)

This is an example of spelling being used to express identity. Use of spelling for that purpose is more obvious when a non-standard variety of the language is involved, especially when it demonstrates that dialect is not inferior language, and that serious literature can be published in dialect, using dialect spelling. It is very affirming. This is illustrated in [9.23]:

[9.23] DANIEL wis jist a wee laddie when King
Nebuchadnezzar took him hostage fae
his hame in Jerusalem. He wis picked oot,
alang wi three o his brainy pals, an taken
aff tae the coort in Babylon. The fower
boys had aw done weel at school an the
king wanted tae train them as coonsellors
in his palace.

(Stuart 1997: 81)

Jamie Stuart's translation of the Bible into Glaswegian was proclaimed in the national press as 'the Scottish publishing event of the year' (*The Glasgow Evening Times* 1992).

9.6 Is speech degenerate writing?

In a literate society like this one, where the written word enjoys such prestige, it is easy to see why people sometimes regard speech as less significant than writing. Normally, if anything needs to be given legal or official status it is 'put in writing'. Some even seem to think that the spoken word in the standard language is derived from the written word, or at any rate validated by a written form. They look down with contempt on languages and dialects that are unwritten.

While it would be foolish to play down the importance of writing, it is necessary to recognise the primacy of speech both in the evolution of our species and in the life of the individual. Whereas writing has been around for only about 5–6,000 years, speech has almost certainly existed since ape-men became human over 40,000 years ago. Furthermore, whereas there are many illiterate individuals in any society, and indeed there are entire linguistic communities which are illiterate, we do not find individuals who fail to acquire the spoken language, except in isolated cases of severe physical or mental deficiency. And, although illiterate linguistic communities with a language that is only spoken are commonplace, speechless but literate linguistic communities where people communicate only by swapping written notes are simply unknown. Looking at language in the life of the individual, the same pattern is observed: speech is acquired before writing.

Nevertheless, the importance of writing should not be underestimated. When writing was first invented, it often involved the visible encoding (on papyrus, cave walls, tree bark etc.) of marks that represented words of the spoken language. That is why an ideal writing system is phonemic. Looking at individual English words, we can often see that the letters of the written word are meant to represent sounds of the spoken word. For instance, we can see that the orthographic word spelt *leg* is a representation of the spoken word with the three sounds represented by *l, e* and *g*.

However, for a highly literate society speech and writing provide two closely related, and often complementary, systems. Writing and speech are parallel, partly overlapping systems that may serve different functions. The language of an auctioneer, and what one says to start off and to end a telephone conversation, are good examples of the domain of the spoken language. It is quite likely that you have never seen either written down. Conversely, there are types of language that are unlikely to be used in speech. Examples include the language of legal contract, bibliographies at the backs of books like this one, and lists in registers of births and deaths.

Once literacy becomes firmly established, it is not always the case that every written word is a record in some sense of the spoken word. Sometimes it is the written word that is primary and the spoken word that is derivative. This is most obviously true of learned words and technical terms coined using roots and affixes of Latin or Greek origin. It is quite likely that a technical word like *morphophonological* (having to do with the study of the relationship between morphology and phonology), which contains the elements *morph(o)-phon-olog-ic-al*, was used in writing before it was used in speech. Its pronunciation would have had to be worked out from its spelling, not the other way round. This process is not marginal. As we saw in Chapter 7, many words of French origin came into the spoken language via the written language.

The upshot of this discussion is that it would be naive to assume that writing always simply attempts to mirror speech (see Giegerich 1999: 151–64). Indeed, it is easy to think of cases of SPELL-ING PRONUNCIATION where pronunciation has changed in order to bring it into line with the spelling. Consider the following, for example:

1 Names whose spelling is not closely related to the pronunciation may be changed so that pronunciation mirrors spelling. Thus, the Scottish name *Menzies* which used to be /mɪŋɪs/ or /meŋɪs/ is nowadays often pronounced /menzɪz/. When spelling and pronunciation diverge, spelling reform is not the only option available: there is always the option of 'reforming speech' to make it fit spelling.

2 Increasingly, the letters *i* and *d* in *often* and *Wednesday* which used to be 'silent' are sounded.

3 The word-initial letter *h* in many words, such as *hotel*, *humour* and *herbs*, which are borrowed from French (where the *h* is normally not pronounced word-initially), is now sounded. Probably this is done because dropping aitches at the beginning of a word is stigmatised in English.

4 Some words with the letter *a* are pronounced with this vowel given the transparent value that it would have in, say, Italian or Spanish. Thus, for example, the older pronunciation of *trauma* as /trɔːmə/ is being edged out by /traumə/ which reflects more clearly the spelling. Similar changes have happened to *gala* and *data*. Instead of, or alongside, /geɪlə/ and /deɪtə/ you will now often hear /gɑːlə/ and /dɑːtə/ (see Wells 1982: 108–9).

5 Acronyms, i.e. words like NATO which are formed from the initial letters of existing words, are an obvious case of going from spelling to pronunciation (see section (8.8)).

Before we get too despondent about the fact that in English spelling does not always quite fit the pronunciation and jump on a radical spelling reform bandwagon, we should bear in mind the fact that the lack of fit between speech and writing is not necessarily an unmitigated disaster, since writing is not merely a pale visual copy of speech.

9.7 Email and text messaging: imo email & txt r gr8

The quickening pace of converging internet and mobile telephone technologies has had a major impact on the way we use written English, especially in the last 10 years. We shall focus here on the narrowing of the gap between speech and writing that has followed the mass adoption of these new technologies.

The impact of email was felt first. Email has revolutionised the ways in which we communicate. It has rightly been the object of intensifying scholarly investigation over the last 10 years. Linguists have been especially interested in the ways in which the boundary between spoken and written language gets blurred in email. Naomi Baron summarises the differences in this fashion:

1 *Social dynamics*
   Email resembles writing. The interlocutors do not communicate face-to-face. Physical separation fosters explicitness since contextual clues are not available to help interlocutors fill in missing information.

2 *Format*
   Like writing, email is durable, unlike speech which is ephemeral (unless recorded). Like speech, email is typically largely unedited. The level of editing tends to correlate with the formality of the message.

3 *Grammar*
   LEXICON: predominantly like speech (e.g. heavy use of first- and second-person pronouns)
   SYNTAX: shares features of both writing and speech (e.g. like writing, email has high type/token ratio, high use of adverbial subordinate clauses, high use of disjunctions, but it resembles speech by using contractions and the present tense frequently).

4 *Style*
   Predominantly like speech (e.g. low level of formality); expression of emotion (flaming) is more common than it normally is in writing.

(Based on Baron 2000: 251)

In the rest of this chapter we will examine some key features of mobile phone (message) texting language, some of which also are found in emails. Texting and email language (and interactive internet language in general, e.g. chatroom discourse) overlap to some extent. But texting language merits a closer look than the rest because, for many users of English, texting has resulted in more radical change, bringing the immediacy of speech to the written medium, and in the process altering significantly the ways in which English is written. Consider the example in [9.24]:

[9.24] My smmr hols wr CWOT. B4, we usd 2go2 NY 2C my bro, his GF & thr 3 :- kds FTF. ILNY, it's a gr8 plc.

Translation: My summer holidays were a complete waste of time. Before, we used to go to New York to see my brother, his girlfriend and their three screaming kids face to face. I love New York, it's a great place.

(From *The Telegraph*, 3 March 2003)

An analysis of the language of this text reveals a number of interesting things:

[9.25] Typically, standard orthography is used for grammatical function words like articles and pronouns.	My, my, we, his, it's, a
Clipping.	hols (general slang too), bro
Abbreviations, especially of compounds and stock phrases, are very common, but other content words (e.g. nouns, verbs, adjectives) may also be abbreviated. In this context the abbreviations yield orthographic words.	CWOT, NY, FTF, ILNY, GF
Omission of vowels (especially, but not exclusively) in content words. Most of the information is carried by the consonants. Hence intelligibility is preserved if vowels are omitted but not if consonants are omitted.	smmr, wr, usd, thr, kds, plc
Abbreviations incorporating numbers 2, 4, 8 whose sounds supply syllables or syllable fragments and thus make it possible to articulate the word.	B4, 2go2, 2C, gr8
Arabic numerals and other symbols (e.g ampersand (&)) are used in a standard fashion.	3, &
Smiley (see below)	:- (meaning screaming)

The screaming smiley is ':-@'

As shown in the text, with the
@ symbol omitted,
'screaming' functions as a
noun modifier rather than the
verbal 'screaming at (someone)'.

Punctuation.   Standard
                                conventions
                                generally
                                observed

One way in which the language of emails and, to a greater extent, texting approximates speech is in having brief turns. Typically, each message is brief. Various conventions (e.g. clipping and abbreviation of words and phrases) are used to condense the message as seen in [9.24]. Most of these methods are also employed elsewhere in the language as we have already seen in Chapter 8, but not to the same degree. In text messages brevity is at a premium.

Unlike the conventional letter which tends to be rather long, and to which the response from the addressee is not instantaneous, the email or text message is normally short. And the writer expects no long delay before a reply comes back; a more or less instant response is expected. This makes possible a rapid exchange of turns as the correspondence develops, almost in real time (if the interlocutors so wish). Thus writing gets close to being like a live dialogue.

Another way in which this form of communication tries to bridge the gap between the spoken and written language is the use of EMOTICONS. These are ordinary characters on the keyboard that are used to indicate emotions and attitudes such as :- in the text above which means 'screaming'. The use of emoticons has added significantly to the range of characters and symbols available in written language, be it texting, email or in cyberspace chat rooms. A conventional figure of a happy smiling face, SMILEY has given its name to the set of symbols that express emotions and attitudes of the kind that are normally carried in speech by PARALINGUISTIC features like facial expression and tone of voice. The traditional standard orthography is poorly equipped to represent these.

Whole dictionaries of smileys have been compiled. Here are a few selections from one of them:

[9.26] Emotions, attitudes

:-) Your basic smiley	This smiley is used to inflect a sarcastic or joking statement since we can't hear voice inflection over email.
:-(Frowning smiley	User did not like that last statement or is upset or depressed about something.
;-) Winky smiley	User just made a flirtatious and/or sarcastic remark. More of a 'don't hit me for what I just said' smiley.

(From *The Unofficial Smiley Dictionary*, http://paul.merton.ox.ac.uk/ascii/smileys.html#basic)

Smileys are also employed to mitigate the effects of distance in written language and the fact that the person reading the message can neither see nor hear the writer of the message. This is done by using characters like those in [9.27]. These smileys describe physical attributes of the writer that would be observable in the spoken language.

[9.27] Physical attributes

:-)-8	User is a Big girl.
{:-)	User wears a toupee.
(-:	User is left handed.

Recently, special visually more expressive fonts have been developed. Unlike the standard smileys which use standard keyboard characters as symbols which have no inherent relation to whatever sentiment or attribute they stand for, the newer ones tend to be iconic. They are images that try to capture visually, albeit in a highly conventionalised form, an aspect of the emotion they represent:

[9.28] *Top 10 smileys*

evolution	obnoxious	yelling	hysterical	together
shocked	disgusted	diva	dead	rebel

Source: From http://www.smileydictionary.com/images/main/emoticons.gif

As we saw in section (9.5), writing is a social institution. Any changes to the orthography do cause a stir. So it has been with the developments we are considering here. Many educators, politicians, journalists and other opinion leaders are appalled by text messaging. Of all the features of texting, it is the smileys – or 'hieroglyphics' as critics call them – that cause the greatest annoyance. Those unaccustomed to the new ways dislike the fact that they cannot make sense of smileys and hence find it difficult to read texts that use them in abundance. (The other characteristics of text messaging cause somewhat less irritation as they only extend the use of familiar ways of writing English.)

The *Telegraph* article from which the text message in [9.24] originally appeared caused a flurry of debate in the press which continued for many months afterwards on the internet. Many found this text message particularly worrying because it formed part of an English essay by a 13-year-old Scottish student. The use of text messaging in an essay provided evidence of declining literacy standards.

The problem highlighted in this article is a real one and it must be addressed urgently. Students need to know the difference between what is appropriate in the written formal variety of the language and what is not. They need to know that the highly informal language of text messaging which incorporates a number of features of the spoken language has its place; but that place is not in an essay.

However, the demand in the same article by a leader of the Scottish Parent Teacher Council that 'There must be rigorous efforts from all quarters of the education system to stamp out the use of texting as a form of written language so far as English study is concerned' is perhaps one that ought not to be heeded. First, it would not work. The text messaging genie cannot be put back in the bottle. Second, texting has enriched our communicative repertoire by introducing some helpful characteristics of the spoken language into the written language and thus making it possible to express certain meanings in writing more easily than we could before. For this reason alone, texting is something that should be celebrated, not repressed.

A preferable course of action, therefore, is to urge educators to intensify their efforts to ensure that pupils and students know from an early age the boundaries between the domains of formal written English and the domains of informal texting language. They should also know the place for the varieties of written English that lie between these two extremes.

9.8 Summary

The chapter started with a survey of writing systems. We classified the English writing system as basically alphabetic: it is founded on the phonemic principle. Ideally, each phoneme should be written with a distinct symbol. However, over the centuries various factors have conspired to subvert the phonemic principle. Consequently, today the spelling of many words (in particular frequent ones like *do* and *night*) lacks phonemic motivation.

In many cases conservatism is to blame. Reluctance to alter spelling as pronunciation has evolved has meant that English is written using a system that is no longer transparent. Nowhere is this more true than in the case of the vowels. For instance, the effects of the Great Vowel Shift are not reflected in the spelling of long vowels.

However, where spelling is not phonemic it is not necessarily arbitrary. In some cases non-phonemic spelling captures morphophonemic patterns. For example, -*s* is used to represent a morpheme whose phonetic realisation may be /s/ (nets), /z/ (beds) or /ɪz/ (roses). In other cases non-phonemic spelling serves to highlight relatedness between words (e.g. sign ~ signal ~ significant) which would be masked by a pure phonemic orthography.

There have been attempts to reform the orthography which have all floundered. The failure is not merely due to inertia; enormous practical difficulties would have to be surmounted for reform to be successful. For instance, since the phoneme systems of dialects do vary, it would be impossible to have a single orthography that represented the phonemes of all dialects phonemically.

The chapter ended with a discussion of recent changes in written English that are due to the widespread use of email, the internet and texting. These technological advances have introduced new ways of writing English that have led to a convergence of spoken and written English.

Exercises

1   Often a sound can be represented in writing by more than one letter or combination of letters.

a   Show the different ways in which the sounds /ə/, /ɪ/, /k/ and /iː/ are spelt in the standard English orthography. Is the choice of letters to represent these sounds totally arbitrary?

b Show the different ways in which the sounds represented by the letters *th*, *u*, *o*, *oo* and *ea* are pronounced in your variety of English.

2 a Translate the text message below into standard English.
 b Explain how you identified the words in the text.

> GR8! U WR THE LST PRSN I KNW 2GET A MOB. FON
> 2MORO B4 L8.
> BFN. GRAN.

3 Referring to plenty of examples, explain how the spelling of the letter *s* as single or double relates to the pronunciation in these positions:

a at the beginning of a word;
b before a consonant letter;
c after a consonant letter;
d between vowel letters;
e at the end of a word.

4 Study the spelling of this passage:

> THE TELLYFONE RINGS IN OUR HOUSE AND MY FATHER PICKS IT UP AND SAYS IN HIS VERY IMPORTANT TELLYFONE VOICE 'SIMPKINS SPEAKING'. THEN HIS FACE GOES WHITE AND HIS VOICE GOES ALL FUNNY AND HE SAYS '*WHAT! WHO?*' AND THEN HE SAYS 'YES SIR I UNDERSTAND SIR BUT SURELY IT IS *ME* YOU IS WISHING TO SPEKE TO SIR NOT MY LITTLE SON?' MY FATHER'S FACE IS GOING FROM WHITE TO DARK PURPEL AND HE IS GULPING LIKE HE HAS A LOBSTER STUCK IN HIS THROTE AND THEN AT LAST HE IS SAYING 'YES SIR VERY WELL SIR I WILL GET HIM SIR' AND HE TURNS TO ME AND HE SAYS IN A RATHER RESPECKFUL VOICE 'IS YOU KNOWING THE PRESIDENT OF THE UNITED STATES?' AND I SAYS 'NO BUT I EXPECT HE IS HEARING ABOUT ME.' THEN I IS HAVING A LONG TALK ON THE FONE AND SAYING THINGS LIKE 'LET ME TAKE CARE OF IT, MR PRESIDENT.

YOU'LL BUNGLE IT ALL UP IF YOU DO IT YOUR WAY'. AND MY FATHER'S EYES IS GOGGLING RIGHT OUT OF HIS HEAD AND THAT IS WHEN I IS HEARING MY FATHER'S REAL VOICE SAYING GET UP YOU LAZY SLOB OR YOU WILL BE LATE FOR SKOOL.

(From *The BFG* by Roald Dahl, pp. 108–9)

Suggest a plausible account for each instance of incorrect spelling in the text from *The BFG*.

5   a   Identify instances of slang and non-standard spelling in the web page on p. 231.

       b   Suggest rules that convert the non-standard spelling into standard spelling.

       c   What features, if any, does the text share with the spoken language?

       d   What motives might lie behind the non-standard spelling?

       e   Should English teachers be concerned about the examples of non-standard language that you have identified?

       f   What are your views about the use of bad language in some of the song lyrics? Should such language be banned?

[9.29]

It's on (Dr. Dre) 187um Killa

See larger picture

 Buy from Amazon.com

Our Price: $11.98

Click here for more information

FREE Super Saver Shipping on most orders over $25. See details

Used and new from $6.00

Customer Rating: ★★★★★
Availability: Usually ships in 24 hours
Search eBay for this item.

Media: Audio CD
Publisher: Ruthless (Red)
Salesrank: 30,496
UPC: 074646944523
Release Date: November 24, 1998
Artist: Eazy-E

freeiPods.com
Click Here for Your Free iPod

Tracks:
1. Exxtra Special Thankz -
2. Real Muthaphuckkin G's - Eazy-E -
3. Any Last Werdz - Eazy-E -
4. Stilla Nigga -
5. Gimmie That Nutt - Eazy-E -
6. It's On - Eazy-E -
7. Boyz-n-the Hood [Remix] [G-Mix] -
8. Down 2 tha Last Roach -

Customer Reviews:

the best eazy ★★★★★
Ok, first of all Eazy killed the doctor lyrically, but the chronic has better beats, even though this was an ep it would have been better with more tracks, and i did prefer the chronic but this cd is just as good. Here is a rundown of the tracks with marks /5
1. Exxtra Special Thankz- An intro similar to the one on the chronic, with a tighter beat 5/5
2. Real Muthaphuckkin G's- Tight beat, tight lyrics, kills dre day 5/5
3. Any Last Werdz- Bangin Track, excellent 5/5
4. Stilla Nigga- Similar to any last werdz, which is a good thing 5/5
5. Gimmie That Nutt- Hilarious, nuf said 5/5
6.- It's On- My personal favourite from the album, tight g-funk beat supplied by cold 187um 5/5
7. Boyz N Tha Hood (G-Mix)- Cold bangin remix of a classic, doesnt match the original, but that would take a miracle, still tight as f
8. Down 2 Tha Last Roach- 7+ minuites long, this is filler, but still kikin, a good track 5/5
As you can see i gave every track full markz, cos every track is bangin, this is a 100% dope record, easily rivalling the chronic and doggystyle.

Although it disses on Dre, its still a good album ★★★★☆
Okay, I am one of the biggest Dr. Dre fans on the planet, but I am also a fan of N.W.A and Gangsta Rap in general, and I have to say this album is sweet. Even though he rips on Dre in almost every song, Eazy made a great CD. The beats are all funky and give a true West Coast vibe. They're almost as good as Dre's beats--and thats saying a lot, coming from me. The best songs are "Real Muthaphuckin' G's" and "Gimme Dat Nutt." I'd have to say that this album's big flaw (the only thing keeping it from 5 stars) is that it only has 8 tracks to listen to. Another 8 would have been nice. Still, its a great album and its "eazily" one of Eazy's greatest albums.

Part IV

Modelling the mental lexicon

The final section is devoted to the role of the MENTAL LEXICON in speech processing. We consider psycholinguistic models of speech recognition in Chapter 10 and conclude with an account of models of speech production in Chapter 11.

Speech recognition

10.1 A mind full of words

We shall now consider the nature of the MENTAL LEXICON – the representation of words in the mind. There are some obvious similarities between the contents of the mental lexicon and the more familiar lexicographer's dictionaries sold in bookshops. Both must contain information about the meaning, grammatical properties, pronunciation (and orthographic representation) of an enormous number of words (see Chapter 5).

The focus in this chapter is on how that information is handled in the mental lexicon. How do we store thousands and thousands of words in the mind? How do we manage to retrieve them correctly and so effortlessly most of the time, both as speakers and as hearers? (This is an achievement that makes finding a needle in the proverbial haystack look like child's play.) How do we manage to associate correctly sound with meaning?

We will restrict ourselves to speech and exclude a detailed discussion of written language so as to keep this book within manageable proportions. The present chapter will deal with speech recognition and the next one speech production.

In speech, the matching of sound with meaning is essential for communication to happen. There would be very little successful communication if the speaker chose a word to express a certain meaning but had no idea of its pronunciation. Conversely, comprehension would not take place if the listener decoded the sounds of a word correctly but had no idea what they meant. However, by itself, a successful match of sound with meaning is not enough. It is also important for the speaker to be able to associate the chosen lexical item with the right set of morphosyntactic properties (e.g.

noun, feminine, singular, present tense, past tense, definite, indefinite etc.) and for the hearer to be able to recognise information about those grammatical properties on hearing the words. It is important, for instance, to know whether the speaker said '*He feared the dog*' or '*He fears dogs*'. The tense, definiteness and number differences between the two sentences are important. We cannot arrive at the right interpretation if they are not grasped.

10.1.1 Types of lexical information

What must a person know about words in order to be able to use them both as a speaker and as a listener?

Phonological information

The mental lexicon must indicate how words and morphemes are pronounced, e.g. *quay* is pronounced /kiː/ (see section (5.4)). In addition, lexical entries for affixes need to indicate the stratum at which they appear, since that reflects some of their properties. So, for instance, the lexicon should indicate that -*esque* and -*ian* are non-neutral suffixes. The former attracts stress to itself, as in *pictu'resque*, and the latter puts stress on the immediately preceding syllable, as in *Ca'nadian*. They contrast with a neutral suffix like -*ful*, as in *con'tainerful*, which has no effect on stress.

Furthermore, for literate speakers the grammar also needs to link orthographic with phonological representations. This is especially important in a language like English where the spelling of a word is not always a totally reliable guide to its pronunciation. Consider these examples:

[10.1] a Orthographic
representation: quay$_{(Noun)}$ key$_{(Noun)}$
Phonological
representation: /kiː/   /kiː/

   b Orthographic
representation: *read*$_{(Verb, Pres.)}$ *read*$_{(Verb, Past)}$ red$_{(Adj.)}$
Phonological
representation: /riːd/   /red/   /red/

Different letters may represent the same sound as in *key* ~ *quay* and *read* ~ *red*. Conversely, the same sequence of letters can represent different pronunciations as in the case of *read* (present tense) vs. read (past tense). Interpretative rules are needed to link orthographic words to phonological words.

Grammatical information

Grammatical information must also form part of entries in the mental lexicon. It may seem natural that *bitter* and *delicious* are adjectives because they attribute qualities or predicate states of entities. However, in some other languages, e.g. Luganda *kukaawa* and *kuwoooma*, the words which express corresponding meanings are verbs. Word-class membership is not determined by meaning; it is fixed by the conventions of a particular language. So, word-class information must be included in lexical entries.

The lexicon must also list any idiosyncratic grammatical properties of a word that do not follow from general principles. For instance, there is no way of predicting from their meanings why some verbs allow a complement clause that begins with either the infinitive marker *to* or the conjunction *that* while other verbs only allow *to*. Contrast [10.2] with [10.3]:

[10.2] a Chris expected that John would play another match.
　　　　b Chris expected John to play another match.

[10.3] a Chris persuaded John to play another match.
　　　　b *Chris persuaded that John would play another match.

So, our lexical entry for a verb will have to specify the kind of complements that a verb is allowed (Chomsky 1965, 1986).

Certain types of morphological information also have to be entered in the lexicon. For instance, some words are indigenous and others are borrowed. This may affect how they behave. Usually affixes of foreign origin have to be used with foreign loans and native affixes with native stems, which is why the plural of Greek loan *phenomenon* is *phenomena* not **phenomenons*.

Also, if a word is an exception to a general rule, we need to flag it with an exception feature in the lexicon. For instance, non-count nouns like *gold* and *jazz* have to be expressly marked as not being eligible for the plural inflection.

Meaning

Obviously, the lexicon would be of little use if it contained phonological and grammatical information but said nothing about
meaning. The whole point of having words is to be able to mean.
We look up in lexicographers' dictionaries the meanings of words
we do not know. Yet, interestingly, even the best standard dictionaries provide only a very bare and selective statement of meaning.
They are a very pale reflection of the meanings contained in the
mental lexicon. (See Fodor (1981), Hudson (1984) and Aitchison
(2003) for more detailed discussion.)

Let us consider the word *dog*. *Webster's Dictionary* says that a
dog is 'any of a large group of domesticated animals belonging to
the same family as the fox, wolf, jackal, etc.', but your mental representation of 'dog' is much more elaborate. It includes all sorts of
information – that the prototypical dog is like a Labrador rather
than a Great Dane or chihuahua; that it barks; that it is carnivorous; that it can be a good companion or a fierce guard; that dog
mess is an urban hazard; and that *dog* normally collocates with (i.e.
occurs in the company of) words like bark, walk, eat, bite, puppy,
lead and not with rhyme, equation, sing etc.

By contrast, the specification of the meaning of a word in a lexicographer's dictionary tends to convey the most salient aspects of
its cognitive meaning and to omit important aspects like other words
to which it is related, its semantic associations and connotations,
and its typical collocations (see sections (6.1) and (10.4.1)).

In sum, both the mental lexicon and the lexicographer's dictionary
must contain orthographic, phonological, grammatical and semantic
information. The various kinds of information outlined here must
be instantaneously retrievable by both speakers and hearers from
their mental lexicon.

10.1.2 The organisation of the mental lexicon

The similarities between the mental lexicon and the lexicographer's
lexicon are important. But so are the differences. The mental lexicon
differs in at least two important ways: in structure and in content.

Whereas lexicographers' dictionaries list words alphabetically, we
do not keep words in an alphabetical list in the mind. That is why
it is extremely unlikely that a speech error would involve mistak-
enly retrieving a word starting with a letter near that found at the

start of the target word in an alphabetical dictionary. We do not find slips of the tongue like *He broke the jaw (meaning He broke the law).

The mind is crammed all the way up to the rafters with words. Soon after the age of two, the average infant has a vocabulary of more than 200 words. By age seven, the figure has risen to over 1,300 words. Oldfield (1963) estimated that the average Oxford undergraduate has a vocabulary of about 75,000 words. Other studies (see Seashore and Eckerson (1940); Diller (1978)) claim that a college-educated adult's mental lexicon may range from a conservative but still very substantial 50,000–250,000 words. The estimates vary widely in part due to a number of methodological difficulties. There are problems in agreeing on what units count as distinct words. There are also problems in determining what 'knowing a word' means and so on.

But everyone agrees that the mental lexicon is vast. So how does the mind store all those words? Our starting assumption is that words are stored in a very orderly manner in the mind. Without your mental lexicon being very systematically organised you would have a better chance of finding the proverbial needle in a haystack than of finding the word you wanted. We have thousands and thousands of words in our minds and yet we are able to find them in a flash. If they were all piled in the mind like old clothes on a jumble sale table, it would take hours, if not days, to find the right word.

Human memory works most efficiently when it deals with structured information rather than a pot-pourri of facts and information. You can verify this by reading and trying to remember the same telephone number presented in two ways, in [10.4a] and in [10.4b]:

[10.4] a (254) 326–4121
        b 2543264121

Although the same digits are presented to you in both cases, they are not equally easy to remember. It is much easier to recall [10.4a], where the area code (254) is bracketed off and the district code 326 is separated from the specific account number (4121) (see Gregg 1986). It is reasonable to assume that the speed of lexical retrieval is possible only because lexical information is highly structured in the mind. So, just finding the correct word time after time (never mind making sense, which we manage to do as well a good bit of the time) is a great accomplishment. (See also p. 276 in Chapter 11.)

10.2 Modelling the mental lexicon

Models of the mental lexicon fall into two broad types: those that have attempted to characterise words in the mind from the speaker's perspective and those that have done so from the hearer's perspective. The former have attempted to represent speech production and the latter speech comprehension. In this chapter we consider models that focus on how we perceive speech. (For a solid textbook providing a more detailed discussion of the language processing issues outlined in this book see Harley (2001).)

10.2.1 Morphological parsing

One of the topics that have attracted a lot of interest is the mental storage and retrieval of morphologically complex words. In this chapter we only deal with successful retrieval (speech errors are discussed in the next chapter). The literature on this subject is quite extensive. I summarise the main issues below drawing on the survey by Hankamer (1989).

One model of the way in which words are stored in the mind is that of Taft and Foster (1975), which was refined by Taft (1979, 1981). In this model roots (including bound ones) and prefixes are stored separately in the mind: complex words are not stored in a pre-assembled state. Word recognition crucially involves MORPHO-LOGICAL PARSING. According to Taft and Foster, the dictionary in the mind engages in PREFIX STRIPPING, a process where a word is parsed and all the prefixes are identified. This is followed by looking up the root in the dictionary. Stanners *et al.* (1979) took the logical step of extending the same model to inflectional suffixes. This is the model that has been loosely assumed and implicitly used so far in this book.

10.2.2 The Full Listing Hypothesis

An alternative model, and one that has won the approval of most psycholinguists, is that of Butterworth (1983). It is called the Full Listing Hypothesis (FLH). Advocates of FLH assume that familiar words are entered in the lexicon already fully assembled, but if confronted with unfamiliar words, one might resort to parsing. Routinely, speech recognition need not entail any morphological parsing. In other words, normally there is no affix stripping.

There are two versions of FLH. Version 1 assumes full listing, with information of morphologically complex entries spelt out. A complex word like *recovering* is listed, complete with its morphological analysis. So it would appear in the lexicon as (re(cover)ing). Version 2 of FLH assumes that every word has a separate entry in the dictionary. But the entries of related complex words are linked as SATELLITES forming part of a constellation whose nucleus is a simple un-affixed bound root or word (see Bradley 1978, 1980; Bybee 1987). For example, the dictionary would indicate that there is the word *cover* which functions as the nucleus of the constellation containing the satellites listed in [10.5]

[10.5] cover	covers	covering	coverings
covered	uncover	uncovers	uncovered
recovered	recovering	coverable	recoverable
recovery	uncovering	recoverability	

As already mentioned, parsing is not entirely ruled out in this model. Butterworth (1983) suggests that it is resorted to, *in extremis*, when a hearer needs to cope with a novel or unfamiliar word such as *Lebanonisation* or *deprofessionalisation*.

Frequency has an important place in this model (see section (11.3.1)). It is the key factor that affects how long people take to process a word. No processing difference is expected depending on whether a word is a simple, unaffixed form or a complex form that can be decomposed into a stem and one or more affixes. So, for example, it is expected that a very frequent word like *sitting* which contains an affix should be processed faster than the less frequent word *satin* that contains no affix.

A theme that has run through this book is that listing of totally unpredictable lexical items is essential. But many lexical items are compositional and hence not unpredictable. Such items need not be listed in the lexicon. FLH takes the opposite view and assumes that the morphological parser is used sparingly: listing of pre-assembled words is the norm. I am inclined to disagree. In the remainder of this section, following Hankamer (1989), I will argue that FLH is not an entirely plausible model of how to produce or recognise words, especially in the case of an AGGLUTINATING language where words are formed by chaining together many morphemes, as in the Turkish word *ev-ler-imiz-de* (house-plural-our-in) which means 'in our houses' (see [10.6]).

Hankamer examines the morphological complexity of Turkish, a typical agglutinating language. He shows that the number of word-forms corresponding to a single lexeme is so large that, even assuming that a speaker has a very modest word-hoard, it is simply impossible that they would have the storage space to store the billions of word-forms they know. This is how Hankamer puts it:

> It seems that agglutinative morphology is even more productive than has been thought. Given a lexicon containing 20,000 noun roots and 10,000 verb roots, which does not seem unreasonable for an educated speaker of Turkish, the FLH would require over 200 billion entries. Furthermore, most of the entries would necessarily be complex, and thus would take up significant storage space in the human brain.
>
> (Hankamer 1989: 403)

Hankamer shows that this is what the word-cluster containing some of the satellites of the nucleus *ev* 'house' would look like:

[10.6] ev   'house'
       evler   'houses'
       evlerimiz   'our houses'
       evlerimizde   'in our houses'
       evlerimizdeki   'the one in our houses'
       evlerimizdekiler   'the ones in our houses'
       evlerimizdekilerin   'of the ones in our houses'
       evlerimizdekilerinki   'the one of (belonging to) the ones in
                                     our houses'

We have here already eight forms, some of them quite complex, without going through all the grammatical cases and without listing the various persons (*my*, *your*, *her* etc.). Since house is pretty much an everyday word, presumably it would have to reside permanently in the mental lexicon, all pre-assembled. That would require a lot of storage space.

The storage implications make the FLH untenable. The human brain is estimated by Sagan (1985) to have a storage capacity of 12,500,000,000,000 (12.5 billion) bytes. This estimate is based on the number of neurons in the brain. If the storage of a fairly simple word takes, say, 10 bytes (and that of complex words like *evlerimizdekilerinki* requires considerably more), it would be possible to store a maximum of 125 billion word-forms. And that would only be possible if the brain was exclusively dedicated to storing words. Since at a conservative estimate educated speakers of Turkish would need to store 200 billion word-forms, the FLH model fails to account for how these speakers manage to list the words they know. But, of course, a bigger problem is the fact that, even to cope with the lower figure of 125 billion words, the FLH would need to make the absurd assumption that our Turkish speaker uses the brain exclusively as a word-store.

While conceding that the FLH cannot work for Turkish, one might say that as English is not an agglutinating language like Turkish (we established in Chapter 3 that English is essentially an isolating language), there is no reason to be pessimistic about the chances of the FLH accounting for the storage of English words in the mind. The problem is that English does have a sizeable number of words, many of them not rare by any means, which contain several affixes. When we listed the satellites of the nucleus *cover* in [10.5], we stopped at 14 word-forms. We could have gone on. In this respect *cover* is not particularly unusual. Clearly, even in English there is quite a big number of agglutinative words. If we take the vocabulary of an educated speaker, any attempt to apply the FLH would mean listing millions of word-forms, many of them quite complex, in the mental lexicon. Again the pressure this would exert on storage space would be intolerable.

If the human mind is equipped with a morphological parsing device to cope with extensive agglutinating languages like Turkish, there is no reason to assume that it cannot be turned on whenever the need arises to deal with morphologically complex words in a language like English. Given the existence of words like those in [10.5], it is reasonable to assume that morphological parsing is needed fairly often in English.

Marslen-Wilson *et al.* (1994) conducted an important study of how words are recognised. These psychologists set up six experiments in which they probed the processing of morphologically complex words in English. The aim of that study was to see whether lexical entries of words containing derivational prefixes and suffixes were actually decomposed by English speakers and whether they had some awareness of the morphological structure of such words. If evidence of morphological decomposition was unearthed, they wanted to know if it showed a correlation with the semantic and phonological transparency of the surface relationship between the stem and the affix.

Their findings were interesting. It was clear that speakers parse words that are semantically transparent. Furthermore, where the meaning of the complex word is transparent, the parsing is done regardless of whether the form is phonologically transparent (as *wash-able, govern-ment* etc.) or phonologically opaque in that the base is modified when the affix is added, as in *negotiate ~ negoti-able* (**negoti(ate)-able*) or *tenacious ~ tenacity* (**tenaci(ous)-ity*). This suggests that morphemic representations are phonologically abstract. So, phonological complications do not get in the way. By contrast, semantically opaque forms (e.g. *fragment, lemonade*), are regarded as unanalysable monomorphemic words despite the fact that they are phonologically transparent (*frag-ment, lemon-ade* etc.).

10.3 Speech recognition

What part is played by the mental lexicon in speech comprehension? Marslen-Wilson provides this answer:

> The role of the mental lexicon in human speech comprehension is to mediate between two fundamentally distinct representational and computational domains: the acoustic-phonetic analysis of the incoming speech signal, and the syntactic and semantic interpretation of the message being communicated.
>
> (1989: 3)

Marslen-Wilson observes that the central problem in speech recognition is that the hearer is simultaneously faced with two tasks. One task is decoding the acoustic signal that hits the eardrums; the other task is untangling the higher levels of word meaning, grammatical structure, sentence meaning and the meaning that the speaker intended to convey. In other words, the task is one of deciphering noises and attaching meanings to them. As we noted above, just the ability to do this is in itself remarkable. What is even more amazing is the speed with which it is done. Normally, we understand speech instantaneously. When someone says something to us, we do not go away for half an hour and do all the necessary acoustic-phonetic computations, followed afterwards by the syntactic-semantic analysis before coming up with an interpretation. Native speakers of English have been shown to be able to recognise a word within about one fifth of a second from the moment the speaker begins uttering it. If all goes well, in normal conversation you literally figure out the words and their meaning before they are out of your interlocutor's mouth. On average, words are recognised in context 200 milliseconds from the moment the speaker utters the first sound of the word, even though at that point there are insufficient auditory clues to identify the word (Marslen-Wilson 1987, 1989). Clearly, sensory input plays a role in identifying the words heard, but it is not the only factor. The listener must be able to use other means. A lot of intelligent guessing goes on. A particular auditory cue is tested for goodness of fit in the linguistic and non-linguistic context. With the minimal phonetic clues obtained in the first 200 milliseconds, which word is most likely to make sense?

10.3.1 Phonetic and phonological decoding

Let us take a closer look at the acoustic decoding task first. To recognise a word it helps if one can identify the individual sounds which represent that word. So, the hearer goes through a PHONETIC STAGE. This involves the identification of noises. To this end, the hearer looks out for the acoustic clues which help to identify segments. For instance, to identify the first two sounds in the word *spin* the hearer, among other things, detects the turbulence of the fricative [s] and the fact that it is followed by a stop. It is quite likely that initially it will be impossible to determine whether the stop is [p] or [b] because acoustically it will be very unclear which it is.

The next stage in sound Recognition is the PHONOLOGICAL STAGE. It is at this stage that it will become clear that the sound in question is /p/, not /b/. If you are a speaker of English, you know how sounds in your language function. You know the phonotactic constraints on the positions where sounds can appear:

1   You know that, if a word-initial fricative is followed by a stop, that fricative must be /s/. Only /s/ is allowed to occur at the beginning of a word if the second sound of the word is a consonant. No English word can begin with /zk/, /fm/, /fk/ etc.
2   You also know that, if the word begins with /s/ and the sound following /s/ is a stop, that stop must be voiceless. There are words like *spin, spoon, stick, skin* etc. where /s/ is followed by a voiceless stop. But there are no words like **sbin, *sboon, *sdick* or **sgin* where /s/ is followed by a voiced stop. This is a phonotactic constraint on the combination of fricatives with

stops in English phonology. It is not something simply determined by their acoustic properties. If the /s/ of *spin* is electronically spliced, you would probably hear the word left behind as [bɪn], not [pɪn]. Why is this? It is because the main cue for distinguishing between [p] and [b] occurring initially in a stressed syllable is aspiration. If you detect aspiration, you assume it is [pʰ]; if you do not you assume it is [b]. As the sound in *spin* was preceded by /s/ before splicing off the [s], it was not initial and so it was unaspirated. So it is perceived as [b]. Obviously, linguistic knowledge of this kind, this COMPETENCE, lies hidden deep in the mind and you are unlikely to be conscious of it without taking a course in linguistics.

10.3.2 The role of high-level information

Understanding speech is not simply a matter of attending to phonetic and phonological detail. Ganong (1980) provided experimental evidence showing that speech recognition depends crucially on high-level information about a word. Participants in the experiment were given ambiguous auditory stimuli that in themselves were inadequate to identify whether the initial sound in a word was /p/ or /b/ at the start of forms like *-eace* [-iːs] vs. *eef* [-iːf]. Despite receiving an ambiguous auditory signal, the participants in the experiment did not perceive the words as **beace* and **peef*, but rather as the real English words *peace* and *beef*. This suggests that judging the goodness of fit between the auditory signals that impinge on our ear drums and the actual words stored in the mental lexicon plays a significant role in deciphering speech.

Cognitive psychologists have also shown experimentally the important role played by context in the PHONEME RESTORATION EFFECT, which bolsters the claim that the identification of sounds goes beyond individual sounds. Warren and Warren (1970) conducted a fascinating study entitled 'Auditory illusions and confusions'. They carried out experiments in which participants listened to tapes with sets of sentences which were identical in every respect, apart from the last word. The sentences had been doctored. A sound in one word had been replaced by the noise of a cough (shown by an asterisk) in **eel* ([iːl]):

[10.7] a It was found that the *eel was on the orange.
       b It was found that the *eel was on the axle.

c It was found that the *eel was on the shoe.
d It was found that the *eel was on the table.

The extraneous noise did not impede word recognition. The participants restored the masked phoneme and identified the words correctly as (a) *peel*, (b) *wheel*, (c) *heel* and (d) *meal*.

How did they do it? To restore the masked sound, they used the semantic information provided by the last word. Interestingly, the listeners did not even notice that they had not actually heard the masked phoneme. This finding contrasted with a finding in an earlier study by Broadbent and Ladefoged (1960) in which an extraneous brief noise in the form of a click or hiss was introduced in utterances without masking any of the phonemes. In these cases the participants were not fooled. They spotted the intrusive sound and no phoneme restoration occurred.

Listening is an active, not a passive activity. The perception of continuous speech is not a simple matter of deciphering raw noises that impinge on the eardrums. The classic example of SELECTIVE LISTENING is the so-called 'cocktail party phenomenon' where the listener's role in creating meaning is vital. You can choose to home in on a specific conversation when a dozen loud conversations are going on in the room. This shows the importance of selection. The listener constructs meaning from a specific set of auditory signals – and ignores the rest.

Psychologists have explored the nature of selective listening by usung SHADOWING experiments where participants repeat instantaneously a taped utterance, word for word, as they listen to it. Meanwhile, the participants listen simultaneously, in one ear, to another message which they are told to ignore. The experiment is set up in such a way that the two messages that are listened to are equally clear and have the same tempo and volume.

In these experiments people easily manage to focus on the utterance that they are shadowing and to ignore the utterance that they are not shadowing. They might not even notice that the utterance which they are not shadowing is in a foreign language, or whether the speaker was a man or a woman (Cherry 1953).

We have established that there is no one-to-one match between acoustic-phonetic cues and the phonological interpretation we give them. What is perceived as the 'same' sound is not physically the same sound in all contexts. Very much depends on the context in which the auditory cues are perceived and on what we know to be permissible in that context in the language.

10.3.3 Relevance theory

Clearly, the perception of individual speech sounds is far from straightforward. But the perception of running speech presents an even greater challenge. A major problem (which people are most acutely aware of when listening to a language in which they have little competence) is that, in fluent speech, words come out in a gushing stream. In purely physical terms, it is normally impossible to hear where one word ends and the next one begins. Looking up each word in the mental lexicon as it is heard is not a credible strategy.

But even if it were possible to separate out words, which clearly it is not, there would be the additional problem of NOISE, in a very broad sense. In many real-life situations, there is not a perfect hush around us as we speak or listen. There is noise. In a pub, at a party, at work, in a railway station or in the home, there are often other people talking, banging, operating noisy machines, playing loud music etc. So, we hear some of the words only partially – if at all. Yet we manage to work out what the other person is saying. How do we do it? Knowing what is relevant in the context helps. We can make intelligent guesses.

In cases where we communicate using almost fixed formulas, GUESSING is relatively easy. Imagine you drop in at a friend's house at 11 a.m. and, shortly after welcoming you, your host says:

[10.8] Would you like *** or ***?

You do not hear the bits marked by asterisks because a loud heavy goods lorry goes past the open window as she says ***. I expect you would have no problem guessing that the words you did not hear were *tea* and *coffee*. Experience tells you that in this situation they are the most likely words to be used.

The notion of RELEVANCE plays a prominent role in speech understanding in the theory of pragmatics called Relevance Theory (Sperber and Wilson 1995). A relevant utterance is one that delivers fresh information or supports a proposition that is still being entertained in a conversation. If we are in a particular situation, and can determine what is relevant in that situation, we can discard some of the possible words we might think we hear. We can also reject homophonous words which are inappropriate in the circumstances, and select the more plausible, relevant word:

[10.9] [vɪkəz ər ən straɪk]

If you live in the English shipbuilding town of Barrow, where most of the working population are employed in weapons factories and the shipyard belonging to Vickers, the defence company, and you have seen a very militant crowd of protestors, a thousand strong, demonstrating outside the gate of the shipyard, you would probably recognise the first word as referring to workers at *Vickers*, the arms manufacturer and not the dog-collared *vicars* from the town's churches. Your interpretation would also be steered in the right direction by knowledge that priests do not strike and that, even if they did, they could not muster a crowd of more than a dozen or so people (since there are not that many churches), and that, even if demonstrating priests' numbers could be augmented by flying pickets from other towns, their demonstration would probably be meek rather than militant. So, you use your world knowledge to eliminate *vicars*. Context and relevance are vitally important when the meaning of the words perceived is to some extent unclear.

10.3.4 Psycholinguistic models of context

In the study of lexical retrieval, lexical ambiguity (see section (6.4.4)) has been a focal point and there are psycholinguistic models of ambiguous word-processing that would support the claims for relevance made above. Advocates of CONTEXT-DEPENDENT models (Simpson 1984; Gluksberg *et al.* 1986) hypothesise that, when an ambiguous word occurs (as in the case of [vɪkəz] above), only the one meaning that is appropriate in that context is activated in the mental lexicon.

However, there is an alternative approach which claims that the initial activation of the words stored in the mental lexicon is CONTEXT-INDEPENDENT. This model claims that it is relative frequency, not relevance, that triggers the initial activation of the meaning of a particular word. A more frequent lexical item (e.g. *key* is retrieved first) is immediately rejected if it turns out to be inappropriate (as in *The houseboat was stolen from the quay* [ðə haʊsbəʊt wəz stəʊlən frɒm ðə kiː]). A less frequent form, in this case *quay* (which is the appropriate word) is then accessed. If there is multiple ambiguity, this process may be repeated many times before the right word is finally retrieved. But, normally, retrieving the most frequent meaning will yield the right word for the context (see Hogaboam and Perfetti 1975).

A third theory, the MULTIPLE ACCESS MODEL (Tanenhaus and Lucas 1987) deduces from the evidence surveyed that syntactic context does not normally influence prelexical processing. Rather, all meanings of an ambiguous word are activated without taking into account either the context where the word occurs or its relative frequency in the language. After all meanings have been activated, the meaning that is most appropriate in the context is then selected.

10.3.5 Exploiting syntactic and semantic clues

Do you have a friend or acquaintance who has that most infuriating habit of finishing your sentences for you? Both the syntactic and semantic aspects of the utterance may be so predictable that the listener knows what you are going to say even before the words come out:

[10.10] *A*: Do you know what? She has threatened to . . .
         B: . . . sue the police.

The syntactic semantic context plays a role in speech comprehension. Listeners use frames provided by the syntax to retrieve a word with the appropriate meaning from the mental lexicon.

This is easily seen in the handling of ANAPHORIC EXPRESSIONS (i.e. grammatical elements that refer back to something already mentioned), which are only interpretable in a specific syntactic context. To interpret anaphoric expressions the hearer must be able to identify the element that has already been mentioned and which is being referred back to. Imagine reading the following sentence in a recipe book:

[10.11] Add cream to the meat casserole and leave *it* in the oven for 10 minutes.

How do you work out what *it* refers to? In this sentence *it* could conceivably refer to the *meat* or the *cream*. But you do not even consider the *cream*. This sentence is not ambiguous. Our knowledge of the world rules out the *cream*. It would be crazy to leave the cream cooking in the oven. But it is reasonable to leave *meat* cooking in a casserole in the oven.

A similar point can be made with regard to STRUCTURAL AMBIGUITY (i.e. situations where a string of words has different interpretations depending on how we group together the words following the verb) (see section (6.7)). Let us consider the example in [10.12a]:

[10.12] a I bought some new shirts and jumpers.
         b [some new shirts and jumpers]$_{NP}$
         c [some new shirts]$_{NP}$ and [jumpers]$_{NP}$

The sentence can be paraphrased as 'I bought some shirts and jumpers all of which were new', in which case words are bracketed as one NP as shown in [10.12b] or, 'I bought some new shirts and some jumpers which may not be new'. This latter interpretation is reflected in the parsing in [10.12c] where we have two distinct NPs. Clearly, in some situations comprehension is impossible without correct parsing. In order to understand speech, the listener needs to work out which words go together syntactically as part of the process of determining the meaning of an utterance.

Sometimes, parsing is complicated. The listener makes a provisional analysis which has to be revised immediately as more information becomes available. A key feature of the speech comprehension process is the way in which listeners constantly update and revise their putative analyses. Nowhere is this clearer than in the analysis of so-called GARDEN PATH SENTENCES. These sentences metaphorically lead you down the garden path. You start doing a parse that looks plausible, but it turns out to be flawed when you get more information:

[10.13] a After taking the *right* turn at the lights, we rejoined the highway.
         b After taking the *right* turn at the lights, we rejoined the highway, but soon we realised that it was the wrong turn.

The sentence in [10.13a] is ambiguous. *Right turn* may mean 'right-hand turn' or 'correct turn'. You need more information to resolve the ambiguity. If the sentence continued as in [10.13b], you would realise that *right* is to be interpreted as 'right-hand' rather than 'correct'.

How much of a sentence does a listener need to hear in order to be able to make intelligent guesses? Not a lot. I suspect that as soon as you hear '*but*' you immediately suspect that *right* does not mean 'correct' here. Everything that comes after that confirms your guess.

The point is driven home by this famous example of a garden path:

[10.14] The horse raced past the barn fell.

This sentence is as clumsy as it is bizarre. Working out its meaning requires a number of attempts at syntactic analysis and semantic interpretation. *The horse raced past the barn* would be a problem-free sentence. This is the interpretation that initially springs to mind. But the verb *fell* at the end jolts us. It looks as if it should go with *the barn fell*. But that would make a nonsense of the whole sentence. So, we go back to the drawing board. This time we interpret *The horse raced past the barn* as a reduced relative clause which we paraphrase as *The horse that was raced past the barn fell*. And it works – which goes to show that syntactic parsing is done and updated continually by the listener in the light of inferences that make sense. Speech comprehension is not simply a matter of associating sounds with the meanings of words.

Two types of structural ambiguity are recognised, namely LOCAL AMBIGUITY and GLOBAL AMBIGUITY. The former type of ambiguity evaporates once the sentence is heard in its entirety, but the latter persists even after the entire sentence has been heard.

Consider 'The wise plan . . .' in [10.15]:

[10.15]   a   The wise plan$_{(Noun)}$ impressed everyone.
            b   The wise plan$_{(Verb)}$ carefully for their children's education.

As seen in [10.15], *plan* can be a noun or a verb. Until you hear what follows, you do not know how 'The wise plan . . .' is to be interpreted. But it is not necessary to hear the whole sentence before you know which interpretation is appropriate. Garden path sentences typically involve local ambiguity.

By contrast, in cases of global ambiguity, you are none the wiser even after hearing the whole sentence. Consider [10.16]:

[10.16]   a   Hamish loves fast cars more than his wife.
            b   She has worked with more talented people than you.

Both of the readings in [10.17a, b] remain viable even after the entire sentence in each case has been processed:

[10.17]   a   'Hamish loves fast cars more than he loves his wife' or
                'Hamish loves fast cars more than his wife does.'
            b   'She has worked with more talented people than you
                have done' or 'She has worked with people who are
                more talented than you.'

These are examples of global ambiguity whose resolution requires more contextual information. We are all both speakers and hearers.

10.4 Speech recognition models

Speech recognition is a field of inquiry which is model-driven to a very large extent. Some major models are presented in this section of the chapter. But, before we consider them, it will be useful to highlight the factors that affect speech recognition which any model must take into account.

10.4.1 Factors influencing speech recognition

There is broad agreement about the factors that influence speech recognition. A key factor already alluded to is FREQUENCY. High-frequency words are easier to identify than low-frequency words (e.g. *drink* vs. *imbibe*). Frequency, however, has to be considered in context as it interacts with other parameters. One of these is the phonological environment. High-frequency words are easier to recognise when they appear near low-frequency words which they resemble (e.g. *life* – *rife*; *took* – *rook* etc.) and conversely low-frequency words are more difficult to recognise if they are in the company of high-frequency lookalikes (e.g. *dimple* – *simple*, *left* – *deft* etc.)

Certain other phonological properties are also important. For example, short words are easier to recognise than longer words (e.g. *show* vs. *demonstrate*). Phonologically unique words (e.g. *igloo*, *zebra*) are easier to recognise than words with numerous look-alikes (e.g. *pan*, *plan*, *plank*, *plant*, *plantation*, *plantain*, *planet* etc.).

Against all that has to be set the role of pragmatic context. A rare word may have a high degree of probability of occurring in a particular situation which makes it easier to recognise. For instance, 'sporran' may be a rare word, but in the context of *Archibald bought a new sporran to go with his kilt* it is easy to recognise 'sporran' as soon as you hear the initial /s/ phoneme if you know that a Scotsman wearing a kilt is likely to have sporran as an accessory.

Collocation also can counter the effect of infrequency. *Addled* is an uncommon word. But it is very common if the next word is *egg* as in *addled egg*. *Bow* may not be all that frequent, but it is very common in collocation with *arrow* as in *bow and arrow*; and *row* is likely to occur with *boat* rather than *bike* etc.

Syntactic environment may also mitigate the effects of low frequency: it is easier to recognise a word when it is used in the context of a sentence than it is to recognise a word uttered in isolation, as collocation increases the probability of certain lexical choices. Thus, though *parsnip* is a low-frequency word, it is easy to recognise it in a sentence like *They had roast beef, potatoes and parsnips for lunch*. A higher frequency word like *parcel* would not be a likely lexical choice in the context of a meal.

Finally, there are two other factors that are obvious and require no comment. Familiarity with the accent and the voice of the speaker facilitates word recognition; clear diction aids speech recognition and mumbled speech hampers it.

Models have a central place in the study of speech processing. While there is a consensus about the broad range of factors that influence speech recognition, there is less agreement about how speech recognition should be modelled. A number of speech recognition models have been proposed over the years.

An early model was TEMPLATE MATCHING. This model claimed that speech recognition was essentially a matter of matching the words and phrases that are heard with templates of target words stored in the mental lexicon; the assumption being that each word or phrase is stored as a separate template and each template is an exact phonological representation of a word. The hearer selects the template that best matches each word in the utterance heard, performing a word-by-word comparison of the speech sample with stored targets. There is a predetermined level of divergence with the target that triggers the rejection of a word as a bad match.

It did not take long before problems with this model were pointed out. First, given the fact that the store of words is indefinitely large (see the discussion of the Full Listing Hypothesis in section (10.2.2.)), it is not plausible to assume that all the words one knows are stored in the mental lexicon with their phonological representations fully specified.

Moreover, variation in the manifestation of words makes the idea of using target words in the mind untenable. The physical acoustic signal emitted when words are uttered varies enormously. There is no way that anyone could store templates for all the sounds that correspond exactly to the ways in which a particular word is produced by a single speaker on different occasions, let alone the ways in which the same word is produced by speakers of different dialects, genders, ages etc. in different situations.

Another early model of speech recognition was ANALYSIS BY SYNTHESIS (see Halle and Stevens 1962; Studdert-Kennedy 1974, 1976; Stevens and House 1972). Its proponents claim that hearers recognise speech sounds uttered by speakers by matching them with speech sounds that are synthesised in their heads. Specifically, the synthesising is said to involve modelling the articulatory gestures that the speaker makes to produce those sounds. In the light of what was said above concerning the incredible speed of word recognition, it is implausible to expect hearers to perform the analysis by synthesis routine. So, many reject this model.

Three models that have gained currency more recently are the Cohort model, proposed by Marslen-Wilson and Welsh (1978); Marslen-Wilson (1989, 1990), TRACE, presented by McClelland and Elman (1986), and SHORTLIST (Norris 1994).

10.4.2 The Cohort model

The model focuses on the fact that speech is recognised in real time. As we listen to speech, we draw up a COHORT, i.e. a list of all candidates that the word we hear might be (see [10.19]). For most forms life in the cohort is brief. As more evidence becomes available the field is narrowed. The process begins with the identification of the initial part of the word being processed and progresses linearly through its syllables. This aspect of the process is bottom-up, going from phonetic input to phonological properties and subsequently to grammar and meaning. Initially, the most frequent forms are lined up in the cohort, focusing on sound without regard to syntactic or semantic appropriateness. Later the top-down approach is activated. Forms that are grammatically, semantically or pragmatically inappropriate are eliminated, as more of the word is processed more and more of the candidates in the cohort are eliminated. Eventually, the right word is the only candidate left. For instance /s/ could lead to the marshalling of a cohort containing words like those in [10.18a]. If the next sound is /k/ all the candidates apart from those whose initial syllable has an onset containing the phonemes /sk/ would be eliminated (as in [10.18b]); and so on till *scram-* was reached. That is the point at which the recognition point is reached. The only word remaining in the cohort would be *scramble*.

[10.18] a /s/   see, so, sit, sun, sky soap sap sale, speed,
                     skate, swim, slender, ski, step, seal snip,
                     snake, smarmy, scribe, scrap, scratch,
                     scrabble, scramble, school, screw,
                     scrumptious psycho, squeal, scope etc.
       b /sk/   school, sky, skip, screw, scrumptious,
                     scrap, scratch, scrabble, scribe, scramble,
                     scroll, squeal, scope etc.
       c /skr/   scribe, screw, scrumptious, scrap, scratch,
                     scrabble, scramble, scroll
       d /skræ/   scrap, scratch, scrabble, scramble
          /skræm/ scramble

[10.19]

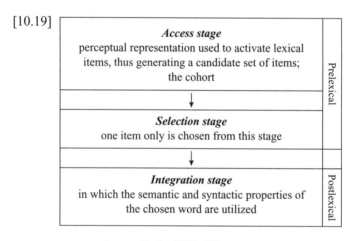

Source: Harley (2001: 229)

Later, in response to criticism based on empirical findings from experimental studies, the theory was modified. The original 1978 version had allowed context to influence the initial consideration of candidates at the access stage. However, experimental evidence showed that this was not the case. So, the revised 1987 version gives context a diminished role in that it is not involved in the initial activation that first marshals the cohort. It only plays a part at the selection stage after phonetically plausible candidates have been identified.

In the original version of the theory a form was always either 100 per cent a candidate or not at all a candidate, with no gradation of candidature allowed. Any failed candidates were swiftly ejected from the cohort. However, in the 1987 version a more relaxed view was taken. Non-optimum candidates were allowed to linger after they had been activated until it became very clear, as more evidence became available, that they were incompatible with the requirements of the slot that they were being considered for. This took care of the fact that listeners constantly update their lexical searches as more evidence becomes available and what might have appeared a non-optimum candidate might turn out to be the word that is eventually selected.

Some problems still remain. For instance, identifying the first segment of a word is crucial in getting a cohort assembled. This turns out not to be a trivial task. In connected speech there are no gaps between words. Words overlap due to processes such as elision and assimilation (e.g. *Fay's handbag* /feɪz hænd bæg/ → /feɪz hæn bæg/ → [feɪz hambæg]). No reliable procedure for identifying where words begin has been found yet.

10.4.3 The TRACE and SHORTLIST models

The TRACE model is a highly interactive connectionist activation network model of spoken word recognition that was proposed by McClelland and Elman (1986). CONNECTIONISM is a model that is widely employed by psychologists and other cognitive scientists. There are a number of important features of connectionism that should be noted at the outset:

1   it uses a battery of simple processing units that are arranged in hierarchical levels;
2   its advocates make intensive use of computer simulations implementing the theory;
3   it assumes that knowledge is acquired through the inductive learning of statistical patterns that emerge from the data rather than by mastering a set of rigid, categorical rules.

TRACE employs a vast number of simple processing units that are joined together by two-way connections that allow information to flow in both directions (see [10.20]). The entire network of units is referred to as the TRACE. Incoming information activates processing units in one unit and activation spreads along the connections to other units. Activation makes units live just like turning on the electric current does.

[10.20] The TRACE model

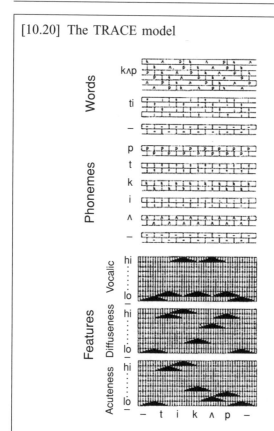

FIG. 2. A subset of the units in TRACE II. Each rectangle represents a different unit. The labels indicate the item for which the unit stands, and the horizontal edges of the rectangle indicate the portion of the Trace spanned by each unit. The input feature specifications for the phrase "tea cup," preceded and followed by silence, are indicated for the three illustrated dimensions by the blackening of the corresponding feature units.

Source: J. M. McClelland and J. L. Elman (1986) 'The TRACE model of speech perception', *Cognitive Psychology* 18: 9.

The theory envisages processing units organised on three levels: the DISTINCTIVE FEATURE level that deals with sub-phonemic units of contrast in phonology (e.g. [+nasal], [–voice] etc.), the PHONEME level and the WORD level. Each unit in a TRACE (see [10.20])

represents some object (e.g. feature or phoneme) that is perceived
as an element of the utterance. The units are rolled out in linear
sequence in real time.

The importance of frequency is fully recognised. The threshold
of activation that has to be reached before an element is recognised
depends on its frequency. In other words the more frequent a word
is the faster it is in getting activated. It is also acknowledged that
the phonemes at the start of a word are particularly important in
getting a word activated. In addition, the model allows information
to flow in both directions. Both bottom-up and top-down information is used to activate units. This makes it possible for top-down
information (e.g. context) to influence the activation of lower-level
units (features and phonemes). But it is not assumed that all
processing is top-down. As well as making use of pragmatic contextual information, for example, it is also possible to make use of raw
phonetic input in the signal while processing contextual information.
Consider the words in [10.21]:

[10.21] plan   plank   planimetry
        plant   plantain   plangent
        planet   plankton   Plantagenet

When as you hear speech, words compete with each other for activation. Activation is cyclic. It cycles around in the network until
the activation of a given word rises above a threshold. And the
competition to be activated is fierce and only the fittest survives.
When you hear a word starting with /pl/, *plan*, *plant* and *planet* will
have the edge as they are more frequent than their rivals. They will
be strongly activated very early, with *plank* not too far behind. The
activation of the less frequent words such as *Plantagenet* and
planimetry (assuming you have them in your lexicon) will happen
later and will be feeble.

To account for this it is assumed that connections between units
at the same level have an inhibitory effect: they hamper or even
stall other connections at that level. The strong activation of *plan*
and *planet* will drown out the activation of the weakly activated
forms. But the opposite is true of connections between units on
different levels. They have an excitatory effect – they stimulate
the flow of information. So, if /pl .../ appears in the context
of astronomy, the activation of *planet* will be strengthened; but if
the context is one of architecture it will be *plan* that will receive

the boost. There is a virtuous circle: words that are activated reinforce the activation of their component phonemes. Eventually only one candidate survives and that is the word that is recognised.

It is generally accepted that the TRACE model is very good at handling context effects in spoken word recognition. Its strength is that it is a bi-directional bottom-up and top-down model. It is able to handle variability in the acoustic input and the robustness of the recognition system seen in facts like the phoneme restoration effects, because acoustic signals that the hearer receives are always reinterpreted not only in the light of phonological-level information but also of the higher-level grammatical and pragmatic context which feeds back to the raw phonetic data. Access to context enables TRACE to cope well in noisy situations where the acoustic signal is not clear. TRACE has also proved successful at determining word boundaries. This is important since, normally, the initial sound of a word has an important function in word identification.

But TRACE is not entirely without problems. Critics have suggested that there is excessive use of top-down contextual information, especially in the very initial stages of recognising a word. Experimental studies show that, normally, we only resort to heavy use of context if the speech we hear is very unclear due to noise or other factors (McQueen 1991).

SHORTLIST is another connectionist model of word recognition. It differs from TRACE in being interactive. TRACE allows information to go in both directions; it allows use of top-down and bottom-up information. So, for example, context can help resolve phonetic ambiguities and conversely information about sound structure can clarify syntactic or semantic issues. SHORTLIST by contrast allows unidirectional flow of information from the prelexical computation of the signal to the lexicon, but the reverse is not permitted. There is no bottom-up backtracking from the lexicon to the prelexical phase that might contain relevant contextual information.

Another difference between the models is that, while both models assume competition between candidate words for selection, the scope of the competition is different. TRACE envisages competition among all the words in one's vocabulary; SHORTLIST only envisages competition between members of a 'shortlist'. Members of the initial shortlist are generated on the basis of bottom-up raw phonetic data alone. Computationally, this is a less daunting task than simulating competition among all the thousands of words in the entire vocabulary, as TRACE expects (Cutler 1999).

10.5 Summary

We have explored the nature of the mental lexicon. We have seen that people store tens of thousands of words in the mind and are able to retrieve them instantaneously. This achievement is facilitated by the fact that the storage system is highly structured. Lexical items are listed in the mental lexicon with the information about their meaning, pronunciation and grammatical and morphological properties. When retrieval is successful, all these facets of a word are recalled in a perfectly synchronised manner.

Research into speech recognition relies heavily on models. Some psychologists have proposed that words are stored fully formed (Full Listing Hypothesis) and others have argued against that position and put forward instead a claim that complex words are parsed and stripped of their affixes in the lexicon. We have reviewed evidence for and against both positions.

Then we have considered the contribution to speech recognition made by phonetic and phonological decoding, as well as high-level contextual information in the light of phenomena such as phoneme restoration and selective listening, which show clearly that raw phonetic data is not all that is taken into account when we recognise words in speech.

Context is highly significant in speech recognition. So, we considered approaches to the role of context in linguistics, in particular Relevance Theory in pragmatics and syntactic analyses of garden path sentences.

The chapter ended with a review of speech recognition models. First we sketched two early models, namely template matching and analysis by synthesis of speech, before focusing on two current models, the Cohort model and the TRACE model. In a nutshell, the Cohort model hypothesises that, as we hear speech, we marshal a cohort of likely candidate words which are plausible candidates for a given slot in the utterance we hear. All members of the cohort but one are eventually rejected and the survivor is the word recognised.

The TRACE model is highly interactive and it highlights the interplay of context (top-down) information with raw acoustic data (bottom-up) processing in word recognition.

Exercises

1   What are the main similarities and differences between the organisation of the mental lexicon and that of the dictionaries sold in bookshops?

2   Explain in detail how the meaning of *it* and *his* is inferred in the following sentence which you might encounter next time you read a detective story:

The murderer put the arsenic in his glass and took *it* to *his* table.

3   a   What is the case for and against entering each of the words below as an unanalysed whole in the lexicon?
    b   What is the case for stripping the following words of affixes and storing them in the lexicon decomposed into simple morphemes? How would each word be segmented if the need to segment was accepted?

    i   act actual activism actionable deactivate react reaction reactivate reactionary
    ii   charmer painter walker astrologer driller seller tailor doctor author advisor
    iii peaceful colourful careful rueful wistful bagful joyful merciful bashful
    iv   navigate navigator navigation navigable circumnavigate navigationally
    v   happy unhappy happiness hapless happily haphazard happen happening

4   a   Clarify the garden path sentences below by adding a few extra words and appropriate punctuation marks where necessary.
    b   Explain how the syntactic ambiguity in each of these sentences is resolved in order to obtain an appropriate interpretation.

    i   Fat people eat accumulates.
    ii   The cotton clothing is usually made of grows in Mississippi.
    iii The man who whistles tunes pianos.
    iv   The man who hunts ducks out on weekends.
    v   When Fred eats food gets thrown.

    vi The girl told the story cried.

    vii I know the words to that song about the queen don't rhyme.

    viii She told me a little white lie will come back to haunt me.

    ix The dog that I had really loved bones.

    x The raft floated down the river sank.

(From http://www.fun-with-words.com/
ambiguous_garden_path.html)

5   Suggest how the Cohort model and the TRACE model might account for how we recognise the italicised words in the following sentences:

   a   I need a new *mouse* for the computer.
      The cat caught the *mouse* quite easily.

   b   'Sergeant *Pepper*' is her favourite Beatles album.
      Add more salt and *pepper* to the meat.

   c   Get some two-inch *nails* from the hardware store.
      I am seeing a chiropodist about my ingrown *nails*.

Chapter 11

Speech production

11.1 Modelling speech production

The seminal papers by Garrett (1975, 1976) proposed a two-stage model of speech production. In a nutshell, in the first stage a lexical item with the appropriate meaning is selected and grammatically encoded. In the second stage the speaker accesses and retrieves the appropriate phonological word-form.

Stage one begins with CONCEPTUALISATION. You decide on a concept that you want to turn into a message and select suitable words to employ. The next step, still at stage one, is FORMULATION. This entails syntactic planning: you decide the order of words, the relationships between them and the morphological inflections and function words (e.g. prepositions and conjunctions) that will signal appropriately the intended relationships between the words.

The action then moves to stage two: ARTICULATION. First, the phonological properties of the abstract words assembled by the syntactic and morphological operations during the formulation exercise are determined. Then you implement a detailed phonetic plan for articulating each word.

This model has been very influential. In what follows I present the elaboration of the two-stage model by Levelt and his collaborators (Levelt 1989; Bock and Levelt 1994; Levelt *et al.* 1999).

Let us now consider the different levels in the figure in more detail. Stage one is the MESSAGE LEVEL: you determine CONCEPTUALIZATION. As a speaker, your first task is to decide on the intended meaning. At this stage you deal in disembowelled, pre-linguistic concepts. There is no grammar. There are no words. There are no speech sounds. The conceptual message is pre-linguistic and so is unaffected by the idiosyncrasies of your language. Rigorous

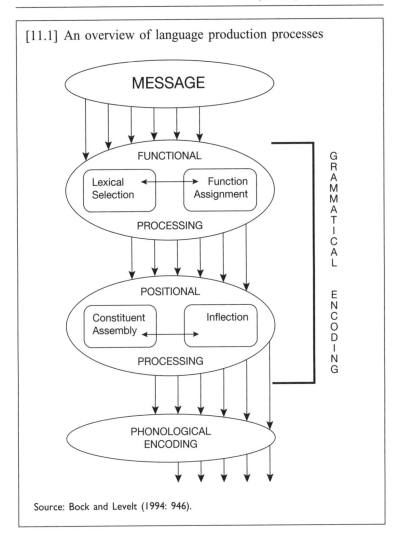

[11.1] An overview of language production processes

MESSAGE

FUNCTIONAL

Lexical Selection ← → Function Assignment

PROCESSING

POSITIONAL

Constituent Assembly ← → Inflection

PROCESSING

PHONOLOGICAL ENCODING

GRAMMATICAL ENCODING

Source: Bock and Levelt (1994: 946).

scientific investigations of what happens at this pre-linguistic stage are not feasible yet. Conceptualisation remains a mystery.

The next phase at stage two is GRAMMATICAL ENCODING (also known as FORMULATION). It deals with lexical selection and syntactic planning and is divided into two parts: FUNCTIONAL PROCESSING and POSITIONAL PROCESSING. Functional processing is itself divided into two parts. One part is LEXICAL SELECTION (or LEMMA SELECTION). To produce speech, the first task we perform is to select lexical items to express the intended meaning; the next task is to assemble lemmas. A LEMMA is an abstract lexical representation whose semantic and syntactic properties are specified, but which lacks any phonological properties. The notion of the lemma allows us to capture the fact that syntax is phonology-free. Phonetic articulation is not relevant to grammar. For instance, the fact that your articulation of a word may vary, e.g. you may say *finance* as [faɪnænts] or [fɪnænts], is of no relevance at the level of grammatical encoding. You have the same lemma; the variation is at the level of phonological encoding. The relevance of lemmas to sentence meaning is obvious. Sentences like *The baby cried* and *The dog yelped* have the same syntactical structure, but of course they mean very different things because different lemmas have been selected.

The other sub-component of the functional component is FUNCTION ASSIGNMENT. This subcomponent performs two functions. First, it assigns the SYNTACTIC FUNCTIONS (also known as GRAMMATICAL RELATIONS), which show the relationship between the verb and various noun phrases in a sentence (e.g. subject, object, indirect object etc.); and, second, it specifies ARGUMENT STRUCTURE by indicating the SEMANTIC ROLES of the various entities involved in the action, process or state indicated by the verb. By semantic roles we mean, for example:

AGENT: the entity that initiates the action, process etc.;
THEME: the entity that undergoes movement;
PATIENT: the entity that undergoes the action;
RECIPIENT: the entity that receives something.

Function assignment is exemplified in [11.2]:

[11.2] a S   O
           Ravi$_{<Agent>}$ washed   the baby $_{<Patient>}$
        b S   O
           Ravi$_{<Agent>}$ rowed   the canoe$_{<Theme>}$
        c S   IO   O
           Shruti$_{<Agent>}$ sent   Ravi$_{<Recipient>}$ a card$_{<Patient>}$
        d S   O
           Ravi$_{<Recipient>}$ received a card$_{<Patient>}$

Note: S = subject, O = object, IO = indirect object; semantic roles are enclosed in angled brackets < >.

As seen in [11.2c] and [11.2d], grammatical functions are distinct from semantic roles. Ravi is the recipient in both cases, but he is an indirect object NP in one case and a subject NP in the other. The selection of the lexical item *send* vs. *receive* has implications for the syntactic functions that are assigned.

POSITIONAL PROCESSING is an aspect of syntactic planning. The speaker decides (in an extremely skeletal fashion) on a syntactic frame and selects the words that will fill the slots occupied by content words (nouns, verbs, adjectives and adverbs):

[11.3] a   b

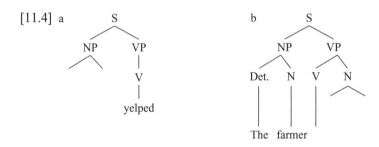

The next task is CONSTITUENT ASSEMBLY, e.g.:

[11.4] a

Effectively this involves determining the CONSTITUENT STRUC-TURE, e.g. which words belong to the noun phrase in subject position, the object noun phrase, the verb phrase etc., and in what order they appear. When constituent assembly is complete, the speaker has syntactic trees like those in [11.5]:

[11.5] a

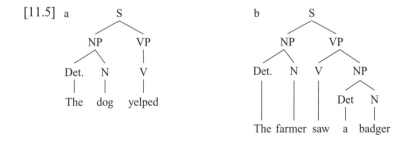

Positional processing has a separate FUNCTION ASSIGNMENT sub-component that selects not only function words (such as preposi-tions, e.g. *to*, *for*, and conjunctions, e.g. *and*, *or*) but also inflectional affixes (e.g. plural -*s*, past tense -*ed*).

[11.6]

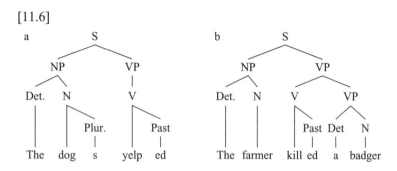

The output of stage one, grammatical encoding, is lemmas – lexical items fully specified for meaning and syntactic and morpho-logical properties, but lacking any indication as to how they will be realised in speech.

Next, stage two, PHONOLOGICAL ENCODING (also known as ARTICULATION), begins (see also Fromkin 1971, 1973; Butterworth 1983, 1989). During this stage the speaker determines in great detail not only how the vowel and consonant sounds in each word are to be articulated, but also the stress, loudness, rhythm and intonation properties of the utterance (see section (11.2.3)).

11.2 Slips of the tongue as evidence for the model

A problem we face in investigating language processing is that it takes place on the sly. People cannot explain to the psycholinguist how exactly they produce and understand speech because they have no explicit knowledge of how they do it. Speech production errors (and failures of comprehension) provide a useful window on how the mind processes language (Fromkin 1971, 1973, 1980; Garrett 1975; Cutler 1988). This is because the errors are for the most part sys-tematic. Normal speech production is subject to strong constraints, the violation of which results in speech peppered with specific types of error. The model of normal speech production presented here is informed by the considerable body of research on speech errors.

11.2.1 Grammatical encoding errors

There are many errors that arise when grammatical encoding goes awry. Some errors such as those illustrated in [11.7] result from the simultaneous selection of two words during the lexical selection stage at the functional level. These errors are called BLENDS (see section (8.11)).

[11.7] a didn't bother me in the *sleast*
(from *slightest* + *least*) (Boomer and Laver 1968)
b Don't *frowl* (*frown* + *scowl*) like that! (Aitchison 2003: 18–21)
c *dreeze* (*draft* + *breeze*) (Fromkin 1973)

The confusion resulting in blends stems from the fact that words are retrieved from the mental lexicon on the basis of their phonological and semantic properties. Usually blends involve two words that are phonologically and semantically similar.

However, as Fromkin (1971) points out, many errors have no basis in phonology. They involve getting one's wires crossed when selecting words that share certain *semantic properties*. For instance, the relationship may be one of antonymy (oppositeness) (see section (6.4.3)), as in [11.8]:

[11.8] Utterance: This room is too damn *hot – cold*.
Target: This room is too damn *cold*.

Or it may involve some other semantic property (e.g. co-hyponymy (see section (6.4.1)) or membership of the same semantic field (see section (6.5)):

[11.9] a Utterance: I'd better give you a *calendar*.
Target: I'd better give you a *map*.
b Utterance: He has to pay her *rent*, I mean alimony.
Target: He has to pay her *alimony*.
c Utterance: They're doing some experiments with the four *blind* – deaf children.
Target: They're doing some experiments with the four *deaf* children.

Consider the further examples of semantic substitution from Fromkin (1971). In [11.10a] the oppositeness in meaning of *hate* and *love* is the important property and in [11.10b] *oral* and *written* belong to the same semantic field and are complementary:

[11.10] a I *like* to – *hate* to get up in the morning.
       b The *oral* – *written* part of the exam.

The reason for the confusion of meaning in [11.11] is also equally easy to see:

[11.11] a Utterance: I'm going to *April* in *May*.
            Target: I'm going to *England* in *May*.
         b Utterance: Are my *legs*, I mean tires, touching the kerb?
            Target: Are my *tires* touching the kerb?

(From Fromkin 1973)

As seen, typically, substitutions affect words belonging to the same word-class (e.g. noun, adjective, verb, preposition etc.) and which have similar meanings. This is in keeping with a finding by Stemberger (1985) who showed in a corpus-based study that 99.7 per cent of words that figured in lexical substitutions belonged to the same word-class as the intended word.

Following Freud, many psychologists regard as FREUDIAN SLIPS those speech errors that arise from lexical substitutions. Freud claimed that lexical substitutions reflect an underlying tension between the intentions of the speaker's conscious mind and what the subconscious mind wishes to say. Normally, the conscious mind wins and things the unconscious mind would like to put us up to are not allowed to surface. But occasionally something unintended does slip through, with embarrassing consequences. Freudian slips of this kind cause a few sniggers or raised eyebrows:

[11.12] a The psychology of sex – success.
         b (From a politician) I like Heath. He's tough – like Hitler. (Shocked silence from reporters) – Did I say Hitler? I meant Churchill.

(From Ellis 1980)

In successful word retrieval, embarrassment of this kind is avoided. Only the word with the intended meaning, which is selected by the conscious mind, is slotted into the sentence. Any other words that are looked up are suppressed.

To sum up, processing faults within the lexical selection sub-component may result in blends or semantic substitutions. It seems this is because in normal speech speakers tend to line up several words in the target semantic area before homing in on the one that they finally select.

We shall now turn to errors that arise at the stage of syntactic function assignment. (Refer to the figure in [11.1].) In [11.13] the right words were selected. But incorrect assignment of argument structure resulted in the target meaning not being expressed:

[11.13] a Utterance:

S		IO	O
Mum$_{<Agent>}$	bought	Helen$_{<Recipient>}$	flowers$_{<Patient>}$

       b Target:

S		IO	O
Helen$_{<Agent>}$	bought	Mum$_{<Recipient>}$	flowers$_{<Patient>}$

If during grammatical encoding function assignment goes wrong, positional processing (constituent assembly and inflection) may also misfire:

[11.14] a Utterance:

S		IO	O
He$_{<Agent>}$	gave	him$_{<Recipient>}$	a skirt$_{<Patient>}$

       b Target:

S		IO	O
He$_{<Agent>}$	gave	her$_{<Recipient>}$	a skirt$_{<Patient>}$

The intended meaning to be encoded by the grammar is that a male individual, who is the agent and subject of the verb, does the giving; a female individual is the recipient and the syntactic function of the indirect object is associated with the NP referring to her. So the pronoun found in that NP slot must be inflected with both feminine gender and accusative case so that it comes out as *her*. Grammatical encoding is done correctly in [11.14b], but in [11.14a] the grammatical encoding has gone off beam. The result is wrong function assignment and wrong inflection.

11.2.2 Grammatical encoding errors: inflection infelicities

The errors affecting inflections and function words provide evidence of the workings of the function assignment sub-component (see figure in [11.1]). Let us begin by observing that, with respect to surfacing in the wrong place, the behaviour of inflectional morphemes and function words differs from that of content words. For instance, when function words are shunted round by mistake, the word that is moved normally takes with it its stress:

[11.15] a Utterance: Can I turn *off* this.
          Target: Can I turn this *off.*
        b Utterance: Well I *much* would have preferred the owl.
          Target: Well I would have *much* preferred the owl.
                                          (From Cutler and Isard 1980,
                                            cited in Butterworth 1980)

This evidence suggests that content words differ from function words in the way in which they are processed in speech production.

In addition to providing insights into prosodic processing, speech errors also give us a window on the storage and retrieval of grammatical elements. Some errors show that grammatical function morphemes are stored in a very abstract manner. This can be clearly seen in errors involving NEG TRANSPORTATION. A disembodied notion of negation is stored separately from the specific morphemes that represent it (e.g. *in-*, *un-*, *non-*, *dis-*, *any-*). Neg transportation is a process whereby some negative prefix (e.g. *in-*, *un-*, *non-*, *dis-*, *any-*) is moved from its normal, intended position and appears incorrectly in a different position where a different negative prefix may be substituted for it. Fromkin (1973) gives this example:

[11.16] Utterance: I *dis*regard this as precise.
         Target: I regard this as *im*precise.

Sometimes the negative morpheme is not transported to a new position in the sentence, but a different, incorrect negative morpheme is used instead of the target one. Thus, in the sentence in [11.17], the clitic *-n't* attached to *was* replaces the correct negative prefix, *un-*, that should appear before *plugged*:

[11.17] Utterance: I was unplugged in . . . .
         Target: I wasn't plugged in for a second.

Neg transportation lends further support to the assumption that content words are stored separately from affixes. That is why you may succeed in retrieving the correct content word (*plug*) and produce an incorrect sentence in the end if the wires get crossed so that the affix with the meaning you want (*neg*) appears on a different site in the sentence (after *was*) from the one intended (as a prefix (*un-*) attached to *plugged*).

The claim that grammatical, functional morphemes are stored and retrieved separately from content morphemes is further buttressed by additional instances of the uncoupling of affixes from stems and bases. An interesting morphological error results in the root morphemes in different words exchanging places, leaving behind the affixes that should have been attached to them. This phenomenon is called AFFIX STRANDING. It can be seen in the following examples from Garrett (1980) (where the stranded suffixes appear in upper case letters):

[11.18] a Utterance: You have to *square* it *face*LY.
        b Target: You have to face it squarely.

[11.19] a Utterance: I've got a load of *cook*EN *chick*ED.
        b Target: I've got a load of cooked chicken.

Garrett claims that affix stranding shows that affixes are not stored with stems as integrated wholes, but that they are stored in separate places. The insertion of stems in syntactic 'positional frames' by syntactic rules is distinct from morphological operations that attach affixes to stems. When all goes well these two processes are fully synchronised. But a slight hitch may cause a mismatch between stems and affixes.

But, as Butterworth (1989) points out, there are problems with Garrett's account. In irregular morphology there are examples of a word being placed in the wrong position with its correct irregular inflected form, as in the following:

[11.20] a Utterance: I don't know that I'd *hear* one if I *knew* it.
        b Target: I don't know that I'd *know* one if I *heard* it.

The expected form according to Garrett's theory is:

[11.21] Utterance: I don't know that I'd *hear* one if I *knowed* it.

In this case the stranding predicted by Garrett does not materialise. Instead, whole-word movement takes place. Butterworth (1989) argues that the evidence for a separation of roots from affixes in the manner proposed by Garrett is not so strong. In [11.21] the inflectional affix is integrated with the stem and moves with it.

Arguably, Garrett's position can be defended. If we assume a lexical morphology model with a distinction between essentially irregular stratum 1 affixes and the regular stratum 2 affixes, we can hazard the prediction that stranding only applies at stratum 2. Irregular inflection in verbs like *knew*, *sang* and *rode* and nouns like *feet* and *mice* is integrated so early and so firmly into the stem that there is no chance of the affixes being left stranded on the beach when the stem is moved elsewhere.

11.2.3 Phonological encoding errors

As we have seen the first stage of speech production is concerned with grammatical encoding and the second stage with phonological encoding. Many things can also go wrong with the phonological encoding process. For instance, a word with a similar pronunciation and belonging to the same word-class but having an unrelated meaning may be substituted for the right word. Fromkin (1971) cites many examples of phonological muddles caused by phonetic similarity, e.g.:

[11.22] *Substitution of phonologically similar words*
    a Utterance: bottle of page five
       Target: bottom of page five
    b Utterance: while the present – pressure indicates
       Target: while the pressure indicates
    c Utterance: it spread like wild flower
       Target: it spread like wild fire

Fromkin recognises a number of different phonological errors, e.g.:

[11.23] a *Phonological anticipations*
             Utterance: bake my bike
             Target: take my bike
         b *Phonological preservations*
             Utterance: pulled a pantrum
             Target: pulled a tantrum

In [11.23a] we see the replacement of the initial consonant of the first content word with that of the second. But in [11.23b] the opposite happens. The initial consonant of the second word is replaced with that of the first.

It is not always entire sounds that are substituted. Sometimes it is the DISTINCTIVE FEATURES of which phonemes are made up that are exchanged or confused:

[11.24] a Utterance: Cedars of Lemadon
       Target: Cedars of Lebanon
    b Utterance: flesh queer water
       Target: fresh clear water
    c Utterance: blake fluid
       Target: brake fluid

(Fromkin 1971)

What is involved in [11.24a] is the changing of oral [b] into nasal [m] and nasal [n] into oral [d]. The phonetic feature [± nasal] is present in the word, but appears as part of the wrong segment in each case. In [11.24b] and [11.24c] it is the feature [± lateral] that is swapped round and appears in the wrong word.

The phonological behaviour displayed in SPOONERISMS lends further support to the two-stage model of lexical retrieval. In a spoonerism, typically there is a transposition of sounds. The result is often an (un)intentional comic effect. The errors in [11.25] are attributed to the Revd William A. Spooner (1844–1930), Warden of New College, Oxford, who is eponymous with this tongue slip.

[11.25] a Utterance: *queer* old *dean*
       Target: *dear* old *queen*
    b Utterance: Is the bean dizzy?
       Target: Is the dean busy?
    c Utterance: The weight of rages will press hard upon the employer.
       Target: The rate of wages will press hard upon the employer.

Morphemes and even words may sometimes be transposed, as in the example below that I heard in a conversation with a school-teacher friend of mine:

[11.26] Utterance: I told them to open their *desks* and leave them on the *books*.
     Target: I told them to open their *books* and leave them on the *desks*.

Spoonerisms are not totally random, but are subject to various constraints. For instance, consonant substitutions tend to occur in equivalent positions in syllables. Normally, there is a transposition of initial consonants or syllables in a pair of words. Furthermore, the transposition tends to occur within a single syntactic constituent or intonation unit but does not affect the pattern of sentence stress. If entire words are swapped, the exchange involves forms with similar sounds and stress patterns, as in [11.26]. This suggests that assigning stress to a sentence is done separately from inserting content words.

11.3 Selecting words

The question we will now consider is how all the information about a word is retrieved successfully in normal speech. One possibility could be that the speaker retrieves words going in a straight line, doing one thing at a time: (1) selecting the meaning; (2) doing the requisite grammatical analysis and selecting the inflectional morphemes and grammatical function words; and (3) finally mapping the morphemes making up the word on to a phonological representation. This is implausible. Evidence from speech errors, like blends where semantic confusion seems to be triggered by phonological resemblance, suggests that retrieval does not go step by step; pronunciation is not considered in isolation from semantic choices and grammatical encoding.

11.3.1 Networked lexical access

A superior model that has been proposed is the networked SPREAD-ING ACTIVATION MODEL (Dell and Reich 1980; Dell 1986; Hörmann 1986; Levelt 1989; Matthei and Roeper 1983; Aitchison 2003). This model assumes that information about the semantic, grammatical and phonological properties of a word is stored at three levels of representation and each piece of semantic syntactic and phonological representation corresponds to a node in the framework. Together the nodes form a big lexical network. Selecting a word involves whizzing round the network and progressively activating the various nodes. The most strongly activated node is selected in each case. The similarity with the TRACE model of speech recognition which we saw in the last chapter is not accidental. Both are connectionist theories (see p. 257).

Finding a word begins at the conceptual level. You have a concept, say, of a cow. You need to find a word to express it, so you search your mental lexicon for the word. The starting point is the broad area of meaning that the word you want belongs to. So, you look up animals and immediately narrow it to mammals, and then to farm animals: Initially, the SEMANTIC FIELD targeted may be very broad and a lot more words may be activated than you actually need. As well as 'cow', other words like 'goat', 'sheep' or 'pig' may be activated. Any promising candidate is considered before the choice is eventually narrowed to a word whose meaning and phonological shape have the best fit (see Marslen-Wilson 1989).

Proponents of the spreading activation model have envisaged a richer account of word meaning than the typical dictionary definitions of words. They have proposed that encyclopaedic information is stored in the form of an interlocking hierarchical network (see Aitchison 2003; Hörmann 1986; Lipka 1990; and references cited therein). The dominance relation in the hierarchy is expressed in terms of 'X is a Y', e.g. 'a mammal is an animal', 'the cow is a mammal', 'the cow is a farm animal' etc. This 'X is a Y' relation is called a relation of INCLUSION (see the discussion on hyponymy in section (6.4.1)).

In addition to inclusion, there are many other semantic relations in the network, e.g. 'X gives Y' (e.g. the cow gives milk), 'X has growth of Y' (e.g. the sheep has growth of wool), 'X is offspring of Y' (e.g. the calf is offspring of the cow) etc. An example of a simplified version of the representation of the meaning of *cow* in the mental lexicon is given in the figure in [11.27].

Nodes corresponding to the various properties of the word 'cow' get activated when you start looking it up in the mental lexicon. Activated nodes are, metaphorically speaking, 'hot'. The greater the amount of active consideration a node receives, the greater is its degree of activation – hence the 'hotter' it is. A hot node transfers its heat to nearby nodes that are linked to it. But a node 'cools' as attention shifts elsewhere to activated nodes that are linked to it remotely, or not at all. Typically, a large number of nodes associated with a large number of words are activated but few are considered actively. The heat of rejected nodes dissipates. If all goes well, there is a clear winner that gets selected – the word that is associated with the most strongly activated nodes.

After the selection of the item that matches the intended meaning is completed, attention turns to grammar encoding. Nodes in the

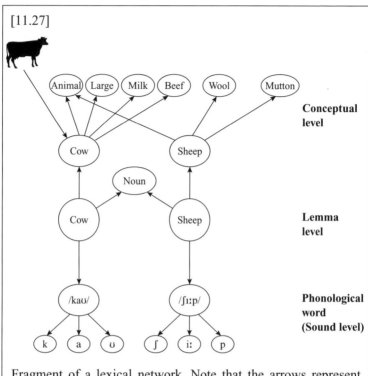

[11.27]

Conceptual level

Lemma level

Phonological word (Sound level)

Fragment of a lexical network. Note that the arrows represent types of connections within the network, not information flow in speech production or comprehension.

Source: Based on Bock and Levelt (1994: 951).

network corresponding to different syntactic and morphological properties are activated and the correct syntactic and morphological representation is assigned to create a lemma (see section (11.1)). Suppose you are intending to say *A cow chased the dog.* The lemma for 'cow' has to be specified as a countable noun, singular number, feminine gender, subject of the verb and agent etc. Activating a syntactic node will also excite closely related nodes, e.g. noun will excite number, gender etc. With 'cow' activated, a number of candidate grammatical words will become hot, e.g. $cow_{\text{[Noun, –Plural, +animate, +feminine]}}$; $cows_{\text{[Noun +Plural, +animate, +feminine]}}$ etc. There will be a competition between the activated lemmas and the hottest will win.

The final stage is assigning phonological form /kaʊ/ to the lemma and producing the spoken word [kʰaʊ]:

Subject

$<cow$ [Noun, –Plural, +animate, + feminine] etc. $>NP$ [Agent].

Normally there is one clear winner at the level of initial lexical selection, lemma selection and at the phonological word level. In those circumstances, the right word with the right meaning, the right grammatical properties and the right pronunciation emerges. But, occasionally, there is no clear winner. Rather there are two very hot candidates which both end up getting selected. Depending on the level where the failure to determine a winner occurs, the word produced has something odd about its meaning, its grammar or its pronunciation (see section (11.2)).

WORD FREQUENCY is a very important factor that affects the speed of retrieval in language processing. Savin (1963) showed that it is easier to recognise frequently used words when they are presented in less than optimum conditions where they are difficult to see or hear. Even in optimum conditions when subjects are presented with both frequent and rare words, they find it easier to identify and classify the more frequent words (see Frederiksen and Kroll 1976). You would expect that. Assuming that words are listed, those that are used very rarely (e.g. *gazebo*, *zymotic*) are put at the bottom of the stack and words that are used several hundred times a day (e.g. *the*, *I*, *am*) are put at the top of the stack for easy access. Frequently used words are more active; they are hot in terms of the spreading activation model; they are always available for use.

This model allows constant movement to and fro between the different sub-components. After having activated a range of words with the desired meaning, you can look up pronunciations then go back to the meanings and narrow the selection of words, then look up the pronunciation again. In between, you may also be sorting out the inflectional morphemes to attach to the stems selected. At any time you may peep back at aspects of the representation of a word and revise them in the light of new information. Alternatively, you may look forward to see what choices are on offer later if a particular path is selected.

It is assumed that, at first, when a whole lot of words are activated, the matching of meaning with phonological representation is done very sketchily – just an indication of the number of syllables, the stress pattern and the initial segment. As a decision about meaning firms up, the phonological representation is also gradually fleshed out. Progress through the lexicon need not be linear.

What is amazing is that all this processing happens in a flash and yet normal fluent speech is remarkably error-free. Though errors give us useful clues about language processing they are not the norm. The error rate in lexical retrieval is estimated at 0.25 per thousand words (Deese 1984). This level of accuracy is no mean achievement given the fact that we have tens of thousands of words in our mental lexicons (Oldfield 1963) (see p. 239); and we talk fast. Typically, we produce two or three words per second (Maclay and Osgood 1959) and are capable of accelerating to a blistering seven words per second (Deese 1984).

11.3.2 It's just on the tip of my tongue

Sometimes you know that you know a word for something but you are unable to retrieve it. Psychologists call that a TIP OF THE TONGUE (TOT) phenomenon. TOT phenomena have been an important area of investigation by psycholinguists studying lexical retrieval. A widely accepted account of what happens in a TOT experience has been based on the notion of BLOCKING that was first proposed by Woodworth (1938) in a study based on an examination of data collected from naturally occurring TOT phenomena. Woodworth noted that, in typical TOT experiences, participants tend to recall words that are similar to the target word – but are frustrated by the inability to access the target word itself. He hypothesised that this situation might be due to the fact that related words act as 'blockers', crowding out the target word and thus inhibiting access to it.

Brown and McNeill (1966) devised an experimental technique for investigating TOT states. The aim was to elicit controlled data that would enable them to investigate systematically the properties of TOT states. They attempted to trigger TOT states by presenting participants in the experiment with the definition of a rare word and getting them to say what the word was. They observed that, if a TOT state was induced, the participant could usually recall many of the phonetic characteristics of the target word – but not enough to fully identify it. If the participants were primed with words phonetically similar to the target word, a TOT experience was normally avoided and recall of the target was successful.

More recently, Burke and associates have taken this line of inquiry further. Burke *et al.* (1991) presented the Transmission Deficit model to account for TOT states. The key claim was that language production depends on the strength of connections linking conceptual and phonological levels within a network. (This study also demonstrated a correlation between TOT experiences and ageing. TOT experiences become more common as we grow older, starting in the mid-thirties; older people are less tenacious in trying to retrieve a word; concrete nouns and especially people's names are more difficult to retrieve than abstract nouns.)

James and Burke (2000) report an experimental investigation that provides evidence of TOT experiences being attributable to weak phonological connections among the words that are stored in the mental lexicon. They suggest that lexical retrieval crucially requires recall of both the semantic and phonological properties of a word. Failure to access both aspects of a lexical representation results in a TOT situation. The authors tested their hypothesis by asking 114 questions to 108 research participants. Some of the questions were general-knowledge questions carefully crafted to bring up target words that are notorious for triggering a large number of TOT incidents. The tasks that were given to the participants included providing answers to questions which were designed to get them to retrieve rare words such as *ornithology* and proper names like *Alcott* and *Nairobi*, as well as giving answers to general-knowledge questions like, 'What word means to formally renounce a throne?' The target word was *abdicate*, a rare word that frequently induces a TOT experience.

In some instances, the participants were primed by being given a series of 10 words which were pronounced before they were asked to take part in the experiment involving the retrieval of TOT-inducing words. Half of the words in the priming set shared at least one phonological characteristic with the target, e.g. for *abdicate* the priming set included *abstract*. The figure in [11.28] gives you the flavour of the task.

This study established that the key factor in TOT situations is not so much blocking as the weakness of the phonological connections among the words that are stored in the mental lexicon. If such connections are strengthened by priming, retrieval is significantly improved.

[11.28]

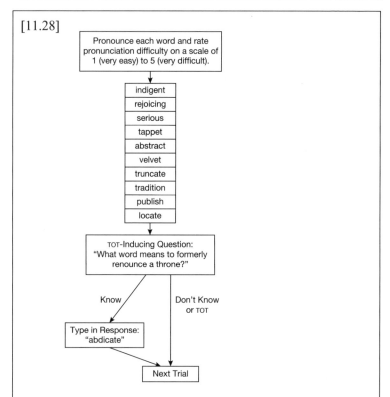

Figure 2. Example of presentation of general knowledge questions and phonological processing task in Experiment 1. A related list of words is displayed, with the phonological components overlapping the target word underlined. They were not underlined in the experiment. TOT = tip-of-the-tongue state.

Source: James and Burke (2000: 1382).

11.3.3 Malapropisms

Some tip-of-the-tongue experiences do not end up in frustrated silence, but in uttering the wrong word. We might say 'oops!', but it is too late. We have confused two words. We have uttered a word which is phonologically, and perhaps also semantically, similar to the word we intended to use. Such a slip is called a MALAPROPISM, after Mrs Malaprop, a character in Sheridan's play *The Rivals*.

Malapropisms occur in real life. Several famous TV sports commentators on British television are notorious for their malapropisms. The publishers of the satirical magazine *Private Eye* were quick to see the commercial potential of these gaffes and produced a series of anthologies called *Colemanballs* (named after David Coleman, the doyen of TV sports commentators). The selection in the 1984 volume of *Private Eye's Colemanballs 2*, edited by Fantoni, includes the cartoon [11.29] in the football section.

[11.29]

Again Mariner and Butcher are trying to work the oracle on the near post.

Martin Tyler

Tyler probably intended to say *miracle*.

Malapropisms support the claim that we store and retrieve words from the mind with the meaning separate from the phonological representation. When retrieval goes wrong, a mismatch of meanings with phonological representations may result.

11.4 Aphasia

Another window on language in the mind is what happens in APHASIA. By aphasia is meant severe damage to a specific part of the brain which plays a role in producing or understanding spoken or written language. The brain damage is usually due to a stroke

[11.30]

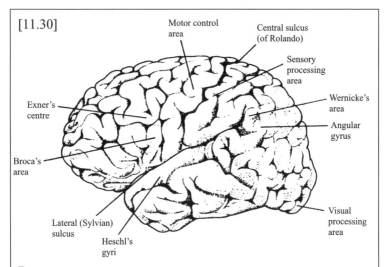

Language areas

The areas which have been proposed for the processing of speaking, listening, reading, writing, and signing are mainly located at or around the Sylvian and Rolandic fissures (p. 250). Several specific areas have been identified.

• The front part of the parietal lobe, along the fissure of Rolando, is primarily involved in the processing of sensation, and may be connected with the speech and auditory areas at the deeper level.
• The area in front of the fissure of Rolando is mainly involved in motor functioning, and is thus relevant to the study of speaking and writing.
• An area in the upper back part of the temporal lobe, extending upwards into the parietal lobe, plays a major part in the comprehension of speech. This is 'Wernicke's area'.
• In the upper part of the temporal lobe is the main area involved in auditory reception, known as 'Heschl's gyri', after the Austrian pathologist R. L. Heschl (1824–81).
• The lower back part of the frontal lobe is primarily involved in the encoding of speech. This is 'Broca's area'.
• Another area towards the back of the frontal lobe may be involved in the motor control of writing. It is known as 'Exner's centre', after the German neurologist Sigmund Exner (1846–1926).

• Part of the left parietal region, close to Wernicke's area, is involved with the control of manual signing.
• The area at the back of the occipital lobe is used mainly for the processing of visual input.

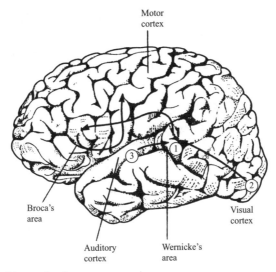

Motor
cortex

Broca's
area

Visual
cortex

Auditory
cortex

Wernicke's
area

Neurolinguistic processing

Some of the neural pathways that are considered to be involved in the processing of spoken language.

1 *Speech production* The basic structure of the utterance is thought to be generated in Wernicke's area and is sent to Broca's area for encoding. The motor programme is then passed on to the adjacent motor area, which governs the articulatory organs.

2 *Reading aloud* The written form is first received by the visual cortex, then transmitted via the angular gyrus to Wernicke's area, where it is thought to be associated with an auditory representation. The utterance structure is then sent on to Broca's area, as in (1).

3 *Speech comprehension* The signals arrive in the auditory cortex from the ear (§25), and are transferred to the adjacent Wernicke's area, where they are interpreted.

Source: Crystal (1997: 263).

or, less frequently, to a horrific head injury caused by an accident or a blow to the head. Aphasia does not wipe out language totally. Rather, a speaker's language faculty is partially impaired; aphasics have some language facility left (see Caplan 1987, 1992; Lecours and Lhermitte 1983).

The left hemisphere of the brain performs most of the linguistic functions. Different types of aphasia are distinguished on the basis of the part of the brain that is damaged, as shown in illustration [11.30] on pp. 284–5 (from Crystal 1997: 263).

11.4.1 Brocha's aphasia

BROCA'S APHASIA (or MOTOR APHASIA) results from damage to Broca's area of the brain. Its symptoms are inability to produce fluent speech:

1   Speech is slow, laboured and minimalist.
2   The patient has reasonably easy access to the content words in the mental lexicon, but finds it very difficult to locate function words and grammatical affixes.

Consequently, this kind of aphasic produces ungrammatical, minimalist (or telegraphic) speech, with content words correctly used, but with few or no inflectional affixes or function words. Hence the label AGRAMMATIC APHASIA is also used for this language disorder (see also Kean 1985; Caramazza and Berndt 1985).

The extract in [11.31] in which an aphasic explains how he returned to the hospital for treatment of his gums is borrowed from Goodglass (1976: 238). It is from the speech of a 28-year-old man. Goodglass points out that not only is this patient's speech syntactically odd, it is also prosodically bizarre (of course, you cannot see that from the transcript). Each chunk followed by a row of dots or by a period is uttered with falling intonation, as though it were a complete utterance.

[11.31]   Ah . . . Monday . . . ah, Dad and Paul Haney [referring to himself by his full name] and Dad . . . hospital. Two . . . ah, doctors . . ., and ah . . . thirty minutes . . . and yes . . . ah . . . hospital. And, er Wednesday . . . nine o'clock. And er Thursday, ten o'clock . . . doctors. Two doctors . . . and ah . . . teeth. Yeah, . . . fine.

The impoverishment of the grammar can be examined systematically by getting patients to describe a picture where the task involves manipulating certain grammatical constructions. The examiner can then probe the extent of the disintegration of their control of grammar. Here is an example from Schwartz *et al.* (1985: 85), where five patients referred to by their initials attempt to describe what is going on in a picture of a boy giving a girl a Valentine:

[11.32] *D.E.*: The boy is gave. . . . The boy is gave the card.
   H.T.: The boy show a Valentine's day. . . . The boy and the girl is Valentine.
   V.S.: The girl . . . the boy is giving a . . . giving is girl friend. The boy Valentine the girl. The boy givin' Valentine to girl.
   P.W.: The boy is Valentine the girl. The boy is giving the Valentine the girl and girl pleased.
   M.W.: Valentine's day and candy. I think Valentine's day. Girl is Valentine's day. . . . Boy is getting with the girl Valentine's candy.

As you can see, these patients cannot produce the dative construction correctly and say *The boy is giving the girl a Valentine*. They also have difficulties with inflectional morphemes. Often, they are either absent (e.g. *The boy show*), or incorrectly used (e.g. *The boy is gave*).

Broca's aphasia lends further support to the claim made by linguists that in morphology and the lexicon it is necessary to distinguish between lexical items (roughly, content words) and grammatical morphemes (function words and inflectional affixes). In morphology this is the motivation for the separation of derivational morphemes which are used to create vocabulary items from inflectional morphemes and grammatical function words whose presence is required by the rules of the syntax. Broca's aphasia shows clearly that damage to the section of the mental lexicon in which grammatical morphemes are kept need not have implications for the storage and retrieval of content words.

11.4.2 Wernicke's aphasia

As you can see in [11.30] on p. 285 WERNICKE'S APHASIA (also called RECEPTIVE APHASIA) is a result of damage to Wernicke's area of the brain. Aphasics who suffer from this disorder show these symptoms:

1　They have very fluent, rapid-fire speech, so no production problem.
2　But they have great difficulty in understanding speech.
3　They find it very difficult, though not totally impossible, to match word meanings with the right phonological representations.
4　Often patients either utter plain nonsense or produce circumlocutions.

These patients very often experience something like an acute version of the tip-of-the-tongue phenomenon we saw earlier. They know the meaning they want to convey but are incapable of finding the right sound envelope for it. They can find reasonably near synonyms, but not the word they want. So they get into horrendously convoluted circumlocutions to paraphrase their intended meaning (e.g. 'what you sleep in' meaning 'bed' or 'something in the mouth that you chew with' meaning 'teeth'). Their speech is generally incoherent, as you can see from this typical example:

[11.33]　Examiner:　Do you like it here in Kansas City?
　　　　　Aphasic:　Yes, I am.
　　　　　Examiner:　I'd like to have you tell me something about your problem.
　　　　　Aphasic:　Yes, I ugh can't hill all of my way. I can't talk all of the things I do, and part of the part I can go alright, but I can't tell from the other people. I usually most of my things. I know what I can talk and know what they are, but I can't always come back even though I know they should be in, and I know I should something eely I should know what I'm doing.
　　　　　　　　　　　　　　　　　　　　(From Bissantz et al. 1985)

A word of caution is in order here. Any evidence from language disorders must be handled with care, since the workings of a malfunctioning brain may not mirror accurately the operation of a normal healthy one. Nonetheless, the difficulties experienced by this type of aphasic are attested in a milder form in the tip-of-the-tongue phenomenon in normal speakers.

To sum up, the tip-of-the-tongue phenomenon and the circumlocution of aphasics with symptoms of Wernicke's aphasia suggest that the meaning of a word and the phonological shape that represents it are stored separately in the mental lexicon. Related meanings are stored together as in a thesaurus and they are not associated with their phonological representations initially. Further, the difficulties, if not total inability, that sufferers from Broca's aphasia have in forming grammatical words (i.e. words where roots have inflectional morphemes) show that grammatical forms are put together at a different stage from content words. Retrieval is successful only if all these facets of the word click into place at the right point.

11.5 Summary

We have considered a two-stage model of speech production (Garrett 1975, 1976; Levelt 1989). The first stage is grammatical encoding. It begins with selecting lexical items appropriate for expressing the initial concept in the mind. A networked spreading activation model has been used for lexical retrieval. In phase two of the grammatical encoding stage the speaker turns conceptual representations into lemmas. Grammatical structure is encoded by assigning syntactic functions, argument structure and constituent structure to words; appropriate inflections and function words are chosen and placed where they are required to go. Stage two is phonological encoding. The speaker decides on the phonological structures to be associated with the lemmas and spells out their exact phonetic realisation.

The model offers an integrated view of speech production. It recognises that things may go wrong at any point in the process. So, it makes provision for speakers going to and fro between the different phases and stages of grammatical and phonological encoding. This enables it to account for any type of lexical error involving meaning, grammar, phonology or phonetics.

As speech production cannot be observed directly, a vital source of evidence of how language is processed by speakers comes from studies of anomalous utterances produced by normal individuals and language disorders in the speech of aphasics. Both sources of evidence are compatible with the model of the mental lexicon presented here.

When observation of how people process language seems to lend support to our theoretical models, we are encouraged to believe that we are on the right track.

Exercises

1　Imagine seeing a bird. You recognise that its plumage is black above and white below. Its legs are bright orange, and so is its bizarrely shaped bill. You do know what that bird is called, but the name just eludes you. You come up with the words *penguin* and *pigeon* but dismiss them immediately. It certainly is not one of those. Half an hour later you remember. It is called a *puffin*.

  a　What is the name of this phenomenon?
  b　How is it accounted for by cognitive psychologists?

2　Study the following sentences and answer the questions below.

  a　'I don't know anyone here that's been killed with a handgun' (Rep. Avery Alexander, D-New Orleans, to the House).
  b　'I can't believe that we are going to let a majority of the people decide what is best for this state' (Rep. John Travis, D-Jackson, to the House)
  c　'This amendment does more damage than it does harm' (Rep. Cynthia Willard-Lewis, D-New Orleans, to the House) (From Jack Wardlaw (2003) *The Little Man Legislative Slips Of The Tongue*, from http://www.humorbin.com/showitem.asp?item=279)

  i　Identify the error (if any) in the data above, as a slip of the tongue, a malapropism, a Freudian slip, a syntactic encoding error etc.
  ii　At what points in the language production process did the malfunction resulting in the error occur?
  iii　Describe in detail what went wrong and how the error could have been avoided.

3　Identify the kinds of error in these sentences. Explain what went wrong in each case.

  a　Utterance:　Don't hide your light under a bush.
  　　Target:　　Don't hide your light under a bushel.

b Utterance: It was a very enjoyful performance.
    Target: It was a very enjoyable performance.

c Utterance: Prosecutors will be trespassed.
    Target: Trespassers will be prosecuted.

4 Account for the errors involving negative morphemes in the data below. What inferences can we make about the organisation of the mental lexicon on the basis of such errors?

    a Utterance: I tell you he's not crazy – I mean, he's insane.
       Target: I tell you he is insane.

    b Utterance: The bonsai didn't die because I watered it.
       Target: The bonsai died because I didn't water it.

    c Utterance: The vowels are not stricted – are unrestricted.
       Target: The vowels are unrestricted.

                               (Data from Fromkin 1973)

5 Many people cannot spell certain words correctly although they can read them correctly. They confuse *their* with *there*, or *weather* with *whether*, or they are not sure if *independent* ends in *-ent* or *-ant* (*independant). What does this tell us about the relation between the production and recognition of words in speech and in writing?

6 Show how the lexical network model can be used to represent in the mental lexicon the meanings of *tulip, palm tree, hill, turkey, zebra, horse, barrister, nurse, desk* and *chair*.

Glossary

Ablaut   A change in a vowel in the root of a word that is used to show a grammatical difference, e.g. *sing* (verb) ~ *song* (noun); *shrink* (present tense) ~ *shrank* (past tense).

Accusative   A case marking for the object of a transitive verb, e.g. *them* in *We ate them*.

Active voice   If the doer of the action is also the subject of the verb the sentence is said to be in the active voice (e.g. The dog bit the man). *See also* **Voice**.

Adjectival phrase   A phrase the head of which is an adjective, e.g. *much quieter*.

Adverbial phrase   A phrase the head of which is an adverb, e.g. *very quietly*.

Affix   A bound morpheme that must occur together with a root to form a word, e.g. *re-, un-, -ing, -ed, -ise*. No word can contain affixes only.

Agent(ive)   The noun phrase indicating who or what brings about the action, state etc. indicated by the verb.

Agrammatism   Loss of the control of some inflectional affixes and syntactic function words usually found in patients suffering from Broca's aphasia. Their speech is like a telegram.

Agreement   A grammatical requirement for words that are in the same syntactic construction to share some morphological marking, e.g. *I am* and *she is* (not **I is* and *she am*).

Allomorph   A variant of a morpheme, i.e. one of the morphs that represent a particular morpheme.

Allophone   A sound representing a given phoneme in certain contexts. Allophones of the same phoneme cannot be used to distinguish the meaning of words, e.g. [1] and [à] are allophones of the phoneme /1/ in English.

Alphabet   A system of writing where letters represent the phonemes of the language.

Alveolar   A speech sound made by raising the tongue so that it makes contact with the alveolar ridge (i.e. teeth ridge), e.g. [d] in *dog*.

Analytic language *see* **Isolating language**

Anaphora   The use of a grammatical device to refer back to something mentioned earlier. Typically this is done using pronouns, e.g. *they* anaphorically refers back to *mice* in *Three blind mice, see how they run*.

Antonym   If words have opposite meanings, they are called antonyms, e.g. *good* and *bad*.

Aphasia   Impairment or loss of the ability to use language caused by damage to the areas of the brain that handle language.

Articulators   Parts of the lips, tongue and throat that play a role in the production of a sound in speech.

Aspect   A grammatical marking in the verb that indicates whether the action or state denoted by a verb is still in progress or completed.

Assimilation   The adjustment in the way a sound is made so that it becomes similar to some other sound or sounds near it.

Asterisk (*)   A linguistic form is asterisked (i.e. 'starred') to show that it is not allowed.

Back-formation   Word-formation involving the dropping of a peripheral part of a word which is wrongly analysed as a suffix, e.g. *lazy*$_{(Adj.)}$ → *laze*$_{(Verb)}$.

Base   Any form to which affixes are appended in word-formation. *See also* **Root** and **Stem**.

Base form *see* **Underlying form**

Blend   A word formed by joining together chunks of two pre-existing words, e.g. *channel* + *tunnel* → *chunnel*.

Borrowing   Adoption of linguistic elements, such as morphemes or words of another language, e.g. English borrowed the word *malaria* from Italian.

Bottom-up   Refers to data-driven processing (e.g. it uses only raw phonetic information in processing speech and does not draw on contextual information).

Bound morpheme   A morpheme which is always appended to some other item because it is incapable of being used on its own as a word, e.g. *-ing* in *coming*.

Broca's area   The lower part of the frontal lobe of the brain responsible for speech.

Calque *see* **Loan translation**

Case   Marking used to indicate the grammatical function of a nominal word, i.e. a noun, pronoun or adjective as in *she/her* and *he/him* in *She saw him* vs. *He saw her.*

Cliché   A hackneyed expression, e.g. *at this point in time*; *that remains to be seen*; *in any shape or form*; *in this day and age.*

Clipping   Word-formation where a long word is shortened to one or two syllables, e.g. *discotheque → disco.*

Cognates   Words of different languages which are to some degree related in meaning and pronunciation because they come from a common historical source.

Collocation   Collocates are words that normally occur together, e.g. *addled egg, salt and pepper.*

Competence   Tacit knowledge of language that lies behind our ability to produce and understand an indefinitely large number of things that can be said or written.

Complementary distribution   If two elements are in complementary distribution, they never occur in identical contexts. So it is not possible to use the difference between them as the sole indicator of a difference in meaning.

Compound word   A word made of two or more words, e.g. *rail + way → railway.*

Connectionism   A model of cognition that uses intensive computer simulations in which many simple units participate in a complex web of interactions. In this approach knowledge is acquired by inductive inference of patterns from statistical regularities rather than by gaining mastery of categorical rules.

Content word *see* **Lexical item** and **Function word**

Denominal   A word 'derived from a noun', e.g. *bookish* (from the noun *book*) is a denominal adjective.

Dental   A consonant made with the tip of the tongue against the upper front teeth, e.g. [t] in French *théâtre* 'theatre'.

Derivation   A word-formation process that is used to create new vocabulary items, e.g. by adding suffixes as in *walk → walker.*

Deverbal   A word 'derived from a verb', e.g. *teacher* (from the verb *teach*) is a deverbal noun.

Digraph   A combination of letters representing a single sound, e.g. *ea* represents [e] in *bread*, *sh* represents [ʃ] in *shin* etc.

Distribution The distribution of a linguistic item refers to all contexts where a linguistic form occurs taken together.

Environment Refers to the context where a linguistic element occurs.

Free morpheme A morpheme capable of occurring on its own (i.e. a word).

Fricative A consonant produced by narrowing the gap between the articulators so that there is audible turbulence as the air squeezes through the narrow gap left for it, e.g. [s] in *see*.

Function word A word mainly serving a grammatical function in a sentence, e.g. *the, with, to* and *a*, as in *The man with a beard gave the milk to the baby*.

Generative rule A rule that specifies an indefinitely large set of the structures that are well-formed members of a class of linguistic structures, e.g. S → NP VP. (A structure where a noun phrase is followed by a verb phrase is a permissible sentence.)

Genitive A marking in noun phrases used to show grammatical subordination. The meaning of genitive constructions includes possession, e.g. *Jane's money*, duration, e.g. *a day's journey* etc.

Glottal stop A consonant produced with a narrowed or closed glottis.

Glottis The space between the vocal cords in the larynx.

Grammatical word This refers to the word as a morphological and syntactic entity, e.g. we can say that '*sat* is the past tense form of the verb *sit*'. *See also* **Function word**.

Head The principal, obligatory element of a construction.

Homonyms Words that are in all ways identical in speech and writing but have unrelated meanings, e.g. *bat* 'little flying mammal' and *bat* 'wooden implement for hitting cricket balls'.

Homophones Words that sound the same but have different meanings, e.g. *male* and *mail*.

Icon A sign which mirrors to some degree the object that it stands for: the link between an iconic sign and whatever it stands for is not totally arbitrary.

Indo-European The language reconstructed by linguists which is assumed to be the ancestor of most European languages (e.g. English, Latin, French, German, Russian) and some Asian languages (e.g. Sanskrit, Hindi, Persian).

Infix   An affix placed inside a root.

Inflection   Affixation that modifies a word to give it the appropriate form when it occurs in some grammatical context.

Inkhorn   The phrase 'inkhorn term' came into English in the first part of the sixteenth century. It was pejoratively applied to 'hard words' which were incomprehensible to ordinary people and which were borrowed in large numbers from classical languages by scholarly gentlemen who were eager to transform English from a vernacular into a major language of culture and scholarship.

Instrument   The noun phrase referring to the entity used to carry out the action indicated by the verb.

Isolating language   Normally in an isolating language (e.g. Vietnamese) a word is realised by just one morph. There are virtually no bound morphemes. Typically, words do not contain several meaningful units.

Labial   An articulation involving one or both the lips.

Latinate   This refers to words borrowed from classical languages and from Romance languages, especially French.

Lemma   A lexical representation whose semantic and grammatical properties are fully specified but which has not yet been associated with a phonological word-form.

Lexeme   A word in the sense of an item of vocabulary that can be listed in the dictionary. A lexeme is a lexical item. *See also* **Lexical item**.

Lexical item   A word belonging to one of the major word-classes (i.e. noun, adjective, verb, adverb) which is listable in the dictionary with an identifiable meaning and is capable of occurring independently, e.g. *girl*, *think*, *quick* etc. (Syntactically, prepositions are also lexical items since they function as lexical heads of prepositional phrases. *See also* **Phrase**.)

Lexicon   The part of the grammar that contains the rules of word-formation and a list of lexical items. *See also* **Mental lexicon**.

Loan translation   A concept is borrowed but is rendered using the words of the language doing the borrowing, e.g. *ça va sans dire* → *it goes without saying*.

Loanword   A word adopted from another language, e.g. *garage* from French.

Macron   A short straight line placed above a vowel to indicate that it is pronounced long.

Malapropism Use of the wrong word which resembles phonologically the intended word, e.g. the use of *progeny* instead of *prodigy* in 'I would by no means wish a daughter of mine to be a progeny of learning' (Sheridan, *The Rivals*).

Mental lexicon The dictionary in the speaker's mind. It contains a list of words as well as rules for generating words that are not listed.

Morph A physical form that represents some morpheme.

Morphophonemic Having to do with the interaction of phonology and morphology.

Morphophonological *see* **Morphophonemic**

Nasal A sound like [m] [n] [ŋ] which is made with the soft palate lowered so that air goes out through the nose.

Nonce word A word that is coined and used just one time.

Noun phrase A phrase whose head is a noun (or pronoun), e.g. *The new students, They*.

Onomatopoeia A word that mirrors an aspect of its meaning, e.g. *cuckoo*, *bang*, is onomatopoeic.

Orthographic word This refers to the word in the written language which appears with a space on either side of it.

Orthography The conventional way of writing a language.

Parsing Analysing a sentence (or word) into its grammatical elements and providing a label for each element identified.

Passive voice If the individual that 'suffers' the action indicated by the verb functions as the subject of the verb, the sentence is said to be in the passive voice (e.g. *The man was bitten by the dog*).

Patient The noun phrase referring to the individual or thing that undergoes the action indicated by the verb.

Perfective aspect A form of the verb indicating completed action.

Person A grammatical form indicating a participant's role in a conversation or in writing. First person (*I*) is the speaker, second person (*you*) is the addressee and third person (*he/she/it*) is neither speaker nor addressee.

Phoneme A sound that is used to distinguish the meaning of words in a particular language. E.g. /t/ and /d/ are different phonemes of English. They distinguish *ten* /ten/ from *den* /den/.

Phonemic transcription A representation of speech showing the vowel and consonant sounds that are used to distinguish word meaning.

Phonological word   The word in the spoken language which can be potentially preceded and followed by a pause.

Phonology   The branch of linguistics concerned with the study of the properties, patterns, functions and representations of speech sounds in a particular language and in language in general.

Phonotactics   The sub-domain of phonology concerned with constraints on the combination of speech sounds.

Phrase   A syntactic constituent headed by a lexical category, i.e. a noun, adjective, verb, adverb or preposition. *See also* **Noun phrase**, **Adjectival phrase** etc.

Place of articulation   The position in the mouth or throat where the obstruction involved in the producing of a consonant takes place. *See also* **Velar**.

Polysemy   A word in the dictionary is said to be polysemous if it has more than one sense, i.e. if it has several related meanings, e.g. *bridge* meaning (1) a structure forming or carrying a road over a river, a ravine etc.; (2) a raised platform extending from side to side of a ship, for the officer in command; (3) the curved central part of spectacles; (4) in a violin etc., a thin upright piece of wood over which the strings are stretched (definitions based on *OED*).

Prefix   An affix that goes before the stem, e.g. *re-* in *re-write*. *See also* **Affix**.

Prepositional phrase   A phrase headed by a preposition, e.g. *on the table*.

Productivity   The capacity of language users to produce and understand a limitless number of words and sentences, many of them novel, in their language.

Progressive aspect   A form of the verb indicating that an action is still continuing.

Received Pronunciation   The prestige accent of spoken British English.

Root   The morpheme at the core of a word to which affixes are added. Such a morpheme is always a member of a lexical category, i.e. noun, verb etc. *See also* **Base** and **Stem**.

Schwa   The central vowel represented by the symbol [ə].

Semantic field   An area of meaning containing words with interlocking senses such that normally you cannot understand one properly without understanding at least some of the others, e.g. the kinship terms (father, mother, sister, daughter, son, uncle, aunt, grandmother, grandfather, cousin etc.) constitute a semantic field.

Spoonerism A type of speech error where by accident (or sometimes by design, one suspects) initial sounds in syllables of neighbouring words swap places, e.g. *The Lord is a shoving leopard to his flock* (Revd William Spooner).

Stem Any form to which *inflectional affixes* can be attached. *See also* **Root** and **Base**.

Stop A consonant made by closing the path of the airstream at the place where the articulators meet so that air is not allowed to go through the centre of the mouth past the obstruction, e.g. [p], [b].

Stress The relative auditory prominence of a syllable.

Subject The part of the sentence containing a noun phrase which precedes the verb and agrees with the verb in number, e.g. '*Her daughter* is a firefighter' vs. '*Her daughters* are brilliant'. Typically, the rest of the sentence (called the predicate) says something about the subject.

Suffix An affix that goes after the stem, e.g. *-er* in *tall-er*. *See also* **Affix**.

Suppletion A case of morphological alternation where forms representing the root morpheme bear no phonological resemblance to each other, e.g. *good ~ better*.

Syllabic consonant A consonant which functions as a syllable nucleus as though it were a vowel, e.g. the [n̩] in *cotton* or the final [l̩] of *metal*.

Synonymy If two words are synonymous they have the same meaning (in some specific situations), e.g. *big*, *large*.

Tense Inflectional marking on the verb used to show the time when some action, event or state takes place (e.g. as 'past', 'present' or 'future') in relation to the moment of speaking.

Top-down A model of language processing using higher-level information (e.g. context) to resolve lower-level problems involving sound structure.

Transitive verb A verb that takes a direct object, e.g. *kick*, in *She kicked the ball*.

Underlying form A form entered in the lexicon from which actual phonetic forms heard in speech are derived.

Velar A sound articulated using the back of the tongue and the soft palate or velum. Consonants like [k] (as in *kayak*) and [g] (as in *go*) are velar.

Verb phrase A phrase headed by a verb, e.g. *They might have been going.*

Voice A marking in grammar (usually done by inflectional endings) that indicates the relation of the subject and verb in the action indicated by the verb. *See also* **Active voice** and **Passive voice**.

Voiced A sound produced with the vocal cords vibrating. In English, all the vowels as well as some consonants like [l m d z] are voiced.

Voiceless A sound produced without vibration of the vocal cords. Consonants like [f s t h ʔ] are voiceless.

Wernicke's area The part of the brain that deals with understanding speech and finding vocabulary items for use in sentence production.

Word The smallest linguistic unit capable of standing meaningfully on its own in the grammar of a language. *See also* **Grammatical word, Lexical item** and **Word-form**.

Word-class This refers to what is more traditionally called 'parts of speech', i.e. a set of words that can occupy the same syntactic positions, e.g. determiners, nouns, verbs, adjectives, adverbs, prepositions.

Word-form A form realising a word in speech (*see* **Phonological word**) or writing (*see* **Orthographic word**).

Notes

8 Words galore: innovation and change

1 The data and the account of Australian diminutives is borrowed from the *Language Talkback* Project at the University of Queensland (http://www.cltr.uq.edu.au/languagetalkback/Projects/Diminutives-types.html).

This source is supplemented with data from the *Australian English Glossary from A to Zed* by David Stybr, MaestroDJS@aol.com, revised to 13 August 1996 (http://www.travel-library.com/pacific/Australia/stybr-language.html).

2 The material on internet jargon and slang is from two sources: *Free On-Line Dictionary of Computing* (http://www.nightflight.com/foldoc) and *NetLingo: The Internet dictionary*, created by Erin Jansen and Vincent James, Ojai, California, Netlingo Inc. (2002) (http://www.netlingo.com/images/netlingobookcover.gif). You may also consult S. H. Gookin and D. Gookin (2000) *Illustrated Computer Dictionary for Dummies* (Foster City, CA: IDG Books Worldwide).

9 Should English be spelt as she is spoke?

1 After the change of long /oː/ to /uː/ a subsequent fifteenth century development shortened some instances of long /uː/ to /ʊ/. So *fooda* is /fʊd/ today, except in a few northern English dialects where it remains /fuːd/. The effect of shortening was not reflected in the spelling.

Bibliography

Adams, V. (1973) *An Introduction to Modern English Word-formation*. London: Longman.

Adams, V. (2001) *Complex Words in English*. London: Pearson/Longman.

Aitchison, J. (2003) *Words in the Mind*. Oxford: Basil Blackwell.

Albrow, K. H. (1972) *The English Writing System: Notes Towards a Description*. London: Longman.

Algeo, J. (1972) *Problems in the Origins and Development of the English Language*, 2nd edn. New York: Harcourt Brace Jovanovich.

Allen, M. (1978) 'Morphological investigations'. Doctoral dissertation, University of Connecticut.

Aronoff, M. (1976) *Word-formation in Generative Grammar*. Cambridge, MA: MIT Press.

AskOxford.com (2002) *Frequently Asked Questions: The English Language*. At http://www.askoxford.com/asktheexperts/faq/aboutenglish/proportion.

Ayto, J. (1999) *20th Century Words*. Oxford: Oxford University Press.

Ayto, J. (ed.) (2002) *The Oxford Dictionary of Rhyming Slang*. Oxford: Oxford University Press.

Baker, P. (2002) *Polari: the Lost Language of Gay Men*. London: Routledge.

Barber, C. (1964) *Linguistic Change in Present-day English*. London: Oliver & Boyd.

Baron, N. S. (2000) *Alphabet to Email*. London: Routledge.

Bauer, L. (1983) *English Word-formation*. Cambridge: Cambridge University Press.

Bauer, L. (1994) *Watching English Change*. London: Longman.

Bauer, L. (2001) *Morphological Productivity*. Cambridge: Cambridge University Press.

Bauer, L. (2002) *An Introduction to International Varieties of English*. Edinburgh: Edinburgh University Press.

Bauer, L. M. (2003) *Introducing Morphology*, 2nd edn. Edinburgh: Edinburgh University Press.

Baugh, A. C. and Cable, T. (2002) *A History of the English Language*. London: Routledge.

BBC Radio 4 (2003) *Routes of English*. At http://www.bbc.co.uk/radio4/routesofenglish/storysofar/programme3_1.shtml.

Beale, P. (1985) *Eric Partridge: A Dictionary of Catch-phrases*, 2nd edn. London: Routledge & Kegan Paul.

Beattie, W. and Meikle, H. W. (eds) (1972) *Robert Burns Poems*. Harmondsworth: Penguin.

Bissantz, A. S., Johnson, K. A., Godby, C. J., Wallace, R., Jolley, C., Schaffer, D. B., Perkins, J. W., Latta, F. C. and Geoghegan, S. G. (1985) *Language Files: Materials for an Introduction to Language*, 3rd edn. Ohio: Department of Linguistics, Ohio State University/Advocate Publishing Group.

Bliss, A. J. (1966) *Dictionary of Foreign Words and Phrases in Current English*. London: Routledge & Kegan Paul.

Bloomfield, L. (1926) 'A set of postulates for the science of language'. *Language* 2: 142–64.

Bloomfield, L. (1933) *Language*. New York: Holt, Rinehart & Winston.

Bock, J. K. and Levelt, W. J. M. (1994) 'Language production: grammatical encoding'. In M. A. Gernsbacher (ed.) *Handbook of Psycholinguistics*. San Diego: Academic Press, pp. 945–84.

Boomer, D. S. and Laver, J. (1968) 'Slips of the tongue'. *British Journal of Disorders of Communication* 3: 1–12.

Bradley, D. C. (1978) 'Computational distinctions of vocabulary type'. Doctoral dissertation, MIT, Cambridge, MA.

Bradley, D. C. (1980) 'Lexical representation of derivational relation'. In M. Aronoff and M.-L. Kean (eds) *Juncture*. Saratoga, CA: Anima Libri.

Bresnan, J. (1982) 'The passive in lexical theory'. In J. Bresnan (ed.) *The Mental Representation of Grammatical Relations*. Cambridge, MA: MIT Press.

Broadbent, D. E. and Ladefoged, P. (1960) 'Vowel judgements and adaptation level'. *Proceedings of the Royal Society*, Series B (Biological Science) 151: 384–99.

Brown, R. and McNeill, D. (1966). 'The "tip of the tongue" phenomenon'. *Journal of Verbal Learning and Verbal Behavior* 5: 325–37.

Burke, D. M., MacKay, D. G., Worthley, J. S. and Wade, E. (1991) 'On the tip of the tongue: what causes word finding failures in young and older adults'. *Journal of Memory and Language* 30: 542–79.

Butterworth, B. L. (ed) (1980) *Language Production, vol. 1*. New York: Academic Press.

Butterworth, B. L. (1983) 'Lexical representation'. In B. L. Butterworth (ed.) *Language Production, Vol. 2: Development, Writing and Other Language Processes*. London: Academic Press.

Butterworth, B. L. (1989) 'Lexical access in speech production'. In W. D. Marslen-Wilson (ed.) *Lexical Representation and Process*. Cambridge, MA: MIT Press, pp. 108–35.

Bybee, J. L. (1987) *Morphology as Lexical Organisation*. Working Papers in Linguistics, Buffalo, NY: State University of New York.

Cambridge Learner's Dictionary (2001). Cambridge: Cambridge University Press.

Caplan, D. (1987) *Neurolinguistics and Linguistic Aphasiology: An Introduction*. Cambridge: Cambridge University Press.

Caplan, D. (1992) *Language: Structure, Processing, and Disorders*. Cambridge, MA: MIT Press.

Caramazza, A. and Berndt, R. S. (1985) 'A multicomponent deficit view of agrammatic Broca's aphasia'. In M.-L. Kean (ed.) *Agrammatism*. New York: Academic Press.

Carney, E. (1994) *A Survey of English Spelling*. London: Routledge.

Carroll, L. (1982) *Alice's Adventures in Wonderland and Through the Looking-Glass*. Harmondsworth: Penguin Books. (First published in 1865 and 1872 respectively.)

Carstairs-McCarthy, A. (2001) *An Introduction to English Morphology*. Edinburgh: Edinburgh University Press.

Cherry, E. C. (1953) 'Some experiments on the recognition of speech, with one and with two ears'. *Journal of the Acoustic Society of America* 25: 975–9.

Chirol, L. (1973) *Les 'mots français' et le mythe de la France en anglais contemporain*. Paris: Éditions Klincksieck.

Chomsky, N. (1965) *Aspects of the Theory of Syntax*. Cambridge, MA: MIT Press.

Chomsky, N. (1986) *Knowledge of Language*. New York: Praeger.

Chomsky, N. and Halle, M. (1968) *The Sound Pattern of English*. New York: Harper & Row.

Clark, H. H. and Clark, E. V. (1977) *Psychology of Language*. New York: Harcourt Brace Jovanovich.

Copley, J. (1961) *Shift of Meaning*. London: Oxford University Press.

Crystal, D. (1997) *The Cambridge Encyclopaedia of Language*, 2nd edn. Cambridge: Cambridge University Press.

Crystal, D. (1988) *The English Language*. Harmondsworth: Penguin Books.

Crystal, D. (1991) *A Dictionary of Linguistics and Phonetics*. Oxford: Blackwell.

Crystal, D. (1997) *English as a Global Language*. Cambridge: Cambridge University Press.

Crystal, D. (2001) *Language and the Internet*. Cambridge: Cambridge University Press.

Crystal, D. (2002) *A Dictionary of Linguistics and Phonetics*, 5th edn. Oxford: Blackwell.

Cutler, A. (1988) 'The Perfect Speech Error'. In L. Hyman and C. Li (eds), *Language, Speech, and Mind*. New York: Routledge.

Cutler, A. (1999) 'Spoken-word recognition'. In R. A. Wilson and F. C. Keil (eds), *MIT Encyclopedia of the Cognitive Sciences*. Cambridge, MA: MIT Press, pp. 677–9.

Cutler, A. and Isard, S. (1980) 'The production of prosody'. In B. L. Butterworth (ed.) *Language Production, Vol. 1: Speech and Talk*. London: Academic Press.

Dahl, R. (1982) *The BFG*. London: Jonathan Cape.

Deese, J. (1984) *Thought into Speech: The Psychology of a Language*. Englewood Cliffs, NJ: Prentice Hall.

DeFrancis, J. (1989) *Visible Speech: The Diverse Oneness of Writing Systems*. Honolulu: University of Hawaii Press.

Dell. G. S. (1986) 'A spreading-activation theory of retrieval in sentence production'. *Psychological Review* 93: 283–321.

Dell, G. S. and Reich, P. A. (1980) 'Toward a unified model of slips of the tongue'. In V. Fromkin (ed.) *Errors in Linguistic Performance: Slips of the Tongue, Ear, Pen, and Hand*. New York: Academic Press.

Diller, K. C. (1978) *The Language Teaching Controversy*. Rowley, MA: Newbury House.

Diringer, D. (1968) *The Alphabet: A Key to the History of Mankind*, 3rd edn. London: Hutchinson.

Di Sciullo, A.-M. and Williams, E. (1987) *On Defining the Word*. Cambridge, MA: MIT Press.

Eliot, T. S. (1963) *Selected Poems*. London: Faber & Faber.

Ellis, A. (1980) 'On the Freudian theory of speech errors'. In V. Fromkin (ed.). *Errors in Linguistic Performance: Slips of the Tongue, Ear, Pen, and Hand*. New York: Academic Press.

Fantoni, B. (1984) *Private Eye's Colemanballs 2*. London: *Private Eye/* André Deutsch.

Fodor, J. A. (1981) *Representations: Philosophical Essays on the Foundations of Cognitive Science*. Cambridge, MA: MIT Press.

Franklin, J. (1960) *A Dictionary of Rhyming Slang*. London: Routledge & Kegan Paul.

Frederiksen, J. and Kroll, J. (1976) 'Spelling and sound: approaches to the internal lexicon'. *Journal of Experimental Psychology: Human Perception and Performance* 2: 361–79.

Fromkin, V. (1971) 'The nonanomalous nature of anomalous utterances'. *Language* 47: 27–52.

Fromkin, V. (ed.) (1973) *Speech Errors as Linguistic Evidence*. The Hague: Mouton.

Fromkin, V. (1980) *Errors in Linguistic Performance: Slips of the Tongue, Ear, Pen, and Hand*. New York: Academic Press.

Gairdner, J. (ed.) (1983) *The Paston Letters*. Gloucester: Alan Sutton.

Ganong, W. F. (1980) 'Phonetic categorisation in auditory word perception'. *Journal of Experimental Psychology: Human Perception and Performance* 6: 110–25.

Garrett, M. F. (1975) 'The analysis of sentence production'. In G. Bower (ed.) *The Psychology of Learning and Motivation, Vol. 9*. New York: Academic Press, pp. 133–77.

Garrett, M. F. (1976) 'Syntactic processes in sentence production'. In R. J. Wales and E. C. T. Walker (eds) *New Approaches to Language Mechanisms*. Amsterdam: North Holland, pp. 231–55.

Garrett, M. F. (1980) 'Levels of processing in sentence production'. In B. L. Butterworth (ed.) *Language Production, Vol. 1: Speech and Talk*. London: Academic Press.

Geipel, J. (1971) *The Viking Legacy: The Scandinavian Influence on the English and Gaelic Languages*. Newton Abbot: David & Charles.

Gelb, I. J. (1963) *A Study of Writing*, 2nd edn. Chicago, IL: University of Chicago Press.

Giegerich, H. (1999) *Lexical Strata in English*. Cambridge: Cambridge University Press.

Glucksberg, S., Kreuz, R. and Rho, S. H. (1986) 'Context can constrain lexical access: implications for models of language comprehension'. *Journal of Experimental Psychology: Learning, Memory, and Cognition* 12: 323–35.

Goldsmith, J. (1990) *Autosegmental and Metrical Phonology*. Oxford: Basil Blackwell.

Goodglass, H. (1976) 'Agrammatism'. In H. Whitaker and H. A. Whitaker (eds) *Studies in Neurolinguistics*. New York: Academic Press.

Görlac, M. (1991) *Introduction to Early Modern English*. Cambridge: Cambridge University Press.

Green, J. (1987) *Dictionary of Jargon*. London: Routledge & Kegan Paul.

Gregg, V. H. (1986) *An Introduction to Human Memory*. London: Routledge & Kegan Paul.

Gussmann, E. (1988) 'Review of Mohanan 1986'. *Journal of Linguistics* 24: 232–9.

Halle, M. and Mohanan, K. P. (1985) 'Segmental phonology of modern English'. *Linguistic Inquiry* 16: 57–116.

Halle, M. and Stevens, K. (1962) 'Speech recognition: a model and a program for research'. *IEEE Transactions on Information Theory* 8: 2, 155–60.

Hankamer, J. (1989) 'Morphological parsing and the lexicon'. In W. D. Marslen-Wilson (ed.) *Lexical Representation and Process*. Cambridge, MA: MIT Press, pp. 392–408.

Harley, T. (2001) *The Psychology of Language: From Data to Theory*, 2nd edn. Hove: The Psychology Press.

Harris, Z. (1951) *Methods in Structural Linguistics*. Chicago, IL: University of Chicago Press.

Haugen, E. (1950) 'The analysis of linguistic borrowing'. *Language* 26: 210–35.

Hogaboam, T. W. and Perfetti, C. A. (1975) Lexical ambiguity and sentence comprehension. *Journal of Verbal Learning and Verbal Behavior* 14: 265–75.

Holder, R. W. (1987) *The Faber Dictionary of Euphemisms*. London: Faber & Faber.

Hörmann, H. (1986) *Meaning and Context: An Introduction to the Psychology of Language* (*Cognition and Language: a Series in Psycholinguistics*). Ed. with intro. by R. E. Innis. Trans. of *Einführung in die Psycholinguistik*. New York and London: Plenum Press.

Hudson, R. (1984) *Word Grammar*. Oxford: Basil Blackwell.

Hulst, H. van der and Smith, N. (1982a) *The Structure of Phonological Representations, Part I*. Dordrecht: Foris.

Hulst, H. van der and Smith, N. (1982b) *The Structure of Phonological Representations, Part II*. Dordrecht, Foris.

Hulst, H. van der and Smith, N. (1982c) 'Introduction'. In H. van der Hulst and N. Smith (eds) *The Structure of Phonological Representations, Part I*. Dordrecht: Foris.

Jackson, H. (1988) *Words and their Meaning*. London: Longman.

James, L. E. and Burke, D. M. (2000) 'Phonological Priming Effects on Word Retrieval and Tip-of-the-Tongue Experiences in Young and Older Adults'. *Journal of Experimental Psychology: Learning, Memory and Cognition* 26 (6): 1378–91.

Kakutani, M. (2000) 'When the geeks get snide: computer slang scoffs at wetware (the Humans)'. At http://faculty.plattsburgh.edu/stewart. denenberg/csc372/articles/Jargon.html.

Katamba, F. (1989) *An Introduction to Phonology*. London: Longman.

Katamba, F. (1993) *Morphology*. London: Macmillan.

Kean, M.-L. (ed.) (1985) *Agrammatism*. New York: Academic Press.

Kiparsky, P. (1982a) 'From cyclic phonology to lexical phonology'. In H. van der Hulst and N. Smith (eds) *The Structure of Phonological Representations, Part I*. Dordrecht: Foris.

Kiparsky, P. (1982b) 'Lexical morphology and phonology'. In I.-S. Yang (ed.) *Linguistics in the Morning Calm*. Seoul: Hanshin.

Kiparsky, P. (1983) 'Word formation and the lexicon'. In F. Ingemnn (ed.) *Proceedings of the 1982 Mid-America Linguistics Conference*. Lawrence, KA: University of Kansas.

Klavans, J. (1985) 'The independence of syntax and phonology in cliticisation'. *Language* 61: 95–120.

Labov, W. (1972) *Sociolinguistic Patterns*. Philadelphia: University of Pennsylvania Press.

Lass, R. (1987) *The Shape of English: Structure and History*. London: J. M. Dent.

Lawrence, D. H. (1960) 'Love among the haystacks' (1930). In *Love among the Haystacks and Other Stories*. Harmondsworth: Penguin.

Lecours, A. R. and Lhermitte, F. (1983) 'Clinical forms of aphasia'. In A. R. Lecours, F. Lhermitte and B. Bryans (eds) *Aphasiology*. London: Baillière, Tindall.

Lederer, R. (1989) *Anguished English*. London. Robson Books Ltd.

Levelt, W. J. M. (1989) *Speaking: From Intention to Articulation*. Cambridge, MA: MIT Press.

Levelt, W. J. M., Roelofs, A. and Meyer, A. S. (1999) 'A theory of lexical access in speech production'. *Behavioral and Brain Sciences* 22: 1–75.

Lieber, R. (1983) 'Argument linking and compounding in English'. *Linguistic Inquiry* 14: 251–86.

Lipka, L. (1990) *An Outline of English Lexicology*. Tübingen: Max Niemeyer.

Lyons, J. (1968) *Theoretical Linguistics*. Cambridge: Cambridge University Press.

M & S Magazine, The (1992) August issue, London: Marks & Spencer PLC.

Maclay, H. and Osgood, C. E. (1959) 'Hesitation phenomena in spontaneous English speech'. *Word* 15, 19–44.

McClelland, J. M. and Elman, J. L. (1986) 'The TRACE model of speech perception'. *Cognitive Psychology* 18: 1–86.

McMahon, A. J. (2001) *An Introduction to English Phonology*. Edinburgh: Edinburgh University Press.

McQueen, J. (1991) 'The influence of the lexicon on phonetic categorisation: stimulus quality and word-final ambiguity'. *Journal of Experimental Psychology: Human Perception and Performance* 17: 433–43.

Marchand, H. (1969) *The Categories and Types of Present-day English Word-formation*. Munich: C. H. Beck.

Marslen-Wilson, W. D. (1987) 'Functional parallelism in spoken word-recognition'. *Cognition* 25: 71–102.

Marslen-Wilson, W. D. (1989) 'Access and integration: projecting sound on to meaning'. In W. D. Marslen-Wilson *Lexical Representation and Process*. Cambridge, MA: MIT Press, pp. 3–24.

Marslen-Wilson, W. D. (1990) 'Activation, competition, and frequency in lexical access'. In G. T. M. Altmann (ed.) *Cognitive Models of Speech Processing: Psycholinguistic and Computational Perspectives*. Cambridge, MA: MIT Press.

Marslen-Wilson, W. D. and Welsh, A. (1978) 'Processing interactions and lexical access during word recognition in continuous speech'. *Cognitive Psychology* 10: 29–63.

Marslen-Wilson, W. D., Tyler, L. K., Waksler, R. and Older, L. (1994) 'Morphology and meaning in the English mental lexicon'. *Psychological Review* 101 (1): 3–33.

Matthei, E. and Roeper, T. (1983) *Understanding and Producing Speech*. London: Fontana.

Matthews, P. (1991) *Morphology*, 2nd edn. Cambridge: Cambridge University Press. First published in 1974.

Miller, J. (2001) *An Introduction to English Syntax*. Edinburgh: Edinburgh University Press.

Milligan, Spike (1968) *Silly Verse for Kids*. London: Penguin Books.

Mohanan, K. (1986) *The Theory of Lexical Phonology*. Reidel: Dordrecht.

Norris, D. (1994) 'SHORTLIST: a connectionist model of continuous speech recognition'. *Cognition* 52: 189–234.

O'Grady, W., Dobrovolsky, M. and Katamba, F. (eds) (1997) *Contemporary Linguistics*. London: Addison Wesley Longman.

Oldfield, R. C. (1963) 'Individual vocabulary and semantic currency: a preliminary study'. *British Journal of Social and Clinical Psychology* 2: 122–30.

Opie, I. and Opie, P. (1980) *A Nursery Companion*. Oxford: Oxford University Press.

Partridge, E. (1933) *Slang: Today and Yesterday*. London: Routledge.

Phillips, M. (1993) 'Another day, another scandal'. *The Guardian*, 16 January: 24.

Phythian, B. A. (1982) *A Concise Dictionary of Foreign Expressions*. London: Hodder & Stoughton.

Pyles, T. and Algeo, J. (1982) *The Origins and Development of the English Language*. New York: Harcourt Brace Jovanovich.

Quirk, R. and Greenbaum, S. (1973) *A University Grammar of English*. London: Longman.

Rao, S. G. (1954) *Indian Words in English*. Oxford: Clarendon Press.

Research and Development Unit for English Studies (RDUES) (1999) *Neologisms from 1999: RDUES*. At http://www.rdues.liv.ac.uk/newwds/1999.html.

Roeper, T. and Siegel, D. (1978) 'A lexical transformation for verbal compounds'. *Linguistic Inquiry* 9: 199–260.

Room, A. (1986) *Dictionary of Changes in Meaning*. London: Routledge & Kegan Paul.

Rosch, E. (1973) 'On the internal structure of perceptual and semantic categories'. In T. M. Moore (ed.) *Cognitive Development and the Acquisition of Language*. New York: Academic Press, pp. 111–44.

Rosch, E. (1978) 'Principles of categorization'. In E. Rosch and B. B. Lloyd (eds) *Cognition and Categorization*. Hillsdale, NJ: Erlbaum, pp. 27–48.

Rubach, J. (1984) *Cyclic and Lexical Phonology*. Dordrecht: Foris.

Sagan, C. (1985) *Cosmos*. New York: Ballantine.

Salzman, L. F. (1952) *Building in England Down to 1540: A Documentary History*. Oxford: Clarendon Press.

Sampson, G. (1985) *Writing Systems: A Linguistic Approach.* London: Hutchinson.

Sapir, L. (1921) *Language.* New York: Harcourt Brace & World.

Saussure, F. (1916) *Cours de linguistique générale.* Paris: Payot. (English translation: *A Course in General Linguistics.* London: Duckworth.)

Savin, H. (1963) 'Word-frequency effect and errors in the perception of speech'. *Journal of the Acoustical Society of America* 35: 200–6.

Schwartz, M. F., Linebarger, M. C. and Saffran, E. M. (1985) 'The status of the syntactic deficit in agrammatism'. In M.-L. Kean (ed.) *Agrammatism.* New York: Academic Press.

Scragg, D. G. (1973) *Spelling.* London: André Deutsch. (Revised version of G. H. Vallins, *Spelling*, 1954.)

Seashore, R. H. and Eckerson, L. D. (1940) 'The measurement of individual differences in general English vocabularies'. *Journal of Educational Psychology* 31: 14–38.

Selkirk, E. O. (1982) *The Syntax of Words.* Cambridge, MA: MIT Press.

Sheridan, R. B. *The Rivals* (1775) In C. Price (ed.) (1975) *Sheridan Plays.* London: Oxford University Press.

Siegel, D. (1971) 'Some lexical transderivational constraints in English'. Unpublished MS, Department of Linguistics, MIT, Cambridge, MA.

Siegel, D. (1974) 'Topics in English morphology'. Ph.D. dissertation, MIT, Cambridge, MA. (Published by Garland, New York, 1979.)

Simpson, G. B. (1984) 'Lexical ambiguity and its role in models of word recognition'. *Psychological Bulletin* 96: 316–40.

Simpson, J. M. Y. (1979) *A First Course in Linguistics.* Edinburgh: Edinburgh University Press.

Skeat, W. W. (1982) *Principles of English Etymology.* Oxford: Clarendon Press.

Smitherman, G. (1994) *Black Talk.* New York: Houghton Mifflin.

Spencer, A. (1991) *Morphological Theory.* Oxford: Basil Blackwell.

Sperber, D. and Wilson, D. (1995) *Relevance: Communication and Cognition*, 2nd edn. Oxford: Blackwell.

Stanners, R. F., Neiser, J. J., Hernon, W. P. and Hall, R. (1979) 'Memory representation for morphologically related words'. *Journal of Verbal Learning and Behaviour* 18: 399–412.

Stemberger, J. P. (1985) 'An interactive activation model of language production'. In A. W. Ellis (ed.) *Progress in the Psychology of Language, Vol. 1.* Hove: Lawrence Erlbaum Associates Ltd, pp. 143–86.

Stevens, K. and House, A. S. (1972) 'Speech perception'. In J. V. Tobias (ed.) *Foundations of Modern Auditory Theory, Vol. 2.* New York: Academic Press, pp. 3–62.

Stuart, J. (1997) *A Glasgow Bible.* Edinburgh: St Andrew Press.

Stubbs, M. (1980) *Language and Literacy: The Sociolinguistics of Reading and Writing.* London: Routledge & Kegan Paul.

Stubbs, M. (1998) 'German loanwords and cultural stereotypes'. *English Today* 53 (14) (Jan): 19–26.

Studdert-Kennedy, M. (1974) 'The perception of speech'. In T. A. Sebeok (ed.) *Current Trends in Linguistics, Vol. 12: Linguistics and Adjacent Arts and Sciences*. The Hague: Mouton, pp. 2349–85.

Studdert-Kennedy, M. (1976) 'Speech perception'. In N. Lass (ed.) *Contemporary Issues in Experimental Phonetics*. New York: Academic Press, pp. 213–93.

Swadesh, M. and Voeglin, C. F. (1939) 'A problem in phonological alternation'. *Language* 15: 1–10. (Reprinted in M. Joos (ed.) (1957) *Readings in Linguistics 1*. Chicago, IL: University of Chicago Press.)

Taft, M. (1979) 'Recognition of affixed words and the word frequency effect'. *Memory and Cognition* 7: 263–72.

Taft, M. (1981) 'Prefix stripping revisited'. *Journal of Verbal Learning and Behaviour* 20: 289–97.

Taft, M. and Foster, K. (1975) 'Lexical storage and retrieval of prefixed words'. *Journal of Verbal Learning and Behaviour* 14: 638–47.

Tanenhaus, M. K. and Lucas, M. M. (1987) 'Context effects in lexical processing'. In U. Frauenfelder and L. K. Tyler (eds) *Spoken Word Recognition* (*Cognition* special issue). Cambridge, MA: MIT Press, pp. 213–34.

Thun, N. (1963) *Reduplicative Words in English*. Uppsala: Carl Bloms.

Trevelyan, G. M. (1949) *Illustrated English Social History, Vol. 1: Chaucer's England and the Early Tudors*. London: Longman.

Trudgill, P. and Hannah, J. (1994) *International English*, 3rd edn. London: Arnold.

Vachek, J. (1973) *Written Language: General Problems and Problems of English*. The Hague: Mouton.

Wardlaw, J. (2003) *The Little Man Legislative Slips Of The Tongue*. Extract from http://www.humorbin.com/showitem.asp?item=279.

Warren, R. M. and Warren, R. P. (1970) 'Auditory illusions and confusions'. *Scientific American* 223: 30–6.

Wells, J. C. (1982) *Accents of English I: An Introduction*. Cambridge: Cambridge University Press.

Woodworth, R. S. (1938) *Experimental Psychology*. New York: Holt.

Wordplay website (2003) http://www.fun-with-words.com/ambiguous_garden_path.html.

Young, J. and Young, P. (1981) *The Ladybird Book of Jokes, Riddles and Rhymes*. Loughborough: Ladybird Books.

Zijderveld, C. (1979) *On Clichés: The Supersedure of Meaning by Function*. London: Routledge & Kegan Paul.

Zwicky, A. (1985) 'Clitics and particles'. *Language* 61: 283–305.

Zwicky, A. and Pullum, G. (1983) 'Cliticisation vs. inflection: English *n't*'. *Language* 59: 502–13.

Name index

Adams, V. 66
Aitchison, J. 128, 238, 269, 276, 277
Albrow, K. H. 206
Algeo, J. 151, 208
Allen, M. 91
Aronoff, M. 98, 103

Baker, P. 171
Barber, C. 179
Baron, N. 223
Bradley, D. C. 241
Bauer, L. 53, 66, 73, 100, 103, 144, 160, 174
Baugh, A. C. and Cable, T. 140, 151, 180
Beattie, W. and Meikle, H. W. 191
Berndt, R. S. 286
Bissantz, A. S. 288
Bliss, A. J. 143–4
Bloomfield, L. 11, 101, 171
Bock, J. K. and Levelt, W. J. M. 278
Boole, G. (Boolean) 175
Boomer, D. S. and Laver, J. 269
Bradley, D. C. 241
Bresnan, J. 89
Broadbent, D. E. and Ladefoged, P. 247
Broca, P. 284–7, 289, 292, 294
Brown, R. and McNeill, D. 280
Burke, D. M., MacKay, D. G., Worthley, J. S. and Wade, E. 281

Butterworth, B. L. 240, 241, 268, 272, 273
Bybee, J. L. 241

Campbell, G. 180
Caplan, D. 286
Caramazza, A. 286
Caramazza, A. and Berndt, R. S. 286
Carney, E. 201
Carroll, L. 6
Celsius, A. 175
Cherry, E. C. 247
Chirol, L. 154–9
Chomsky, N. 237
Chomsky, N. and Halle, M. 212
Coleman, D. 283
Copley, J. 174
Crystal, D. 9, 199–200, 204, 215, 216, 218, 284–5, 286
Cutler, A. 261, 268
Cutler, A. and Isard, S. 272

Dahl, R. 54, 55, 229–30
Deese, J. 280
Dell, G. S. 276
Dell, G. S. and Reich, P. A. 276
Diller, K. C. 239
Di Sciullo, A.-M. and Williams, E. 24, 76
Dostoevsky, L. 172

Eliot, T. S. 11–12
Ellis, A. 270
Exner, S. 284

Fodor, J. A. 238
Ford, H. 174
Freud, S. 270
Fromkin, V. 269–70, 272, 274–5, 291

Ganong, W. F. 246
Garrett, M. F. 264, 268, 273–4, 289
Geiger-(Müller), H. 159, 175
Giegerich, H. 50, 105–110, 221
Geipel, J. 150–1
Glucksberg, S., Kreuz, R. and Rho, S. H. 249
Goodglass, H. 286
Green, J. 187, 190

Halle, M. and Mohanan, K. P. 91, 105
Halle, M. and Stevens, K. 255
Hankamer, J. 240, 241–2
Harley, T. 240, 256
Harris, Z. 102
Haugen, E. 137
Henry II (1154–89) 152
Heschl, R. L. 284
Hogaboam, T. W. and Perfetti, C. A. 249
Holder, R. W. 190
Holmes, S. 190
Hoover, W. H. 194
Hörmann, H. 276, 277
House, A. S. 255
Hudson, R. 238
Hulst, van der, H. and Smith, N. 109

Jackson, H. 174
James, L.E. and Burke, D.M. 281–2

Kakutani, M. 186–7
Katamba, F. 64, 66, 76, 91, 103, 109
Kean, M.-L. 286
Kiparsky, P. 91, 93, 105–6

Lass, R. 151, 153
Lawrence, D. H. 82
Lecours, A. R. and Lhermitte, F. 286
Levelt, W. J. M. 264–5, 276, 278, 289
Lipka, L. 277
Lyons, J. 24, 107

M&S Magazine 13
McAdam, J. L. 174
McClelland, J. M. and Elman J. L. 255, 257, 258
Mach, E. 175
Maclay, H. and Osgood, C. E 280
Marchand, T. 66, 69, 185
Marslen-Wilson, W. 243–5, 255, 277, and Welsh , A. 255
Matthei, T. and Siegel, D. 276
Matthews, P. 24
Milligan, S. 46–7, 210
Mohanan, K. 91, 105–6, 109

Norris, D. 255

O'Grady, W., Dobrovolsky, M. and Katamba, F. 188
Oldfield, R. C. 239, 280
Opie, I. and Opie, P. 198
Osgood, C. E. 280

Partridge, E. 169
Paston, J. 153
Phillips, M. 75
Phythian, B. A. 145
Pitman, J. 218
Private Eye 283

Rao, S. G. 260–1
Reed, K. 218
Repps, R. 153
Roeper, T. and Siegel, D. 66
Room, A. 175
Rubach, J. 91
Russell, B. 191–2

Sagan, C. 242
Salzman, L. F. 152

Sampson, G. 197, 199, 206, 218–19
Sapir, L. 72
Sassoon, S. 21
Saussure, F. 148, 173
Savin, H. 279
Schwartz, M. F., Linebarger, M. C. and Saffran, E. M. 287
Scragg, D. G. 199, 203, 219
Seashore, R. H. and Eckerson, L. D. 239
Selkirk, E. O. 66, 69, 72, 108
Shakespeare, W.: (*Anthony and Cleopatra*) 12; (*Henry V*) 12; (*Romeo and Juliet*) 139, 172, 173, 211
Shaw, G. B. 218
Sheridan, R. B. 282, 297
Siegel, D. 91, 103, 104
Simpson, G. B. 249
Simpson, J. Y. M. 126–7
Skeat, W. W. 57
Smith G. D. 171
Smitherman, G. 170
Spencer, A. 91
Spooner, Revd W. A. 275, 299
Stanners, R. F., Neiser, J. J., Hernon, W. P. and Hall, R. 240

Stevens, K. 255; and House, A. 255
Stuart, J. 220
Stubbs, M. 159, 199, 202–3, 215
Studdert-Kennedy, M. 255
Swadesh, M. and Voeglin, C. F. 40
Swift, J. 180

Taft, M. and Foster, K. 240
Tanenhaus, M. K. and Lucas, M. M. 249
Thun, N. 73
Trevelyan, G. M. 151
Tyler, M. 283

Vachek, J. 199

Wernicke, C. 284, 285, 286–9, 300
Wijk, A. 218
Winchester, S. 13
Woodworth, R. S. 280

Young, J. and Young, P. 20–1

Zijderveld, C. 172

Subject index

abbreviations xx, 165, 183–4, 187–8, 224
ablaut 73, 292
ablaut motivated compounds 72–3, 81
access stage 256
acronyms 159, 183–4; *see also* abbreviation
adopted words 159; *see also* borrowing, loanwords
affixation 54, 57–64, 67, 81, 94, 103–10, 296; *see also* affixes
affix-driven stratification 93, 106, 107, 110
affixes 40, 42, 50–3, 81, 136, 221, 236–7, 268, 272–4, 286–7, 292; *see also* back-formation, Broca's
affix stranding 273–4
affix stripping 240; *see also* Full Listing Hypothesis
African American English (AAE) 169–70
agent 59, 69, 89, 100, 129, 266, 278, 292; *see also* agentive noun, passive, subject
agentive noun 37, 97–8, 178
agglutinating language 241–3
agrammatic aphasia 286; *see also* Broca's aphasia
agrammatism 292
allomorphs 31–43, 47–8, 90, 98–100, 149, 212, 292; *see also* morpheme
allophone 18, 148–9, 154, 292

allophonic rules 40–1
alphabet 198, 228, 238, 293
alphabetic writing 188, 197; *see also* roman alphabet, spelling reform
amelioration 176, 194
American English 139, 158–9, 162, 206, 216–17; *see also* African American English
analogy 5, 136, 184–5; *see also* back-formation, false etymology, metaphor
analysis by synthesis 255, 261
analytic language *see* isolating language
anaphora 293
anaphoric expression 250
anglicisation 144–5; *see also* nativisation of loanwords
antonymy 120–1, 269
aphasia 283–9, 293
Arabic 135, 141
arbitrariness (of the linguistic sign) 5, 87, 114, 173–4, 200; *see also* iconic, onomatopoeia
argument structure 266–7, 271, 289
articulation: in phonetics 45, 104, 296; in psycholinguistics 264, 266, 268
assimilation 39–40, 48, 90, 104, 257, 293; *see also* phonological conditioning
Australian English 162, 181, 217

back-clipping 180–1
back-formation 185
base 38, 293
base-driven stratification 105–10
base form *see* underlying
    representation
bilingualism 138–9, 152
Black Talk *see* African American
    English
blends 186, 189, 194, 269, 271,
    276
blocking 96–8, 99, 108–9
Bloomfield 11, 101, 171
borrowing 160–2, 163, 164–5, 293,
    297; *see also* adopted words,
    Latinate, loanwords
bound morphemes 43–4, 47, 51,
    77, 81, 293, 296; *see also* free
    morphemes
bound roots 51–2, 101–2, 107–8,
    241
Broca's aphasia 286–7, 289, 294
Broca's area 284–6

calques *see* loan translations
Canadian pronunciation 209
catch-phrases 172
Celtic 151, 162
Chinese 17, 161
'clear *l*' xix, 17–8
cliché 172, 194, 294
clipping 180–2,189, 194, 224, 225,
    294
clitic 77–81, 272
clitic group 79
closed word classes 54
cocktail party phenomenon *see*
    selective listening
code-switching 139, 145–6, 152
cognate 163, 294
cognitive meaning 15, 44, 80, 195,
    238
cohort model 255–7, 261
co-hyponyms 119, 269
collocation 114, 238, 253–4, 294
competence 246, 294; *see also* tacit
    knowledge
complementary distribution 33–4,
    47, 294

compositionality 69, 74, 81, 87–8,
    98, 107
compounding 54, 64, 66–73, 81,
    105–6, 185–90
comprehension 235–6, 240
conceptualisation 264–5
connectionism 257, 294
connotation 113–4, 130, 176, 182,
    238
conscious mind 270
constituent assembly 265, 267, 271
constituent structure *see* phrase
    structure rules
content words 15–16, 44, 51, 54,
    164, 206, 224, 267, 272–3, 274,
    276, 286–7, 289, 294; *see also*
    open word classes
context 5, 18, 30, 37, 40, 104,
    113–14, 120, 122, 182, 194, 201,
    223; *see also* ambiguity,
    complementary distribution,
    pragmatics, speech recognition
context-dependent models 249
contrast 35–7, 47–8, 149; *see also*
    distinctive features, morpheme,
    phoneme
conversion 54, 64–6, 81, 108, 168
copy cat formations *see* fads
core vocabulary 163
Cornish 151
count noun 88, 237
cranberry words 101–2
cuisine 157
cyberspeak 207–9

'dark *l*' xviii, 17–18
dead metaphors 179
decency *see* euphemism
derivation 53–62, 81, 294
derivational affixes 59, 96, 106–7;
    see also neutral and non-neutral
    affixes, zero derivation
derivational morphology 97, 99,
    102–3; *see also* lexical
    morphology
derivational suffixes 59–62, 63–4,
    93, 96
derivations 93–6; *see also*
    underlying representations

deverbal compound nouns 69–70, 72
dictionary 4–5, 7, 11, 18–20, 28, 30, 58, 69, 75, 80, 122–4, 160, 202, 238–9, 240, 277, 296; *see also* etymological dictionary, lexicon, mental lexicon, smiley dictionary
dictionary entries 37, 88
digraph 199
direct borrowing 135; *see also* borrowing
distinctive features 258–9
distribution 33–5, 37–8, 42, 101–2, 120, 295; *see also* complementary distribution
doublespeak 192–3

Ebonics *see* African American English
email 222–8
emoticons 225–6
endocentric compound 68
Eskimo 142, 181
etymological dictionary 52, 57, 111
euphemism 88, 142–3, 190–4
exocentric compound 68

fads 74, 184–5; *see also* slang
false etymology 136–7
fashion 157–8
FLH *see* Full Listing Hypothesis
fore-clipping 180–1
form 36
formatives 53
formulation 264–5
free morphemes 43–4, 51, 295
free root 101, 108
French 4, 88, 93, 102, 114, 135, 137–8, 140–8, 160, 162, 175–7, 207–8, 213, 219, 221–2, 296; *see also* Latinate, *mots français*, Norman French, Old French
French influence 151–8
frequency 201–2, 241, 249–50, 253–4, 259, 279
Freudian slips 270
fricative 39–40, 148–9, 203, 245, 295

Full Listing Hypothesis 240–4, 254, 261
function 36
function assignment 266, 268, 271–4
function words 15, 16, 44, 164, 206, 244, 264, 268, 289, 202; *see also* Broca's aphasia, grammatical encoding
functional processing 265

garden path sentences 251–2, 261–3; *see also* structural ambiguity
geek-speak *see* internet slang and jargon
generating 72, 256
genitive 40–1, 212, 295; *see also* clitics
German 107, 114, 137, 143, 159, 162, 163, 176, 208, 284
Germanic 162–3
gerundive noun 70, 110
Glaswegian 220
global ambiguity 252
grammatical context 41–2, 53, 64
grammatical effects of borrowing 149
grammatical encoding 265–8, 276, 289
grammatical encoding errors 269–74
grammatical information 237; *see also* syntactic information
grammatical meanings 22
grammatical morphemes 287; *see also* function words, inflectional affixes
grammatical relation 266–7; *see also* syntactic function
grammatical words 21–5, 41, 44, 56, 81, 278, 289, 295; *see also* grammatical encoding, lemma
Greek (or Hellenic) 93, 140, 141, 142, 144, 149, 160, 162, 163, 213, 219, 221, 237
guessing 245, 248–9

head 67–70, 78–80, 118, 142, 295
hierarchical strata 93
high-level information 246
homonym 122–3, 173–4, 295
homophone 122, 124, 295
homophony 125, 173
host 78–80,
host language 147
hot node 277–9

iconic 45, 47–8, 226, 295
identity 139
idioms 75–7, 81, 190
imported words 149, 212; see also
    borrowing
inclusion 119, 277
indefinite article 33, 35, 65
Independent, The 13
Indian languages 160–1, 213
indirect borrowing 135–6, 160
Indo-European 12, 124, 162–4, 295
Indo-Iranian 163
infixes 52–3, 296
inflection 53–6, 62–4, 80–1, 106,
    146, 226, 237, 265; see also
    grammatical encoding
inflectional affixes 42, 63, 100,
    268, 274, 286–7, 292, 299
inflectional allomorphy 98–100
inflectional infelicities 271–4
inflectional morphemes 63–4, 149,
    272–4, 276, 279, 287, 289
inflectional morphology 97–9,
    102
inflectional suffixes 62–4, 90,
    240
initial teaching alphabet (i.t.a.) 218
institutionalised words 74–5, 183
instrument 67, 69–70, 296
integration stage 256
internal structure 30–1, 63, 76, 81
internet slang and jargon 186–90
isolating language 62–3, 343, 296
Italian 138, 143, 156, 158, 162,
    207–8, 215

Japanese 142, 161–2
jargon 168–9; see also internet
    slang and jargon

labelled brackets 56
labial 45, 103, 296
language areas 284–5
language change 162, 171
language contact 150–1; see also
    borrowing
language faculty 286
Latin 52, 93, 99, 124, 137, 140–2,
    144, 149, 151, 153, 160, 162,
    163, 174, 213, 219, 221
Latinate 93, 99, 102, 163–4
lemma 266–8, 278–9, 289, 296; see
    also dictionary, grammatical
    word
lemma selection 266, 279
levels see hierarchical strata
lexeme 18–21; see also lexical
    item, lemma, word
lexical ambiguity 21, 122–5, 249
lexical categories 50–1
lexical conditioning 42
lexical items 21, 52, 54, 56, 64, 76,
    87, 89, 99, 108, 123–5, 127,
    135, 168, 170, 172, 179, 202,
    235–6, 241, 249, 256, 261, 266,
    289, 296; see also compounding,
    content word, lemma, lexeme,
    lexicon
lexical morphology 90–112, 274
lexical phonology (LP); see also
    lexical morphology
lexical retrieval 239, 249–53, 289;
    see also Spoonerisms, TOT
lexical revivals 178–9
lexical selection 265, 269–71,
    279
lexical semantics 113–32; see also
    meaning
lexicographers' dictionaries 238;
    see also dictionary,
lexicon 4, 68, 72, 75, 81, 116, 125,
    129, 135, 145–6, 149, 151, 154,
    160, 162, 163, 169–70, 185, 186,
    187, 194, 201, 223, 238, 296;
    see also dictionary; mental
    lexicon
lingua franca 140, 160, 216
linguistic knowledge 246; see also
    competence

linguistic sign 4–5, 45–6, 48; *see also* arbitrariness
listed (in the lexicon) 4, 7, 9, 28, 50, 68, 74–5, 81, 87, 94, 261; *see also* FLH, idioms, lexical item
literature 21, 155, 220
loanshift 137–8
loan translations 137–8, 159
loanwords 158–62, 164, 296
local ambiguity 252
location 70
loss of words 177–8
love and sexuality 157
Luganda 136, 237

main stress 15–16, 53, 205
malapropism 282–3, 297
manifestation 20, 25, 35, 38, 254; *see also* realisation
manufacturing lexical items 168–94
Maori 142
ME *see* Middle English
meaning 4–5, 7, 11, 14, 15, 21, 24, 27, 28, 35, 69, 75, 87–8, 98, 101–2, 107, 173–80, 189–94, 201, 219, 238, 244–5, 247, 249, 250–5, 261; *see also* arbitrariness, iconic, compositionality, derivation; lexeme, mental lexicon, pragmatics, semantics, word meaning
mental lexicon 4, 9, 87, 235–44, 250, 254, 261, 269, 277, 280–1, 286–7, 289, 296, 297
message 244, 247, 264–5
metaphor 179–80, 186, 190, 194
Middle English 2, 124, 144, 151, 164, 177
minimal free form 23
morph 32–5
morpheme 27–48; *see also* affix, clitic, root
morpheme sequencing 95
morphological objects 75–6
morphological parsing 240, 243
morphological signposts 212–13

morphology 7–8, 9, 27–31; *see also* morpheme, word
morphophonemic rules 38, 40–1; *see also* underlying representations
motor aphasia *see* Broca's aphasia
mots français, les 146–8
MTV 171
multiple access model 249–50
music 140, 155, 156, 158, 169

nasal 17, 147, 148, 258, 275, 297
nativisation of loanwords 144–8
NEG transportation 272–4
neurolinguistic processing 285
neutral and non-neutral affixes 91–3
New Spelling 218–19
New York Times 286–7
noise 248, 260
nonce words 74, 81
non-count noun 88
non-European languages 159–62
Norman French 151–4

obligatoriness 54
OE *see* Old English
OED 9, 11, 13, 219
Old English 12, 138, 148, 149, 150, 151, 163, 175, 177–8, 207–8, 219
Old French 124, 144, 149, 176
Old Norse (ON) 138, 144, 150–1, 163, 177
onomatopoeia 44–8, 114, 173, 297
open lexical classes 138; *see also* open word classes
open word classes 54; *see also* content words
orthographic representation 4, 235, 236; *see also* spelling
orthographic word 12–14, 18, 20, 25, 224, 237, 297; *see also* spelling, word form
Oxford English Dictionary see OED

painting 155
paralinguistic features 225
parsing 240–4, 251–2, 297
passive 60, 88–9, 297
past participle 19, 22, 41, 42,
    89
pejoration 176, 194
phonaesthemes 44–5, 48; *see also*
    onomatopoeia
phoneme xviii, xix, 15, 17–18, 32,
    35, 60–1, 148–9, 154, 197–8,
    201, 207, 228, 253, 255, 258–61,
    275, 292
phoneme restoration effect 246–7,
    260–1
phoneme split 148–9, 154
phonemic transcription 14–15
phonetic representation *see* surface
    representation
phonetic stage 245–6
phonological anticipations 274
phonological conditioned
    allomorphs 37–41, 211
phonological effects of borrowing
    148–9
phonological encoding 265, 266,
    268
phonological encoding errors
    274–6
phonological information 89–90,
    236–7
phonological preservations 274
phonological representation 4, 32,
    197, 236, 254, 276, 279–80, 283,
    288, 289
phonological stage 245–6
phonological words 14, 16, 20, 78,
    104, 237
phonology 4, 40–2, 66. 68, 148,
    154, 164, 205, 207, 221, 226,
    266, 269, 289, 298; *see also*
    distinctive features, lexical
    phonology, phoneme
phonotactics 16–17, 90, 147, 183,
    201, 245–6, 298
phrasal (phonology) rules *see*
    post-lexical rules
phrase structure rules 70–2,
    81

phrase structure trees 72
Polari 171
polysemy 122–5, 129, 173, 174,
    298
positional mobility 23–4
positional processing 265, 267–8,
    271
post-lexical rules 104
potential words 74–5, 104
pragmatics 113, 129–30, 182
prefix 52, 57, 63, 66, 74–5, 81,
    95–6, 298; *see also* NEG
    transportation
prefix stripping 240
prelexical 250, 256, 260
prestige 15, 139
productivity: potential words 81,
    98, 100–4, 107, 109, 298;
    see also nonce words,
progressive aspect 19, 63, 298
punctuation 54, 225, 262

Queen's Christmas speech 171
Queen's English 15, 216–17; *see
    also* Received Pronounciation

RDUES (Research and
    Development Unit for English
    Studies) 13
realisation 20, 40, 212, 218, 289
rebus principle 188
Received Pronunciation xviii–xix,
    15, 298
receptive aphasia *see* Wernicke's
    aphasia
reduplication 72–3
referential meaning *see* cognitive
    meaning
relevance 21, 248–9, 261
representation *see* realisation
rhyme motivated compounds 73
rhyming slang 170–1
Rolando 284
roman alphabet 207
Romance languages 162, 296
root 50–2, 54, 63, 73–4, 81, 88,
    93–6, 98, 100–2, 107–8, 124,
    144, 183, 186, 219, 221, 240–2,
    273, 289, 293; *see also* affix,

base, base-driven stratification, bound roots, stem, underived root
root-based 107–10
RP *see* Received Pronunciation

satellite 241–3
Scandinavian loanwords 150–1
selection stage 256, 269
selective listening 247, 261
semantic field 12–17, 130, 140, 269–70, 277, 299
semantic narrowing 149–50, 175
semantic properties 118, 269
semantic role 129, 266–7
semantics 4, 85, 182; *see also* lexical semantics, meaning
semantic widening 174–5
shadowing 247
Shavian 218
SHORTLIST 260–1
sibilants 39
Simpler Spelling Society 218
slang 169–70, 173, 179, 194, 213, 224; *see also* fads, internet slang and jargon, rhyming slang
Slavic 162
slips of the tongue 268–76
smiley 189, 224–6
smiley dictionary 226
society 156
soft palate 18, 297, 300
Spanish 116, 141, 142, 143, 162, 208
speech community 5, 218
speech production 264–83
speech recognition 244–61; *see also* comprehension
spelling 17, 18, 54–5, 90, 122, 135, 146, 157, 173, 197–230, 236; *see also* orthographic word
spelling pronunciation 221–2
spelling reform 199, 214–22
Spoonerisms 275–6
spreading activation model 276–80, 289
stability *see* positional mobility
stem 38–41, 63–4, 81, 90, 91, 98–9, 107, 204, 241, 243–4, 274

stop xix, 17, 245, 295
stratum *see* hierarchical strata
stress 15–16, 53, 54, 58, 62, 66, 68, 80, 91–7, 103–4, 109, 147, 205–6, 236, 268, 272, 276, 280, 299
Strict Cycle Condition 106
structural ambiguity 129, 250, 252 *see also* garden path sentences
structural linguistics 8
subconscious mind 270
suffix 5, 30–1, 39–42, 52–74, 80, 136, 145, 149, 176, 178, 181, 185, 204–5, 212, 214, 219, 236, 299; *see also* affixes, lexical phonology, zero suffix
suppletion 42–3, 48, 299
surface representation 38–9; *see also* derivations, underlying representation
Swahili 5, 114, 136, 150, 207
syllables 32, 41, 53, 54, 73, 180, 182, 210, 224, 255; *see also* stress
Sylvian and Rolandic fissures 284
synchronic 52, 100–1
syncretism 22–3
syntactic ambiguity *see* structural ambiguity
syntactic and semantic clues 250–3
syntactic constituents 76; *see also* parsing, phrase structure rules
syntactic function 65, 266–7, 271, 289
syntactic information 88–9
syntax 4, 21, 23–4, 47, 69, 72, 81, 104, 118, 148, 223, 250–3, 266–8, 287; *see also* grammatical encoding, grammatical words, inflection
system 148

taboo 190–3
tacit knowledge 30, 294; *see also* competence
Tagalog 52
template matching 254

text messaging 222–8
tip of the tongue 280–2; *see also* malapropisms
TOT *see* tip of the tongue
TRACE 255, 257–61
transcription xvii-xviii, 14–15, 217, 298
transitive verb 89, 299
tree diagrams 56–7
Turkish 135, 241–3

underived root 93–6
underlying representation 38, 43
understanding speech 246–53, 288; *see also* comprehension, speech recognition, Wernicke's aphasia
unlisted syntactic objects 76; *see also* idioms

velarisation 18
vocabulary item 18–21, 28, 54, 122, 137, 200; *see also* lexical item, lexeme
voice assimilation 90; *see also* assimilation

Wernicke's aphasia 287–9
Wernicke's area 284–5, 300
word 10–25, 27–28, 70, 113–14; *see also* lemma, lexeme, lexical item, word forms
Word-and-Paradigm 99
word-based 107–10
word formation 7–8, 30, 38, 50–81, 90, 93–4, 100, 102, 107, 109, 168–94; *see also* inflectional morphemes, derivational morphology, productivity
word forms 12, 14, 43, 77, 173, 175, 183, 186, 194, 214, 242–3; *see also* lexeme, phonological words, orthographic word
word frequency 279–80
word meaning 113–30
WP *see* Word-and-Paradigm

Yiddish 139

zero derivation 64–5; *see also* conversion
zero suffix 42, 99